Cracking the Product Marketing Code

Craft winning go-to-market strategies for market domination

IMAN BAYATRA

BIRMINGHAM—MUMBAI

Cracking the Product Marketing Code

Group Product Manager: Alok Dhuri
Publishing Product Manager: Uzma Sheerin
Book Project Manager: Deeksha Thakkar
Senior Editor: Rounak Kulkarni
Technical Editor: Maran Fernandes
Copy Editor: Safis Editing
Proofreader: Safis Editing
Indexer: Rekha Nair
Production Designer: Nilesh Mohite
DevRel Marketing Coordinator: Deepak Kumar and Mayank Singh
Business Development Executive: Puneet Kaur
Product Development Manager: Ketan Kamble
Design Lead: Joseph Runnacles

First published: October 2023

Production reference: 280923

Published by Packt Publishing Ltd.

Grosvenor House
11 St Paul's Square
Birmingham
B3 1RB, UK

ISBN: 978-1-83763-276-3

www.packtpub.com

To the memory of my beloved mother, Hayat, and my father, Khier, who taught me the true essence of determination and the value of unconditional love. To my extraordinary, unwavering pillars of strength and the embodiment of passion. To my friend, Wala Loubani, for cheering and inspiring me.

To the remarkable publishing team at Packt, your dedication and expertise have brilliantly transformed my words into a polished manuscript, ready to embrace readers across the globe.

To my cherished readers – the driving force behind this incredible journey – thank you for infusing my words with purpose.

With sincere appreciation,
Iman Bayatra

Foreword

As I look back on my journey in the world of marketing, it's hard to believe it all began more than two decades ago, right after I completed my MBA and landed my first job at a small software company in Boston. It marked a significant shift from my previous role as an IT management consulting career at KPMG, to campaigns, demand generation, and trade shows. Over time, I discovered that my passion across marketing spheres focused primarily on translating a product's value into a concise narrative for customers, which is now recognized as a fundamental aspect of Product Marketing.

Once I started calling myself a product marketer, there was no looking back. Each project I led was more exciting than the previous, with products to launch, challenges to tackle, and incumbents to disrupt. I worked with early-stage startups and successful unicorns of the B2B tech space, such as Axcient, MindTickle, and Snowflake, and landed at Atlassian, which combines the magic of **product-led growth** (PLG) with the diligence of traditional sales-led PMM. Through them all, I learned by trial and error how to craft compelling messaging, do sales enablement, and manage product launches. I also created my fair share of visually appealing slides along the way.

This book embodies the blueprint I wish I had at the outset of my career. In this book, Iman dissects all the critical elements that make for a successful product marketer and lays them out in easy-to-follow chapters. From the basic concepts to in-depth frameworks that took me so long to learn, all of it is now neatly laid out within these pages for you. As you journey through the book, you'll uncover the dynamic interplay between inbound strategies and outbound tactics, gaining a deep understanding of their roles in the **Go-to-Market** (GTM) process. This exploration equips you with the knowledge and tools necessary to wield these strategies and tactics with precision, ultimately ensuring a successful launch of your product.

But Iman is more than just a product marketer; she is armed with a diverse blend of sales expertise and insights from both the online and offline realms of advertising—the crucial juncture where the proverbial rubber meets the road, and all marketing materials get tested. Armed with this rich background, she decided to return to product marketing, leaving behind a trail of success, culminating in this compendium of knowledge she now shares with the product marketing community.

Iman, thank you, for distilling essential product marketing knowledge and outlining it in an exciting and instructive format.

Daniel Kuperman

Director of Product Marketing, ITSM at Atlassian

Contributors

About the author

Iman Bayatra comes from a background in product marketing and has successfully managed a career in top global advertising companies alongside an MBA program. She embarked on a transformative journey, transitioning to the nascent world of digital advertising—an industry still in its infancy. Iman was among the pioneers, working on platforms, like Google AdWords, YouTube, Facebook, and LinkedIn, when they were just emerging. This shift allowed her to pivot from focusing on the launch of **consumer packaged goods** (CPG) products to the dynamic tech industry, where she had the privilege of working with both tech B2B and B2C products. She straddled the worlds of product-led growth and sales-led companies, offering a unique vantage point.

This experience ultimately led Iman to make the decision to relocate from Israel to Europe, where Iman joined industry giants, such as Google and Docomo NTT. Later, she found a calling at Microsoft, where she assumed the role of a sales executive. It was there that Iman discovered a true passion for connecting the right product with the right audience at the right time, with the right message.

Armed with a rich blend of sales expertise and insights from the worlds of online and offline advertising, Iman also drew from inbound and outbound product marketing skills honed at leading agencies, like Publicis and BBDO. With this diverse background, Iman decided to return to product marketing, this time as a Product Marketing Director.

Motivated by more than personal fulfillment, Iman aspired to enable others, sparing them the pitfalls of trial and error in crafting messaging, managing product launches, and executing effective sales enablement strategies. This led Iman to become an active member and ambassador of the **Product Marketing Alliance (PMA)**. Within the PMA community, Iman assumed a leadership role in the GTM channel content, contributing extensive experience in bringing new products to market, positioning existing products for expansion, and driving sustainable revenue growth at tech companies.

About the reviewer

Waseem Sayegh boasts a rich history in the technology industry, amassing over two decades of experience. With a decade spent at both Google and TikTok, he's played a significant role in shaping product marketing strategies. Waseem's commitment to excellence motivated him to pursue higher education, earning him a master's degree in software engineering from Northeastern University and an MBA in marketing and strategy from McGill University. Currently, he serves as an invaluable contributor to TikTok, overseeing advertising product marketing across the Middle East, Turkey, Pakistan, Africa, and Eastern Europe.

Waseem's career journey reflects his enduring passion for technology and a commitment to staying on the cutting edge of innovation. His extensive experience and strategic insight have contributed to TikTok's success in these diverse regions, solidifying his status as an influential figure in the tech world.

I extend my heartfelt gratitude to my beloved wife and daughter, who have been unwavering pillars of support throughout every step of this incredible journey. Their boundless love, encouragement, and unwavering belief in me have been the driving force behind my determination and success. Their presence fills my life with strength, purpose, and inspiration, reminding me daily of the profound beauty and joy that exist beyond the professional world. It is their love that fuels my passion, and for that, I am eternally grateful.

Contents

Preface 1

Who this book is for 1
What this book covers 2
Conventions used 4
Get in touch 4
Share Your Thoughts 4

Download a free PDF copy of this book 5

Part 1 Introduction 1

1 3

Introducing Product Marketing 3

Understanding the role of a product marketer 3
Diving deep into the role of a product marketer – key functions and
responsibilities 5

Understanding the impact of company size and structure on the product
marketing role 8

Inbound versus outbound 11

Summary 13

2 15

Inbound Product Marketing – Product Innovation .. 15

What is inbound product marketing? 15
Role of inbound product marketing in driving product development and
fostering innovation 16

Why inbound product marketing? 20
Involving product marketers 21
Applying an outside-in perspective 22

Clearly defining target customers   22

Summary   24

3   25

Outbound Product Marketing – Driving Product Adoption and Growth   25

What is outbound product marketing?   26
    Messaging and creatives   27
        GTM campaign timeline   27
        Marketing plan   28
        Sales enablement plan   29
        Performance and measurement   30

    Outbound product marketing and customer journey   31
    Top of the funnel (TOFU) – the problem/need recognition stage   32
        Middle of the funnel (MOFU) – information search stage   33
        MOFU – evaluation of alternatives   33
        Bottom of the funnel (BOFU) – purchase decision   33
        BOFU – post-purchase behavior   34

    Summary   35

Part 2 Driving Product Enhancement with Inbound Strategies   37

4   39

Market Research and Competitive Analysis - Strategies to Enhance Innovation   39

Market research and benefits   39
    Why market research?   40

    Primary versus secondary research   45
    Primary market research   46
        Quantitative versus qualitative data   48
        Secondary market research   51

    Competitive intelligence   54

Best practices to execute effective competitor analysis   55

Integrating CI throughout the GTM and product launch plan   59
Substitute analysis (part of Porter's five forces)   59
    SWOT analysis   61
    Win/loss analysis   65
    Competitive pricing intelligence   69

Summary   70

5   71

Customer Research – Creating an Effective Voice for Customer Programs   71

Understanding customer research for effective decision-making   71
    Differentiating between market research, customer research, and user research   73
        Types of customer research   74
        The challenge of using customer insights effectively   78
        Guiding product roadmaps and fostering innovation through customer research   79

Enhancing customer understanding through effective VoC programs   81
What exactly does VoC mean?   81
    Building an effective VoC program   83
    Essential principles for a successful VoC program   89

VoC program to create differentiation   92
Turning customer insights into action   92

Boosting ROI with a VoC program   95
What are VoC metrics?   95
    How to measure the ROI of your VoC program?   97

Summary   99

6   101

Influencing the Product Roadmap   101

What is a product roadmap?   102

    The role of product marketing in the roadmap   103

Implementing strategies to influence the product roadmap   104

Communicating the product roadmap   108

Effectively communicating the product roadmap and vision   110

Summary   112

7   113

Customer Segmentation and Personas   113

Segmentation – How to improvecustomer segmentation   113
Understanding why segmenting your customer base is critical   115
Navigating the types of customer segmentation   116
Mastering the customer segmentation process   118
Crafting your ideal customer profile   120

Understanding your personas in detail   122
Navigating persona types – user, buyer, and more   123

Harnessing the power of personas – how to use them effectively   130

Creating effective personas with the JBTD framework   133
JTBD versus personas   134

Summary   135

Part 3 Outbound: Strategies for Product Adoption and
Exponential Growth   137

8   139

Competitive Positioning and Messaging for Growth   139

Driving growth with positioning   140
What are the key components of positioning?   141

Value proposition and competitive positioning   144
How to create a strong value proposition   145

Strategic narrative, narrative design, and positioning   149

Effective product messaging for growth   151
The key elements of effective messaging   152

Messaging automation   160

Summary   162

9   163

GTM Strategies for Exponential Growth   163

Exploring the key components of an effective GTM strategy   164

Identifying your ideal market   169
Determining whether you're in the right market   169
Product–market fit   173

Laying out distribution strategy   178
Exploring common distribution methods   178
B2B versus B2C distribution strategies   180
Summing it up   183

Creating your content strategy   183
Content development   184

Measuring and optimizing your efforts   189

Unveiling the blueprint for a successful product launch   191
Aligning with the launch process   192
A global product launch   202

Summary   204

10   205

Enable Your Sales Team and Maximize Effectiveness   205

Building an effective sales enablement program   206

Building your sales collateral hub   208

Adjusting your sales collateral for every stage of the buying journey   209
Awareness and interest stage   210
Consideration stage   212
Purchase stage   219
Advocacy/post-purchase stage   221

Sales enablement tools   222

Sales enablement success indicators   225

Summary   232

Part 4 – Impactful Collaboration and Value Creation   232

11   233

Ensure Internal Stakeholders Buy-In   233

Collaborating with PMs   233
Building effective collaboration between PMs and PMMs   236

Collaborating with marketing, sales, and customer success teams   238
Aligning product marketing, marketing, sales, and customer success   238
Getting buy-in and earning the trust of each team   239

Engaging the C-suite   241

Summary   243

12   245

Analyst Relations (AR)   245

The role of product marketing in AR   246
How can analysts help?   246
How to create a successful AR program   248

AR program – best practices   249

Summary   251

Index   253

Why subscribe?   263

Other Books You May Enjoy   264

Packt is searching for authors like you   269

Share Your Thoughts   271

Download a free PDF copy of this book   273

Preface

In the modern world, the synergy between crafting the right product and strategically introducing it to the perfect market has never held more importance. Welcome to an exhaustive guide that invites you to plunge into the fusion of creativity and methodology, enabling you to seamlessly bridge the gap between your product and a discerning market, effectively catering to the ever-evolving needs of customers.

In this book, you'll get a solid grasp of product marketing and its key aspects. You'll navigate the dynamic interplay between inbound and outbound strategies, acquiring a profound understanding of their roles throughout the product launch process and how to use them effectively to bring your product to market.

Once you've got the basics down, we'll dive into inbound strategies. These are the ways you can influence your product's direction, making sure it's just what your audience needs. We'll cover everything from conducting market research, engaging with customer insights, scrutinizing the competitive landscape, and refining customer segmentation to sculpting an intricate persona.

Following this, you'll delve into the intricate realm of outbound strategies meticulously designed to propel product adoption and fuel exponential growth. You'll master the nuanced art of crafting and fine-tuning compelling messaging and positioning, architecting a robust go-to-market plan, empowering your sales cadre for optimal efficiency, and nurturing a harmonious product-market resonance across the diverse stages of a buyer's expedition.

The journey concludes with a deep look at collaboration – how working together with people both inside and outside your company creates real value. By the time you finish this book, you'll be a product marketing pro, enhancing your product to meet customer needs, driving product adoption, and accelerating growth.

Who this book is for

If you're a product marketer, product marketing leader, or marketing manager looking to sharpen your product marketing skills, this book is for you. With this book, you'll deep dive into product marketing and identify blind spots in your strategies, primarily in B2B tech. This book is also beneficial for product managers who want to explore key product marketing functions to foster exceptional collaboration and positively impact future solutions.

To get the most out of this book, a basic knowledge of product marketing is recommended.

What this book covers

Chapter 1, Introducing Product Marketing, provides an introduction to product marketing roles, covering outbound and inbound functions.

Chapter 2, Inbound Product Marketing – Driving Innovation, explains the concept of inbound product marketing and provides practical examples of how product marketers use inbound strategies to shape the product roadmap, guide product development, and foster innovation. It offers insights into the key components of inbound marketing, explores the importance of product innovation, and highlights the reasons for choosing an inbound approach, all while clarifying its impact on the organization of the overall product.

Chapter 3, Outbound Product Marketing – Driving Product Adoption and Growth, provides a general overview of outbound product marketing. It explains how outbound activities are used to drive product adoption and expedite growth across the various stages of the buying funnel – awareness, interest, consideration, adoption, and advocacy. Additionally, it shares examples of companies that prioritize outbound strategies, particularly those with a sales-led focus.

Chapter 4, Market Research and Competitive Analysis – Strategies to Enhance Innovation, provides essential strategies involving market research and **competitive intelligence (CI)**. It walks you through diverse market research approaches and analyses, including SWOT analysis, Win/Loss analysis, and Porter's Five Forces analysis. Moreover, it illustrates how these analyses can effectively inform the product roadmap, and validate the right markets to outreach the right segments and audiences. It encompasses primary and secondary market research types, delving extensively into the nuances of both categories.

Chapter 5, Customer Research – Creating Effective Voice of Customer Programs, emphasizes customer research and the skill of crafting an effective **Voice of Customer (VoC)** initiative within your organization. It also provides steps on how to identify customer needs, categorize them into product needs, service needs, and so on, and finally, how to meet those needs.

Chapter 6, Influencing the Product Roadmap, provides an in-depth exploration of the concept of a product roadmap. It encompasses a comprehensive overview of the precise involvement of the product marketer within the roadmap, illustrating its application across the various phases of a product launch. Additionally, it delves into the significance and advantages of sharing the roadmap with customers, coupled with strategies to effectively convey the product roadmap and its overarching vision.

Chapter 7, Customer Segmentation and Personas, comprehensively details customer segmentation, outlining its essence and significance. It presents a spectrum of customer segmentation types, accompanied by tactics to effectively chart out high-performing segments. Following this, the subsequent section delves into various persona variations. It furnishes a meticulous, step-by-step guide on persona construction and their proficient integration throughout the entirety of the product launch process. Furthermore, the concept of the "jobs to be done" principle is elucidated, unveiling its role in addressing the query of why our personas choose your product.

Chapter 8, Competitive Positioning and Messaging for Growth, delves into the concept of positioning, offering a comprehensive understanding. It presents a step-by-step guide to crafting precise positioning, exploring various positioning frameworks, and illustrating how positioning strategies can be harnessed to foster growth. The second part focuses entirely on messaging, detailing how to chart your messaging strategy, which includes a step-by-step walkthrough of the messaging framework. It then delves into the emerging trend of automated messaging and how utilizing tools can simplify and enhance your messaging management, offering greater ease and control.

Chapter 9, GTM Strategies for Exponential Growth, provides a comprehensive understanding of a GTM strategy, encompassing its core definition and the methodical approach to constructing your GTM plan. This chapter delves into the multifaceted components that make up an effective GTM strategy, along with insightful tactics customized for each facet. Additionally, it explores the pivotal concept of "product-market fit," explaining both its significance and how to measure it. The last part focuses on the product launch and how it connects with the GTM strategy. It looks at different aspects of coordinating the launch, such as working with stakeholders, setting goals, planning launch tiers, and tracking metrics.

Chapter 10, Enable Your Sales Team and Maximize Effectiveness, clarifies the concept of sales enablement and outlines the necessary components for a successful program. It provides an overview of a framework designed to build and scale an enablement program. It then explains how to create a hub for sales collateral, highlighting the need to adjust these resources for different buyer stages – awareness, interest, consideration, and adoption. Finally, the focus shifts to evaluating the effectiveness of your enablement program using significant metrics.

Chapter 11, Ensure Internal Stakeholders Buy-In, covers several essential aspects of relationship-building within the product marketing realm. It addresses the dynamics of fostering healthy relationships with internal stakeholders, while ensuring alignment and minimizing friction with other teams to prevent conflicts. The discussion delves into the daily routine of a product manager, outlining the distinct responsibilities of **Product Marketing Managers** (**PMMs**) and **Product Managers** (**PMs**). It elucidates the points of overlap between these roles and emphasizes the potential for collaboration. The chapter also examines collaboration with adjacent teams, such as sales and marketing, outlining methods to secure their buy-in and maintain harmonious relationships to avert friction and disputes. Lastly, this chapter emphasizes the crucial role of connecting with the C-suite and provides guidance on key focus areas when engaging with these high-level executives.

Chapter 12, Analyst Relations (AR), highlights the pivotal role analysts play as influential figures in guiding various decisions for potential customers and investors. It illustrates how analysts can aid product marketers in boosting product adoption. The chapter then provides a comprehensive guide on creating an analyst relations plan, including a killing analyst deck. Lastly, the discussion delves into measurement and the essential metrics that are vital to monitor and ensure the success of your analyst plan.

Conventions used

Get in touch

Feedback from our readers is always welcome.

General feedback: If you have questions about any aspect of this book, email us at customercare@packtpub.com and mention the book title in the subject of your message.

Errata: Although we have taken every care to ensure the accuracy of our content, mistakes do happen. If you have found a mistake in this book, we would be grateful if you would report this to us. Please visit www.packtpub.com/support/errata and fill in the form.

Piracy: If you come across any illegal copies of our works in any form on the internet, we would be grateful if you would provide us with the location address or website name. Please contact us at copyright@packt.com with a link to the material.

If you are interested in becoming an author: If there is a topic that you have expertise in and you are interested in either writing or contributing to a book, please visit authors.packtpub.com.

Share Your Thoughts

Once you've read *Cracking the Product Marketing Code*, we'd love to hear your thoughts! Scan the QR code below to go straight to the Amazon review page for this book and share your feedback.

https://packt.link/r/1837632766

Your review is important to us and the tech community and will help us make sure we're delivering excellent quality content.

Some of the graphics within this title have small text, and therefore where this impacts clarity we encourage the reader to refer to the downloadable graphics package from our registered packt.link. Download the full graphics package from this registered packt.link: https://packt.link/wshHO for all images included in this book.

Download a free PDF copy of this book

Thanks for purchasing this book!

Do you like to read on the go but are unable to carry your print books everywhere?
Is your eBook purchase not compatible with the device of your choice?

Don't worry, now with every Packt book you get a DRM-free PDF version of that book at no cost.

Read anywhere, any place, on any device. Search, copy, and paste code from your favorite technical books directly into your application.

The perks don't stop there, you can get exclusive access to discounts, newsletters, and great free content in your inbox daily

Follow these simple steps to get the benefits:

1. Scan the QR code or visit the link below

https://packt.link/free-ebook/978-1-83763-276-3

2. Submit your proof of purchase
3. That's it! We'll send your free PDF and other benefits to your email directly

Part 1
Introduction

This part serves as an insightful introduction to the pivotal role of product marketing. It provides a clear explanation of what product marketing entails, while distinctly dividing its key function into two sets of functions – *outbound* and *inbound*. Each of these functions is meticulously defined, with real-world examples skillfully incorporated to illustrate when and how to apply them effectively.

This part has the following chapters:

- *Chapter 1, Introducing Product Marketing*
- *Chapter 2, Inbound Product Marketing – Driving Innovation*
- *Chapter 3, Outbound Product Marketing – Driving Product Adoption and Growth*

Introducing Product Marketing 1

In recent years, product marketing has undergone a significant transformation, and has become a vital trend and top role, especially in the field of tech companies operating in a crowded and rapidly changing market. In the past, product marketing was primarily concerned with executing tactical activities such as creating sales and marketing materials, gaining an in-depth understanding of buyer personas, and crafting messaging that resonated with customers. As competition in many industries intensifies, customer journeys become more complex. In addition, with the dynamic nature of customer behavior, which places great emphasis on enhancing customer experience, the product marketing role has evolved into a more strategic function. The modern product marketer must possess strategic thinking abilities to navigate the changing market conditions and leverage new technologies to achieve business objectives. Moreover, product marketers must be skilled in problem-solving, creative communication, and collaboration to lead cross-functional teams and work with stakeholders across the organization, ensuring successful product launches that achieve the business objectives outlined.

In this chapter, we aim to provide an in-depth exploration of the product marketing role, examining the various factors that influence the shape and functions of product marketers. We will gain a comprehensive understanding of the difference between *inbound* and *outbound* product marketing, highlighting the benefits they offer to businesses. We will explore the impact of company size and structure on the product marketing role, including how larger or smaller organizations may have different requirements and expectations for product marketers. In this chapter, we will address several important questions related to the product marketing role:

- What were the primary factors that led to the transformation of the product marketing role?
- How do a company's size and structure affect the key functions of product marketers?
- What distinguishes inbound product marketing from outbound product marketing?

Understanding the role of a product marketer

In today's fast-paced tech industry, product marketing has emerged as a crucial strategic function that drives success for any business. No longer just a tactical role, product marketing is now at the forefront of strategic decision-making in tech companies. This shift has been driven by several key factors, one of which is increasing competition. With the rapid growth of the tech industry, competition has become fierce, making it crucial for companies to strive to develop products that not only align with the overall business objectives but also deliver significant value to customers, ultimately driving the company's bottom line. Product marketing plays a critical role in this process by conducting market and customer research to help companies better understand customer needs and identify gaps in the market, monitoring competitors' activities to identify opportunities, crafting effective go-to-market strategies, and communicating the value of their products to target audiences.

Another key driver is evolving customer expectations. Customers today expect a personalized, seamless, and engaging experience from the products and services they use. Product marketing plays a key role in delivering on these expectations by understanding customer needs and preferences, developing customer-centric products and features, and communicating the value of those products to customers.

Finally, data-driven decision-making has become a key driver of the shift toward more strategic product marketing. With the availability of vast amounts of customer and market data, companies can make more informed decisions about their products and go-to-market strategies. Product marketing plays a critical role in this process by analyzing data and using it to inform product development, enhance customer experience, and optimize the customer journey and overall **Go-to-Market (GTM)** strategies.

Product marketing plays a critical role in the success of businesses. By developing customer-centric products, creating effective go-to-market strategies, and communicating the value of those products to customers, product marketers help their companies differentiate themselves and maintain growth in a highly competitive market. In 2020, a tech company called **Quibi** launched a mobile-only streaming service that offered short-form video content designed to be watched on the go. They invested heavily in developing original content and securing high-profile talent for their platform. However, Quibi failed to consider the changing media landscape and the behavior of its target audience, which was primarily millennials and Gen Z consumers. They also didn't have a strategic approach to product marketing, which led to their failure. They didn't invest in developing targeted marketing campaigns that would resonate with their target audience. As a result, Quibi struggled to attract and retain subscribers. Its product didn't provide enough value to consumers, who could find similar short-form video content on social media platforms for free. Quibi also faced tough competition from established streaming services such as Netflix, Hulu, and Amazon Prime Video. Despite attempts to pivot its product and marketing strategy, Quibi eventually failed to gain traction and shut down in late 2020, just six months after launching.

Quibi's failure demonstrates the importance of having a strategic and customer-centric approach to product marketing, especially in an industry as competitive as streaming services. By not considering the changing media landscape and behavior of its target audience and by not investing in building a strong brand or developing targeted marketing campaigns, Quibi couldn't build a product that provided substantial value to its customers and differentiate itself in a crowded market, leading to its eventual downfall.

Diving deep into the role of a product marketer – key functions and responsibilities

Product marketing involves the crucial task of connecting the dots between the product and the customer. This involves understanding the customer's needs and wants and ensuring that the product addresses those needs. To accomplish this, product marketers conduct market research to identify gaps or opportunities and work with the product development team to shape the product in a way that meets customer demands. Crafting a compelling message that effectively communicates the product's value to the target audience is another key responsibility of the product marketer. This involves identifying the product's key benefits, developing product positioning, and creating effective marketing campaigns that drive customer engagement and adoption. In addition, product marketers must have a deep understanding of the market and competitive landscape. This knowledge allows us to identify trends, anticipate market shifts, and develop strategies to stay ahead of the competition. To ensure a successful product launch, product marketers must build an effective GTM strategy that leverages multiple channels to reach the target audience, equips the sales team with the necessary tools and resources, and continually optimizes based on feedback and data. The GTM strategy is critical to the success of any product launch. Moreover, product marketers must plan, execute, and measure the success of the product launch. This requires careful planning, execution, and measurement to ensure that the product meets customer needs and achieves business objectives. Overall, a product marketer's core responsibilities can be broken down into three key categories: advocating for the customer, effectively communicating the product's value, and driving product distribution to ensure broad reach and accessibility.

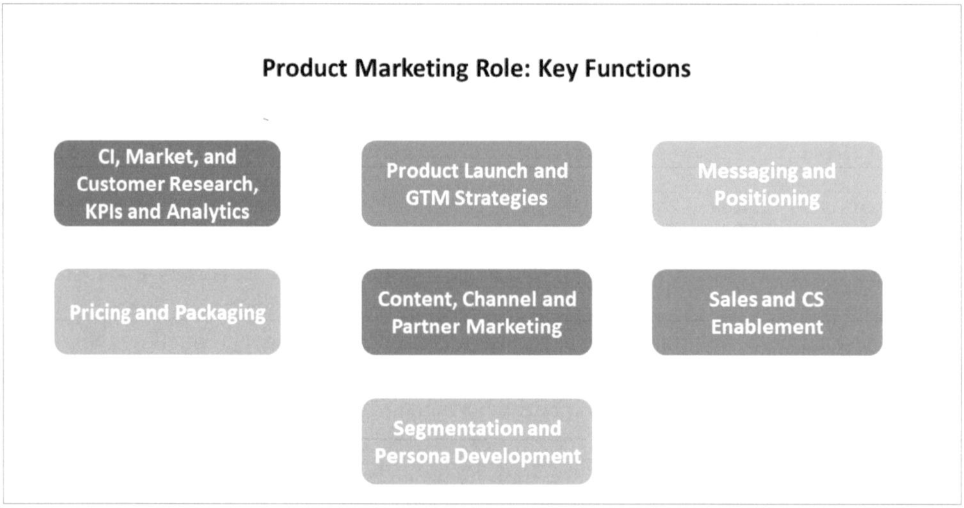

Product Marketing Role: Key Functions

CI, Market, and Customer Research, KPIs and Analytics

Product Launch and GTM Strategies

Messaging and Positioning

Pricing and Packaging

Content, Channel and Partner Marketing

Sales and CS Enablement

Segmentation and Persona Development

Figure 1.1 – Product marketing functions

The responsibilities of product marketers have evolved significantly in recent years, with a greater focus on delivering exceptional customer experiences. Today's customers demand more than just a product or service; they expect a seamless and enjoyable experience throughout their interactions with a company. As such, the role of product marketers has shifted to prioritize enhancing the customer experience across all touchpoints, both online and offline. Looking ahead to 2023, this trend is set to continue, with product marketers placing even greater emphasis on understanding and meeting customer needs in order to drive innovation and accelerate the growth of their companies.

AI and machine learning are transforming the way product marketers reach out and engage with their customers. These technologies enable marketers to analyze vast amounts of customer data, such as demographics, past purchases, and browsing behavior, to uncover insights and create personalized messaging and campaigns that resonate with specific segments of the audience. AI-powered chatbots and other advanced tools also provide valuable customer data that allows marketers to predict demand and market trends, adjust their strategies, and make informed decisions on product positioning, pricing, and messaging. By optimizing their GTM strategies and identifying the most effective channels, messaging, and tactics, product marketers can reach and engage customers in a more personalized and effective way.

With the aid of real-time data and automated **Continuous Integration** (CI) tools, product marketers are now better equipped to identify market gaps and emerging trends. They can track the actions of other players in the market, enabling them to make informed decisions and stay ahead of the competition. The capabilities of analytics tools have also allowed product marketers to track the actions of customers at every stage of the buying journey. They can monitor and analyze customer behavior across various touchpoints, from awareness to adoption. Moreover, product marketers are now tailoring personalized buying and onboarding journeys based on customers' specific use cases, which leads to higher customer satisfaction and product adoption.

Furthermore, in the digital age, businesses have undergone significant transformations in how they connect with customers and engage with them. The advent of social media platforms and chatbots has revolutionized the bond between product marketers and customers, offering novel ways to communicate in real-time and glean valuable insights into their needs and preferences. This allows product marketers to tailor their marketing strategies to better address customer pain points and drive product adoption.

As product marketers, our role involves working on various projects and collaborating with different teams within an organization. For example, we may be tasked with conducting market research to understand customer needs and preferences and then working with the product development team to shape the product accordingly. We may also be responsible for crafting messaging and positioning that effectively communicates the product's value to the target audience, which requires collaborating with the marketing and communications teams. We must stay up to date with industry trends and the competitive landscape, which may involve collaborating with the sales team, conducting market analysis, and attending industry events. We may also work with the customer success team to identify opportunities for upselling and cross-selling to existing customers.

Figure 1.2 – Product marketing: orchestrating cross-functional teams for market success

Collaboration with cross-functional teams is essential for product marketers to apply a customer-centric perspective, build the right customer experience, develop products that align with customer preferences, and remain competitive in a crowded landscape. Given the diverse responsibilities, product marketers need to be versatile and agile, adapting to different projects' and teams' needs while ensuring all stakeholders are working toward a mutual goal. This requires strong communication and collaboration skills and a deep understanding of the company's product and market. Ultimately, the ability to wear multiple hats and switch between projects seamlessly is critical to success as a product marketer.

Considering the external factors outlined earlier, along with others, product marketers are compelled to shift toward a more strategic approach rather than a tactical one. Nowadays, product marketers prioritize a customer-centric perspective and emphasize innovation, identifying gaps in the market while collaborating with cross-functional teams such as product management, sales, engineering, and customer support by bringing in the customer's voice. This collaboration helps to create the right customer experience, develop products that cater to customers' preferences, and maintain a competitive edge. Such strategic focus allows companies to innovate, accelerate growth, and drive revenues. However, internal factors within an organization, such as company size and team structure, can significantly impact the scope, responsibilities, and reporting structure of product marketers. The next part of this chapter delves deeper into how these internal factors shape the role of product marketing.

Understanding the impact of company size and structure on the product marketing role

Product marketing is a critical function in any organization, as it is about connecting the right product with the right audience at the right time with the right message to ensure product adoption and drive growth. However, the scope of product marketers' responsibilities and their involvement in the organization are often defined by the size of the company. In larger organizations with ample resources, product marketers typically have a more specialized role, focusing on specific aspects of product marketing and collaborating with various teams. In contrast, smaller companies with limited resources require product marketers to wear multiple hats and take on diverse tasks. This demands a broad skill set and a deep understanding of the market, the customer, and the product.

In a small company or a start-up, the role of the product marketer is closely tied to the product's growth stage. As the company or product grows and evolves, the product marketer's responsibilities will also shift and expand to align with the product's changing needs. In the early stages of a small company or start-up, the product marketer's role may be focused on market validation, conducting customer research, defining the product's value proposition, and developing a go-to-market strategy. This may involve working closely with the product development team to ensure that the product meets customer needs and that the messaging and positioning align with the product's features and benefits. As the product moves into the growth phase, the product marketer's role may shift toward driving customer acquisition and retention. This may involve developing marketing campaigns, optimizing the sales funnel, and developing customer loyalty programs. The product marketer may also be responsible for analyzing customer data to gain insights into user behavior and preferences. In the maturity phase, the product marketer's role may shift toward optimizing profitability and maintaining market share. This may involve identifying new revenue streams and exploring expansion opportunities.

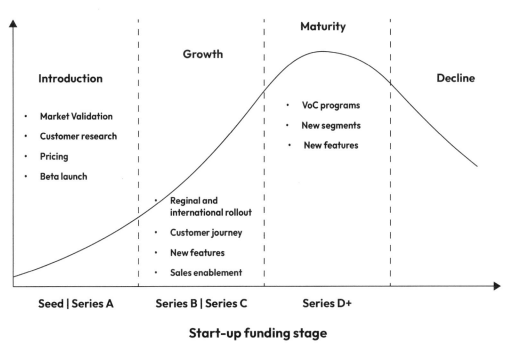

Figure 1.3 – Product marketer's role in the start-up product life cycle: Raymond Vernon *The Product Lifecycle Theory*

As previously mentioned, product marketers in smaller organizations have a broader role that may encompass both the technical aspects of inbound product marketing, which focus on activities around the product, as well as the execution-oriented aspects of outbound product marketing, which involve product adoption. For mid-stage organizations and enterprises, product marketers have a more specific focus on particular aspects, and their roles are more clearly divided between technical, *inbound product marketing* and execution-oriented, *outbound product marketing*. These companies typically have more available resources, including product and sales teams, as well as various marketing teams, such as customer acquisition, content creation, and brand marketing. However, having more resources may make the launch process more complex due to the need to coordinate and enable more teams, which requires additional efforts to ensure effective communication and organization to foster collaboration between different teams. As a result, product marketers tend to focus on developing repeatable processes and clear templates and frameworks to ensure alignment between teams and maximize effectiveness. This includes the use of launch checklists, sales collateral templates, messaging frameworks, and other tools to streamline the launch process.

For mid-stage organizations and enterprises, the role of product marketers is to focus on a handful of key products, typically distributed by region. At this stage, there may be several verticals to consider, and the core goals of the product marketer will be defined by the maturity of the product and the sales and marketing teams. Product marketers also work closely with cross-functional teams, including sales, product management, and customer success, to ensure that the product is effectively positioned and that sales teams have the necessary tools and resources to sell the product. As a result, team enablement becomes critical, with product marketers focusing on developing sales and marketing collaterals at each stage of the customer journey.

Contrasting Product Marketing Roles in Enterprises versus Small Businesses

Start-ups and Small Businesses | versus | **Enterprises**

+ Takes on diverse tasks

+ More direct line of communication with all team members

+ Team enablement is less relevant

+ Processes and frameworks are less relevant

+ Need to be more agile and adaptable due to limited resources

+ Clearly divided roles between inbound and outbound product marketing

+ Launch process more complicated to manage internally

+ Team enablement is critical

+ Structured and repeatable processes

+ More available resources

Figure 1.4 – Contrasting product marketing roles in enterprises versus small businesses

Simultaneously, a company's culture, leadership, and team structure can greatly impact the product marketer's role, and working within the existing culture and structure is equally as important as understanding the market and customer needs. For example, in a company that is *product-led*, such as Facebook, the product is at the core of the company's culture and is the main driver of innovation and growth. In this type of culture, the role of the product marketer is to work closely with the product development team to ensure that the product meets the needs of the target audience and that the messaging effectively communicates the value of the product to users. On the other hand, in a company that is *marketing-led*, such as Apple, the role of the product marketer is to work closely with the marketing team to develop messaging and positioning that resonates with the target audience. In this type of culture, the product marketer must understand the features and benefits of the product and develop messaging that highlights its unique selling proposition. In a company that is *design-led*, such as Airbnb, the role of the product marketer is to work closely with the design team to ensure that the user experience of the product is aligned with the brand and meets the needs of the target audience. In this type of culture, the product marketer must understand the user journey and work with the design team to develop user interfaces that are intuitive and easy to use.

Product marketers play an essential role in ensuring the success of a product in the market. They work closely with cross-functional teams to understand the needs of the target audience and ensure that the product meets those needs while effectively communicating with users to bring the right product to the right audience at the right time with the right message. The activities and responsibilities of product marketers can vary significantly depending on the company culture and team structure. However, they typically fall into two categories: *inbound* and *outbound*.

Inbound versus outbound

Inbound product marketing, also referred to as technical product marketing, encompasses a range of activities that focus on the product itself and the processes involved in bringing it to market. This type of marketing is predominantly internal facing, with key stakeholders including product management, UX teams, and designers. Some examples of activities involved in inbound product marketing include conducting market and user research to gain insights that can inform the product roadmap, overseeing the product launch process, and developing product enablement programs. The primary objective of inbound product marketing is to understand which features to prioritize, how to release them, when to bring them to market, and how to incorporate customer feedback into the product development process. Inbound product marketing and product management are closely aligned, as both functions share the goal of understanding customer needs and preferences and how to create and bring products to market that meet those needs.

Outbound product marketing, in contrast to inbound product marketing, is focused on executing the GTM strategy for a product or solution. This role involves being ultimately responsible for revenue, pipeline, win rate, and the sales cycle and ensuring that the product or solution hits its revenue targets. As an outbound product marketer, you'll work closely with sales, customer success, and business development teams to drive product adoption and customer retention. Unlike inbound product marketing, this role is more external facing, with key stakeholders including analysts, customers, and others who interact with the product in the market. The activities involved in outbound product marketing are numerous and varied, but they often include developing a comprehensive GTM plan, identifying and prioritizing key customer segments and potential markets, and producing effective marketing collateral that supports customer outreach and engagement.

Outbound product marketing is an essential function for ensuring that a product or solution is successful in the market. By working closely with sales and other teams, outbound product marketers help to drive adoption, retention, and revenue growth, while also helping to build the brand and reputation of the product in the market.

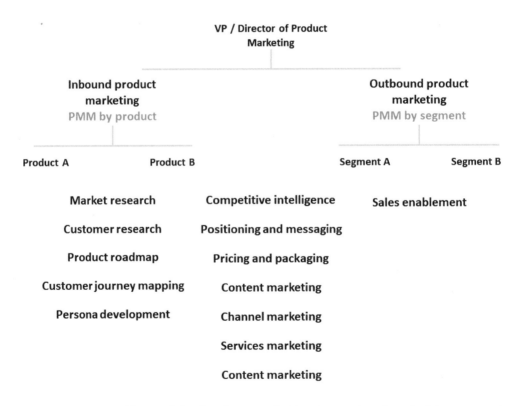

Figure 1.5 – Product marketing team structure in big companies

In an ideal scenario, the product marketing department would take ownership of the entire product marketing process, from end to end. This would involve leading both inbound and outbound marketing efforts to influence both product innovation and GTM strategy. For some companies, this integrated approach can ensure greater efficiency and continuity, particularly when resources are limited. However, not all organizations adopt this approach. Larger companies, such as Google and Amazon, typically split their product marketing functions into inbound and outbound. Inbound product marketing is focused on the product itself and is often split by product line. Outbound product marketing, on the other hand, is focused on the GTM strategy and is often split into segments and verticals.

While the integrated approach may work well for some organizations, the split approach can provide a more focused and specialized approach to product marketing. Ultimately, the approach that a company adopts will depend on a range of factors, including the company's size, culture, and available resources.

Summary

Over the past few years, product marketing has become a critical trend and a top role, especially in tech companies. The key functions of the role are dynamic and can vary significantly between organizations, influenced by internal and external factors. External factors such as real-time data and the rapid growth of technology have a considerable impact on the responsibilities of product marketers, while internal factors such as company size and structure can also shift the focus of the role.

Furthermore, the product marketing role can be divided into two key aspects: inbound and outbound product marketing. Inbound product marketing tends to focus on the product development side, including understanding customer needs, developing value propositions, and driving product roadmaps. Outbound product marketing is more execution-focused, centered around GTM activities such as demand generation, sales enablement, and customer advocacy.

In the upcoming chapter, we will explore inbound product marketing in depth and learn how it can be leveraged to drive innovation.

Inbound Product Marketing – Product Innovation 2

Today, a product's success hinges on more than its appealing features and functionality, especially since we're in a fast-paced and constantly evolving marketplace. To genuinely connect with customers and differentiate them from competitors, businesses must embrace a strategic and customer-centric approach to product marketing. This is precisely where inbound product marketing comes into play.

As mentioned in the previous chapter, the role of product marketing varies across companies and encompasses two key sets of functions: *outbound* activities and *inbound* activities. In this chapter, our primary focus will be on exploring the realm of inbound product marketing.

Inbound product marketing is a powerful methodology that focuses on gathering deep insights into customer needs, preferences, and challenges to inform the development and enhancement of a product. It involves meticulous research, data analysis, and collaboration with product teams to enhance user experience and ensure that the product not only meets but exceeds customer expectations.

In this chapter, we will delve into the world of inbound product marketing, exploring its core principles, tasks, and significance in today's highly competitive landscape. We will uncover the essential components of successful inbound product marketing strategies and discuss how they can drive product excellence and market success.

Throughout this chapter, we will answer the following questions:

- What is inbound product marketing?
- Why inbound product marketing?
- How can inbound product marketing drive product development and foster innovation?

What is inbound product marketing?

Inbound product marketing goes beyond being a theoretical concept; it is a practical and results-driven approach that delivers tangible outcomes. This strategic approach actively informs and influences the development and improvement of products. The focus of inbound product marketing lies in tasks that shape product development and enhancement. This includes conducting thorough market research, gaining an understanding of competition and customer personas, as well as collaborating closely with the product organization. The core tasks of inbound product marketing primarily revolve around customer and market analysis, business case development, and other research-oriented activities. This approach proves most effective when the target customer's definition is challenging, typically determined by the problem they face or the triggering event they are experiencing. The following figure shows some of the key activities of inbound product marketing:

Key Tasks of Inbound Product Marketing

Figure 2.1 – Key tasks of inbound product marketing

One of the key aspects of inbound product marketing is quantitatively tracking product usage. This involves understanding how the product is used, what the job to be done is, and who is using it. Collecting and analyzing usage data provides invaluable insights into customer behavior and preferences, allowing you to integrate the customer's voice throughout the product life cycle.

Gathering qualitative feedback from customers is another critical aspect of inbound product marketing. By actively seeking feedback and engaging with customers, you can identify any potential issues or barriers to usage. This feedback is invaluable in understanding customer sentiments, uncovering pain points, and identifying areas for improvement. By integrating this qualitative feedback into the product development process, you prioritize customer perspectives, leading to a product that is more customer-centric and ultimately more effective.

Let's take a deeper look into the role of inbound product marketing in driving product development.

Role of inbound product marketing in driving product development and fostering innovation

Every year, thousands of tech startups fail because they ignore customer needs and gaps in the market when developing products. This raises the fundamental question: why do companies allocate resources and investment to develop a product if there is no apparent customer demand and a clear market opportunity?

Undoubtedly, the underlying objective of introducing new products, launching innovative features, or enhancing the performance of an existing product is to effectively address customer needs, outpace competitors, and consequently drive accelerated growth. It is precisely within this realm that inbound product marketing thrives. By assuming a pivotal role, inbound product marketing shapes the product roadmap, provides guidance on product direction, and cultivates innovation through the utilization of its distinctive inbound functions.

Inbound product marketing acts as a catalyst for understanding customer desires and preferences, thereby informing the strategic decisions that drive product development. It employs customer-centric methodologies, ensuring products are designed and optimized to deliver exceptional value and address specific pain points. This customer-driven approach not only enhances the product's market fit but also establishes a strong foundation for customer satisfaction and loyalty.

Moreover, inbound product marketing serves as a dynamic force that propels innovation within organizations. Leveraging the power of inbound functions, such as comprehensive market research, customer insights, and data analysis, enables businesses to uncover new opportunities, identify emerging trends, and seize competitive advantages.

Inbound product marketing is not only key to fostering innovation but also plays a pivotal role in propelling growth strategies forward. Ansoff's product-market matrix outlines two approaches for companies to pursue future growth: adjusting the market or adjusting the product. Strategies such as product development and diversification involve modifying the product itself, while market penetration and market development focus on expanding and adjusting the target market:

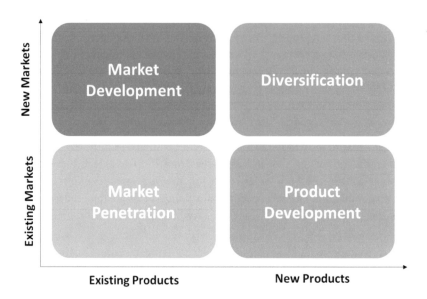

Figure 2.2 – Ansoff's product-market matrix

In the realm of growth strategies, innovation serves as a driving force that empowers companies to strengthen their market presence. It plays a pivotal role in both developing new products for existing markets (product development) and creating novel products for untapped markets (diversification). Innovation excels in identifying and fulfilling the distinctive needs of customers in new markets, thereby driving market penetration. Additionally, it enables companies to enhance their current products, securing a larger market share within their existing market (market penetration).

In this section, we will delve into the second part of the matrix:

- Product development
- Diversification

Let's get started.

Product development

The product development strategy focuses on crafting new and improved products that adeptly meet the demands of an established customer base. This necessitates a deep comprehension of both the current market dynamics and customers' evolving needs. To establish a strong product development strategy, thorough market research and analysis are imperative. These activities aim to identify market gaps and customer pain points, providing valuable insights that can be leveraged to uncover opportunities for developing new products or enhancing existing ones.

Slack, a widely used collaboration and communication platform, exemplified the application of inbound product marketing principles to shape their product roadmap and foster innovation. Their success stemmed from their profound understanding of their target audience's needs within a rapidly evolving workplace landscape. To gather valuable insights and feedback, Slack proactively engaged users through diverse channels, including user surveys, feedback forums, and direct communication. Emphasizing attentive listening to customers' pain points, challenges, and feature requests, they obtained valuable inputs for their product development process. Guided by this customer-centric approach, Slack continuously enhanced and expanded its platform's capabilities, introducing new features, integrations, and enhancements that directly addressed teams' collaborative needs and heightened productivity. By closely aligning its product roadmap with customer feedback and market demands, Slack effectively distinguished itself in the competitive collaboration software market.

Diversification

Diversification is a strategic approach that's employed by companies to broaden their operations and product portfolio. This strategy can take two forms: *related* and *unrelated* diversification.

Related diversification is a strategic approach wherein a company expands into a new market or product category closely tied to its existing business. For instance, Apple began manufacturing personal computers and later ventured into the smartphone market with the iPhone. This expansion qualifies as related diversification as Apple utilized its existing expertise and resources in hardware and software design to create a new product category closely related to its existing business.

On the other hand, unrelated diversification involves expanding into a completely new market or product category with which the company has no prior experience. **Alphabet,** the parent company of Google, is a great example. While Google is widely recognized for its search engine and online advertising, Alphabet expanded its focus to include autonomous vehicles, healthcare, and smart home technology. For instance, **Waymo,** a subsidiary of Alphabet, has taken the lead in the autonomous vehicle industry, showcasing Alphabet's commitment to revolutionizing transportation. Furthermore, **Verily Life Sciences** focuses on healthcare solutions that leverage data analytics and wearable technology to improve patient outcomes. Additionally, Alphabet's strategic acquisitions in the smart home technology sector, including Nest Labs, demonstrate its dedication to providing seamless consumer experiences. These bold moves by Alphabet exemplify its ability to identify new market opportunities and leverage its technological expertise across various industries.

To validate the demand for a new product or service and identify potential challenges and opportunities, companies should engage in market research. Market research allows companies to gather valuable insights about their target customers, the competitive landscape, and overall market trends, which can help confirm the need and mitigate the risks associated with diversification. This is where inbound product marketing plays a significant role.

Data and insights are crucial in inbound product marketing, providing valuable information that guides product strategy and development decisions. Through various methods, such as customer research, including jobs-to-be-done analysis, market segmentation, competitive benchmarking, and more, inbound product marketers can identify market gaps and discern customers' needs and preferences. This process enables them to identify opportunities for new or improved products that better cater to customer needs and preferences.

Inbound product marketing is driven by leveraging data and insights to influence the product strategy effectively. It revolves around key insights that inform the product's direction, ensuring alignment with upcoming opportunities. Additionally, it addresses the question of what products to build and confirms that the right products are being developed for the right customers.

Inbound product marketing addresses the decisions surrounding the product roadmap, a domain that may overlap with product management. In smaller organizations, the product manager assumes numerous traditional inbound product marketing responsibilities, such as identifying target market segments and prioritizing customer types. Similarly, in larger organizations, the product marketer performs many of these same functions. This takes us to the next part of this chapter, where we will delve deeper into the significance of inbound product marketing.

Why inbound product marketing?

Many tech companies are product first; they are busy innovating their products and implementing new features so frequently while assuming this is what customers want, while this is not the case. Product marketing is the right path to help companies make the shift to become customer-centric and infuse customers' needs and demands. This is exactly what happened with Microsoft when they launched Windows 8. The launch was a big failure since Microsoft was *product-first*. Later, this was a great lesson that Microsoft learned from when launching Windows 10, as it involved marketers at the earliest stages of developing the new product. They made sure every step was customer-centric and developed a compelling product with the right features that customers wanted to adopt.

During this time, Microsoft was facing growing competition from Google and Apple and decided to release the new big thing in the industry, Windows 8. The product was packed with countless innovative features to create added value over iOS, Android, and Chrome, making it the ideal product for customers. However, it received negative feedback claiming Windows 8 was *needlessly confusing and hard to use*.

Microsoft invested millions of dollars in **Research and Development (R&D)** and dedicated top engineers to work secretly on the product, who believed they knew what their target audience needed. However, no product marketers were involved in generating insights and understanding the targeted customers' needs.

Like Microsoft when they developed Windows 8, many tech companies are product first, investing all their efforts in developing a new product or implementing new features and ignoring market and customer insights while assuming they can be innovative and accelerate their growth, which, most of the time, drives them to fail. On the other hand, successful tech companies have come to realize that thorough market and customer research, coupled with deep segmentation analysis, is crucial for identifying their top-performing customers' needs. By understanding their customers' needs and preferences, these companies can effectively develop and tailor their products to meet those specific requirements. This customer-centric approach allows them to deliver the right product to the right customers, resulting in increased customer satisfaction, loyalty, and, ultimately, business success.

To be innovative, organizations have no choice but to be customer-centric. Only with the help of product marketers will companies be able to drive an outside-in strategy to guarantee that customer insights are a leading resource to continue reshaping their products, drive innovation, and stay ahead of the competition. The following are the strategic steps that companies need to take and where product marketers play a crucial role in helping these companies ensure success regarding their innovation and get closer to product-market fit when developing new products:

- Involving product marketers in scaling products and shaping future ones
- Applying an outside-in perspective to better understand the jobs to be done (a theory of innovation)
- Clearly defining target customers and focusing on top-performing segments

Let's explore each in a bit more detail.

Involving product marketers

Product marketers play a key role in transforming market and customer insights, including competitive landscape analysis, into product strategies to ensure a product-market fit and, consequently, drive product adoption and maintain growth. Involving product marketers in scaling products and developing new ones helps companies guarantee that budgets and resources are deployed correctly to develop new products. As product marketers, we can help companies stay innovative by doing the following:

- Prioritizing customers over competitors by identifying the wants and needs of customers and creating detailed customer profiles by conducting market research, analyzing customer data, and gathering customer feedback.
- Identifying areas for improvement in the customer experience. After gaining a comprehensive understanding of the customers, determine their expectations and compare them to what they're currently getting. As product marketers, we can help our companies turn gaps in customer experience into opportunities for growth.

- Exploring customers' unmet needs and determining how our company can provide value to them. This might involve developing new features or even products or services that might lead to a new market and differentiate our companies from competitors.

Let's move on to the next strategic step that companies need to take: an *outside-in* perspective.

Applying an outside-in perspective

To apply an outside-in perspective, the jobs-to-be-done analysis is recommended to start with to *uncover desired outcomes* and identify customers' needs. It helps our companies better understand why customers are *hiring* their product or *firing* it. The jobs-to-be-done perspective helps map disruptive and innovative opportunities that can change the direction of the product. In this case, our companies are more likely to win in the marketplace since they'll be able to get their jobs done significantly better and/or even more affordable. When Twitter sought a clear direction for its products and services, it turned to the *jobs-to-be-done* analysis. This approach helped the company pinpoint the top needs of its customers and ultimately played a crucial role in Twitter's transformation. In 2015, CEO Jack Dorsey defined Twitter's strategy with a clear focus on building features and services to meet three core jobs: news, discussion, and helping people get paid. At the time, Twitter faced fierce competition from a wide range of players, including Facebook, TikTok, and the New York Times. By leveraging the jobs-to-be-done perspective, Twitter has achieved impressive results, with over 200 million **daily active users (DAUs)** and over $4 billion in annual revenue for 2021 (source: https://www.statista.com).

It's an excellent approach to observe the market and the competitive landscape to understand customers' pain points, identify their wants and needs, and consequently help improve their lives. Product marketing is the team with the outside-in perspective to run the jobs-to-be-done analysis and convert customer and market research into insights to inform the product roadmap and ensure a product-market fit for new products to drive innovation.

Clearly defining target customers

Companies that stay continuously connected to their customers are better positioned to respond to evolving needs and seize new opportunities as they emerge. Focusing on relevant targets not only helps accelerate growth but it helps the company make the right priorities in terms of product development, pricing, and customer support. In addition, companies will be able to nail more personalized customer journeys and onboarding processes according to the specific segment use cases to build the right customer experience and ensure customer-centric approaches.

With inbound, product marketers can build credibility since they are responsible for gathering market and customer insights, which enables them to help product teams understand the following:

- Where is the market expected to be in the short and long term?
- What are the top market segments, and what are the trends in what delivers value?

- How can we differentiate products from those offered by other players in the market?
- What is the value proposition?

Answering these questions, along with others, can aid product teams in prioritizing the extensive lists of features that engineers believe customers may require. Furthermore, this approach can provide a solid justification for why certain features were selected for the product roadmap, thereby aligning teams and establishing a clear direction for where the product is going. To determine which features should be included in the roadmap, product marketers must identify key functions, analysis, and insights that can assist in defining what should be built.

A great example of a customer-centric company that used inbound product marketing to drive innovation and accelerate growth is Uber. They used a customer segmentation strategy to identify how many out of more than 100 million users on the Uber platform were likely to be business travelers using Uber products in a business context.

As a first step of customer segmentation analysis, Uber identified customers paying by personal credit card versus corporate card. The second data point was analyzing the behaviors of those corporate credit card holders/users by checking how many of them requested rides to and from the airport frequently and how many of them were using the Uber platform internationally. Based on this analysis, Uber found that a significant proportion of its customer base was business travelers. As a next step, Uber decided to analyze the user experience to identify their pain points and gaps in the customer journey to build a product that meets customer needs. But that wasn't enough for Uber to understand the unique behaviors of each customer and the different segments within the business travel area. They spent a lot of time doing interviews and running quantitative and qualitative surveys. Based on this deep analysis, Uber was able to identify the different segments within business travel, including jet setters, road warriors, locals, and techies. In addition, they were able to understand their behaviors: executives and VPs were less price-sensitive and more inclined to spend on premium products for comfort, while road warriors were constantly traveling for work since they were either consultants or salespeople, which made them more interested in getting more information about loyalty programs. Then, some combined business travel with leisure, and so on.

Based on this data, Uber was able to build a detailed profile for each persona, which included their role at the company, their needs, what they value, their highest spending category, their behaviors, and the channels they use to communicate.

Uber wanted to build unique solutions that included the right features for each segment, create a personalized experience for each persona, and allow them to plan for the type of ride they wanted. For example, Uber enabled its business riders who used Uber frequently to automate the whole process of expending receipts to make their lives easier and save them time.

By leveraging the insights and data gathered from their customer segmentation analysis and detailed persona profiles, Uber was able to create value propositions and narratives for each customer segment across the diverse markets they targeted.

Through their effective inbound strategies, Uber successfully created millions of new business profiles and drove growth in the total volume of business trips and revenue. This success was rooted in their deep understanding of their audience, as well as the rigorous experimentation they conducted across all channels and content.

Summary

The product market in the 21st century holds significant importance as it requires collaboration across diverse, specialized teams, including product, marketing, and sales. These teams work together to ensure companies maintain a customer-centric approach and continually innovate to meet the ever-evolving needs of their customers. In this context, inbound programs play a crucial role by facilitating these collaborative efforts and driving customer-focused initiatives.

Inbound product marketers play a key role in helping companies gain a competitive advantage by identifying market gaps and understanding the jobs to be done regarding their products. By conducting in-depth market research and analyzing customer data, they can uncover unmet customer needs, pain points, and preferences.

Moreover, inbound product marketers closely examine the top market segments and personas. By doing so, they can help the product team prioritize the features and use cases that align with the needs of these segments, developing products that meet customers' needs.

In the next chapter, we'll talk about outbound product marketing and how it enables product marketers to drive product adoption and accelerate growth.

Outbound Product Marketing – Driving Product Adoption and Growth

3

In the dynamic realm of business, the significance of product marketing cannot be overstated when it comes to fostering growth and achieving success. Within the broader scope of product marketing, outbound product marketing stands out as a prominent strategy that encompasses strategic tactics, positioning, and market expansion. It revolves around proactive outreach to untapped markets, leveraging proven achievements in existing markets as a foundation. Additionally, outbound product marketing emphasizes the iterative process of refining messaging based on valuable feedback, along with the art of crafting compelling go-to-market (GTM) strategies for upcoming products.

At its core, outbound product marketing encompasses a proactive and customer-centric approach. It delves into understanding the unique needs and preferences of target audiences, identifying opportunities for market expansion, and crafting compelling messaging that resonates with potential customers. By utilizing a variety of channels and tools, outbound product marketers aim to capture the attention and interest of prospects, enticing them to explore and embrace the offered solutions.

The success of outbound product marketing lies in its ability to drive adoption and revenue growth. By effectively positioning products, highlighting their value propositions, and reaching the right audience at the right time, organizations can create a powerful impact in the market. Metrics such as sales effectiveness, marketing impact, and product adoption serve as benchmarks for evaluating the effectiveness of outbound product marketing efforts.

In this chapter, we will take a closer look at the pivotal role of outbound product marketing in driving product adoption and revenue growth. We will explore the various aspects of outbound product marketing and discuss key functions at each stage of the GTM strategy. Our focus will be on the different stages of the buyer journey, starting at awareness and ending at adoption.

You'll find answers to key questions in this chapter:

- What is outbound product marketing?
- What are the primary functions of outbound product marketing?
- How does the role of the outbound product marketer evolve across the different stages of the buyer journey?

What is outbound product marketing?

The role of a product marketer is highly dynamic and can vary significantly depending on the size and structure of a company. In many organizations, product marketing is primarily focused on outbound marketing. This involves developing a GTM strategy, crafting messaging that resonates with different personas, and collaborating with stakeholders to launch products successfully.

As an outbound product marketer, you essentially act as a **General Manager (GM)** for the product, assuming ultimate responsibility for its revenue and success. This includes overseeing the product's pipeline, win rate, sales cycle, and other key metrics to ensure it is meeting its revenue targets. To achieve these objectives, you must work closely with sales and customer success teams to ensure the product or segment you support is achieving its goals.

Overall, being an outbound product marketer requires a deep understanding of the target market and the ability to identify the different levers that can drive a product or solution to market. As an outbound product marketer, a deep understanding of the target market and the various factors that can drive a product's success in the market is critical. Additionally, outstanding communication and collaboration skills are necessary to effectively work with cross-functional teams both internally and externally. Being the product's representative entails presenting it on stage, engaging with analysts, and conversing with customers, essentially becoming the face of the product.

Outbound product marketers tackle crucial questions to drive a product's success:

- What is the optimal market or geography to target?
- Which segments or buyer personas align best with the product?
- What does the competitive landscape look like?
- What is the unique positioning and messaging that will resonate with the audience in the new product area?
- What are the most effective marketing and sales enablement strategies/activities?

As previously noted, the outbound product marketer plays a crucial role in building effective GTM plans and strategies to drive product adoption and achieve revenue targets. To accomplish this, the outbound product marketer engages in a range of key activities throughout the GTM process. These activities may include conducting deep competitive analysis and customer research to identify the right segments and their needs, developing value propositions and messaging that resonate with these audiences, creating compelling content and marketing materials, coordinating cross-functional teams across departments, and establishing partnerships with key stakeholders internally and externally, and more. Each of these activities is essential to ensure successful product adoption. Let's take a high-level overview of some of the following critical activities that the outbound product marketer must undertake to bring a product to market effectively:

- Messages and creatives
- GTM campaign timeline
- Marketing plan
- Sales enablement plan
- Performance and measurement

Let's explore each of these in more detail.

Messaging and creatives

Crafting effective product messaging is a critical responsibility for outbound product marketers, and achieving alignment among different stakeholders is crucial for ensuring consistency. Therefore, outbound product marketers work closely with different stakeholders to understand their perspectives and collaborate to develop messaging that resonates with the target audience. Outbound product marketers are responsible for creating messaging documents and reviewing final campaign elements to ensure they align with the product's messaging and goals.

To create compelling messaging, outbound product marketers employ various research techniques, including quantitative surveys and qualitative interviews, to collect data and identify what messages are most effective. Outbound product marketers also test messaging and creatives in real-life scenarios across multiple channels. For example, they may conduct A/B tests of creative, text messages, and landing pages on the company website or through paid advertising on platforms such as Google AdWords or Facebook, as well as on email, social media, and in-product or in-app experiences.

By measuring key metrics such as **conversion rate (CVR)**, **lifetime value (LTV)**, and **average order value (AOV)**, outbound product marketers can determine whether the messaging is resonating with the target audience and adjust their approach accordingly. This may involve modifying their **call-to-actions (CTAs)**, ad content, or headline, among other things. Overall, the goal is to continuously refine and improve the messaging to ensure that it effectively communicates the product's value proposition and drives customer engagement and revenue growth.

GTM campaign timeline

The GTM campaign timeline is part of the outbound product marketer's responsibilities as it provides a structured and strategic approach to bringing products to market and achieving revenue goals. It's a strategic plan that outlines the entire marketing activities timeline, including which channels to use and what type of promotion to offer during each stage of the buyer's journey. For instance, the timeline may specify that a product launch event should occur on a particular date, followed by email campaigns, social media advertising, and a series of webinars. The timeline may also include details such as the specific messaging to be used in each channel and the target audience for each promotion. The timeline also includes a plan for targeting specific geographies at each stage of the campaign. *Figure 3.1* shows a high-level example of a GTM campaign timeline:

Campaign Timeline

Figure 3.1 – Example of a campaign timeline

While outbound product marketers are not responsible for executing specific campaigns, they play a vital role in supporting marketing efforts. This includes working closely with the marketing team to provide guidance on the timing of product releases, key features, and their benefits.

Marketing plan

Effective marketing channels are crucial for reaching your target audience, but the mix of channels will depend on your marketing goals. For example, if your objective is to increase awareness, different channels may be needed than if your goal is to drive adoption. Marketing channels can range from almost-free options, such as building a community or collecting email lists, to targeted paid platforms, such as Google AdWords and Facebook.

As a product marketer, you can build the most effective channel strategy by using surveys and focus groups, among other research tools on platforms such as Google AdWords, to better understand the communication channels each persona group prefers to use or to learn about new products. By gathering these insights, you can create a robust channel strategy that resonates with your target audience, boosting engagement and driving conversions.

In addition to choosing the right channels, a successful marketing plan also requires working closely with the content team to ensure consistent messaging and developing the right content for each stage of the buying journey. As an outbound product marketer, it is critical to acquire users to hit revenue targets, and content plays a vital role in achieving this. When it comes to content marketing, the possibilities are endless, including SEO-led landing pages, social ads, pay-per-click (PPC) text, and guest blogs. However, it is essential to select the right channels and content types that increase product visibility, build credibility and trust, generate traffic and leads, add value, and increase conversions.

Marketing Plan

Demand Generation	Customer Marketing	Content Marketing	Podcasts and Events	Website and SEO	Partner Marketing
• New Campaign • Prospect Email • Web Chat?	• Customer Newsletter • "Company Name" Academy • Video Testimonial • Dedicated Customer Email	• Blog Content • PR • Whitepapers • eBooks*/ Guides • Webinars • Social Campaign • Infographics	• "How to" Video/ Tutorials • Product Video • Thought Leadership Events • Hosted/ Sponsored Events	• Product page • Solutions Pages • Chatbot • Landing Pages	• Newsletter • Partner Portal • Webinar • Joint Blog Content • Campaign

Figure 3.2 – Example of a marketing plan

Overall, a successful marketing plan involves selecting the most effective marketing channels based on your goals and using research tools to understand your target audience's communication preferences. Working closely with the content team to develop the right content for each stage of the buying journey is also critical for achieving revenue targets. By focusing on the right channels and content types, you can increase your product's visibility, build credibility, and drive conversions.

Sales enablement plan

In B2B organizations, the outbound product marketer plays a crucial role in driving sales enablement, particularly in large enterprises with complex purchasing processes and long sales cycles. Their primary responsibility is to collaborate with sales leadership to align goals and develop programs and strategies to meet those goals.

The outbound product marketer works closely with various sales teams to define and implement a sales enablement program that spans the entire customer journey. This includes equipping sales professionals with different types of assets, such as product training and external and internal sales collaterals.

One of the critical aspects of sales enablement is building an effective program that monitors key metrics such as win rate, sales cycle, and so on and running different types of analysis, such as win/loss analysis. By monitoring different metrics and analyzing data, the outbound product marketer can improve the sales process and drive more sales for the organization.

Sales Enablement Plan

Internal Assets	Training	External Collateral
• Product Notification • Roadmap Updates • Sales Email Templates • Sales Scripts • Battlecards • Cheat / Comparison Sheets • Sales / CS Email Signature Updates	• Sales, CS and partner Training • Video Demo • Demo scripts	• Sales One-Pager • Case Studies • Sales Playbook • Sales Pitch Decks • Product Comparison Page

Figure 3.3 – Example of a sales enablement plan

There are several benefits of having a well-designed sales enablement program. By equipping the sales team with the right tools and resources, the program can bring in more customers and help them navigate through the buyer's journey with confidence. Additionally, a successful sales enablement program can help ensure that the product hits its revenue target.

Performance and measurement

To ensure the success of your product marketing efforts, it is crucial to establish appropriate **Objectives and Key Results (OKRs)** and **Key Performance Indicators (KPIs)**. These metrics help you clarify the purpose of your product or feature, devise effective strategies, and execute your plans toward the OKRs. However, it is not sufficient to simply set these goals and measures. To truly gauge the performance of your project over time, you need to carefully select and define the right KPIs to evaluate its success.

While it is true that we strive towards lofty goals and measure their success with standard KPIs and metrics such as product adoption or target revenue, achieving such objectives requires a granular approach. In order to realize our ambitious targets, we must carefully define and pursue a range of activities, including clear and concise OKRs and KPIs that align with our overarching aims. To illustrate, let's consider the scenario of launching a new feature in a specific product category. The ultimate objective is to achieve a high feature adoption rate within a targeted customer segment and generate a specific revenue target within a defined timeframe. To attain this objective, it is crucial to meticulously identify and execute several activities, such as launching tailored ad campaigns on appropriate channels, such as social media and email marketing. Alongside these activities, a set of clearly defined and measurable OKRs is crucial, such as achieving a feature *adoption rate* of 30% within the specified customer segment, with key results comprising increasing the number of positive reviews for the new feature on social media channels by 50% within the stipulated timeframe. Additionally, pertinent KPIs for this objective might include enhancing the **Customer Lifetime Value (CLTV)** of the targeted customer segment by 10% within the specified time frame or curbing the *churn rate* of the designated segment by 5% during the same period.

The key to successful outbound product marketing lies in defining appropriate OKRs and KPIs. These metrics provide clarity and direction for outbound product marketing strategies and guide execution toward achieving the established goals. However, the selection and definition of KPIs must be done carefully to accurately evaluate performance over time.

As previously discussed, a critical aspect of the outbound product marketer's role is bringing a product to market, which entails a series of activities that commence in the pre-launch phase. However, it's essential to acknowledge that the outbound product marketer's responsibilities extend beyond devising GTM strategies and plans to ensure a seamless and effective buying journey. From building awareness to fostering loyalty and advocacy, the outbound product marketer is accountable for the entire customer journey to achieve product adoption and meet revenue targets. Through the implementation of tailored strategies and tactics at each stage of the customer journey, the outbound product marketer can drive product adoption, customer retention, and growth acceleration by developing the right programs and processes. In the upcoming section, we'll take a deeper dive into the tactics utilized at each stage of the customer journey to ensure that the product hits its revenue objectives.

Outbound product marketing and customer journey

As an outbound product marketer, a key component of your role is to guide customers through both the buyer journey and the overall customer journey. To accomplish this, you collaborate closely with marketing, sales, and customer success teams to create strategies and plans that provide a series of positive and seamless experiences to move buyers along the funnel.

The buyer journey consists of several stages that a prospect goes through when considering a purchase or subscription, from initial awareness of the product or service to making a final decision. These stages include researching the product, evaluating its features and benefits, comparing it to alternative options in the market, and finally, making the purchase. Your responsibility as an outbound product marketer is to align each of these stages with captivating content that not only grabs the target audience's attention but also converts them into **marketing** qualified leads (MQLs) and sales qualified leads (SQLS) and, ultimately, loyal advocates of your brand.

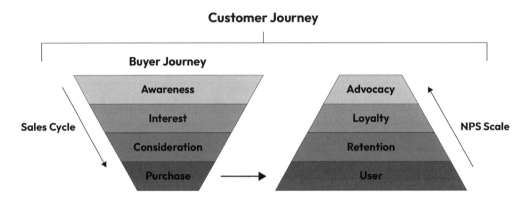

Figure 3.4 – Customer journey

However, your role as an outbound product marketer extends beyond the buyer journey. You also have a crucial responsibility for the entire customer journey, which involves the overall experience that a customer has with a company, from initial awareness and consideration to post-purchase support and advocacy. By providing exceptional customer experiences throughout the entire journey, you can turn customers into brand advocates who promote your products or services and help drive future sales.

You also need to continually monitor and analyze customer data to optimize your efforts and ensure that the customer journey is always evolving and improving.

Let's explore the various stages of the marketing funnel and the decision-making process for buyers while examining the specific role of outbound product marketers in each phase.

Top of the funnel (TOFU) – the problem/need recognition stage

The initial stage of a marketing strategy is critical for engaging the target audience and introducing them to the product and its solution. As an outbound product marketer, your focus should be on identifying the specific need that your product meets and effectively communicating this message to your target audience. Developing a unique value proposition and a compelling selling point is crucial to highlight the ways your product can serve your audience and stand out from competitors.

For example, Amazon Prime's shipping service is a shining example of a value proposition that satisfies customers' need for speed and convenience. By providing a two-day shipping service, Amazon stands out from its competitors, addressing the needs of its customers in a way that resonates with them. As an outbound product marketer, your goal is to create a value proposition that is equally compelling, resonates with your target audience, and sets your product apart in a crowded market.

Middle of the funnel (MOFU) – information search stage

When potential customers recognize that they have a problem that requires a solution, they enter the information-seeking phase. To establish trust with these customers before they make a purchase, it is critical to work closely with your content team to provide them with real value through informative content, such as articles, guides, and e-books. Google is an outstanding example of a company that places a high emphasis on providing potential and existing customers with helpful content. Google provides blogs, guides, and even an academy to enable customers to not only understand how Google's solutions can address their specific needs but also to guide them on how to apply these solutions easily.

By doing so, Google proves that it is offering the best choice, as customers can use the solutions without the need for external support. During this stage, buyers want to ensure they are choosing the right solution. Providing testimonials at various touchpoints, such as the company's website, social media accounts, and emails, will aid buyers in validating their decisions. As an outbound product marketer, it is critical to collaborate with your content team to provide potential customers with informative content that can help establish trust and provide value during the information-seeking phase.

MOFU – evaluation of alternatives

As buyers seek to determine whether a specific product is the right choice or not, they typically want to explore other alternatives. This is a crucial stage in the buying journey where searchable content can help establish your product or service as the preferred solution. As an outbound product marketer, you will need to collaborate with marketing teams, specifically the demand generation and SEO teams, to develop effective targeting strategies that include ads, creatives, and keyword lists while also ensuring SEO-friendliness and being always on.

Simultaneously, you will need to work with third-party blogs and websites, such as G2.com, to provide reviews and endorsements of your products, as well as to compare them with those of your competitors. This approach provides buyers who want to make a decision with testimonials and valuable information to assist them in selecting the most appropriate solution. By working closely with your marketing teams and third-party websites, you can effectively communicate the unique value proposition of your product and establish it as the preferred choice for potential customers during the evaluation stage of the buying journey.

Bottom of the funnel (BOFU) – purchase decision

At this stage, potential buyers are required to make a decision, and this is where you must provide further validation to persuade them to proceed with the purchase. Buyers are likely to withdraw from making a purchase if they are not entirely convinced that your product/solution is the right one for them. As an outbound product marketer, your role is to provide additional content that offers additional testimonials and case studies that demonstrate how your solution has helped other clients, along with positive reviews. This approach provides further validation and supports potential buyers in making an informed decision.

However, at this stage, any negative reviews can have a significant impact on the buyer's decision and cause negative consequences. As a result, it is highly recommended to apply a *flywheel* model to the marketing funnel. The flywheel model can assist you in creating a positive feedback loop that encourages customers to stay engaged with your product, resulting in increased customer satisfaction, loyalty, and advocacy. By focusing on the flywheel model, you can optimize your marketing efforts to cultivate a positive customer experience that will inspire customers to promote your product and become lifelong customers.

To elaborate on the flywheel model, is a marketing approach that emphasizes creating a positive feedback loop that generates momentum and drives growth. In this model, the focus is on delivering a positive customer experience that leads to customer satisfaction, loyalty, and advocacy. By focusing on providing value to customers, the flywheel model encourages customers to stay engaged with your product, resulting in increased customer satisfaction, retention, and acquisition.

The flywheel model involves three key stages:

- **Attract**: This is the first stage. Here, you need to attract potential customers to your product by creating compelling content and promotional campaigns that resonate with your target audience.

- **Engage**: Once you have attracted potential customers, the next step is to engage with them by providing valuable content, personalized messaging, and exceptional customer service.

- **Delight**: The final stage of the flywheel model is to delight your customers by providing them with an exceptional experience that exceeds their expectations. Delighted customers are more likely to become loyal customers and advocates who promote your product to others.

The flywheel model is a customer-centric approach that focuses on creating a positive experience for customers at every stage of the marketing funnel. By prioritizing customer satisfaction and loyalty, the flywheel model can help you build a sustainable marketing strategy that drives long-term growth.

BOFU – post-purchase behavior

In the post-purchase stage, it's essential to prioritize successful retention marketing strategies and deliver a meaningful customer experience. This stage is critical as it helps with retaining customers and driving growth to your business. According to research conducted by Gartner, *"One in three businesses without a loyalty program today will establish one by 2027 to retain high-priority customers."* As an outbound product marketer, your focus should be to collaborate with

CX teams to create personalized experiences and work with the customer loyalty team to build loyalty programs that encourage advocacy and retention.

Creating a referral program for recent buyers is an effective way to build customer loyalty. By growing a group of word-of-mouth marketers through social media platforms or developing your own system, you can incentivize referrals and encourage customers to become advocates for your products. Tesla has successfully integrated a referral program as a core component of their marketing strategy. The program enables customers to share a unique referral code with their acquaintances, and, in return, participants receive a lucrative reward of 1,000 miles of free supercharging with the purchase of a new Tesla car. Additionally, each successful referral also gives them an opportunity to win a Model Y monthly or Roadster supercar quarterly, creating an element of excitement and exclusivity. To make the experience seamless and engaging, Tesla has developed a dedicated app that tracks the entire program and provides users with an effortless and rewarding experience.

By focusing on post-purchase retention marketing strategies and creating loyalty programs, you can not only retain customers but also create product advocates who will inspire other customers to adopt your products. We will discuss post-purchase phases and relevant programs in more depth in *Chapter 11*, *Product–Market Fit – Activation, Engagement, Retention, and Loyalty*.

Summary

A skilled outbound product marketer is like a general manager of a product or segment, tasked with achieving revenue targets amidst a constantly shifting landscape of customer needs. To succeed, they must take a holistic approach to understanding customers, delving beyond their immediate behaviors to uncover the underlying motivations and factors that drive purchasing decisions.

While driving accelerated market outreach and revenue growth is undoubtedly a primary objective, it's important to recognize that developing effective GTM strategies alone isn't sufficient. The outbound product marketer plays a pivotal role in all aspects of the product's post-launch life cycle, tracking its adoption and performance to optimize the customer journey and enhance the overall customer experience. This requires a collaborative approach, working with various teams to develop the right assets, programs, and strategies, ultimately resulting in sustainable growth and customer retention.

The following chapters of the book will delve into essential inbound functions and strategies aimed at fostering innovation.

Part 2
Driving Product Enhancement with Inbound Strategies

This part is dedicated to exploring the essential functions of inbound product marketing, which include market research, customer research, customer segmentation, and buyer persona development. Notably, it also covers how product marketers adeptly influence the product roadmap. Throughout each chapter, we will demonstrate in-depth examples of how these learned strategies are applied to enrich a product, foster innovation, drive higher product adoption rates, and fuel accelerated growth.

This part has the following chapters:

- *Chapter 4, Market Research and Competitive Analysis – Strategies to Enhance Innovation*
- *Chapter 5, Customer Research – Creating Effective Voice of Customer Programs*
- *Chapter 6, Influencing the Product Roadmap*
- *Chapter 7, Customer Segmentation and Personas*

Market Research and Competitive Analysis - Strategies to Enhance Innovation

4

Market research is the science of uncovering hidden truths about a market the secret desires, untapped potential, and unspoken needs of its customers. Through market research, you can explore customer preferences and behaviors, competitor activity, and industry trends. Armed with this knowledge, you can make informed decisions about your products and marketing strategies.

In the upcoming two chapters of this book, we will explore how, as a product marketing manager, you can leverage the data and insights you collect from market research to develop actionable strategies. It's all about working closely with different teams and stakeholders, using this valuable information to make products even better, enhance customer experiences, and maintain a competitive edge.

This chapter will provide answers to essential questions, such as the following:

- What advantages does market research offer, and what are the various types of market research available?
- How can market research help product marketers create effective product marketing strategies?
- How do we leverage competitive analysis to enhance products, improve customer experience, and drive innovation?

Market research and benefits

Companies can struggle to match their products with market demand, risking wasted efforts. Market research helps generate customer-centric ideas and solutions that resonate with the target audience and consequently drive growth. Zendesk, a top-tier provider of customer service software, owes its success to its early adoption of extensive market research. In its early days, the company's founders conducted surveys and interviews with potential customers to gain insight into their customer service struggles and current support request management methods. Through this research, Zendesk was able to identify several key pain points, including the inefficiencies and fragmentation of existing systems to track and address customer inquiries. As a result, Zendesk developed a cloud-based software platform that streamlined the support process, providing a centralized hub to manage customer interactions across multiple channels. Today, Zendesk serves thousands of businesses worldwide as a leading provider of customer service software.

Market research is essential for businesses navigating today's dynamic landscape. It uncovers new opportunities, customer preferences, and competitive insights. By understanding their audience and competitors, companies can tailor products and marketing strategies for growth and customer loyalty. Market research also helps in mitigating risks, testing innovations, and staying competitive. A classic example of a company that overlooked the importance of market research is Blockbuster, a once-dominant player in the home video rental market. With the advent of digital streaming and evolving consumer preferences, Blockbuster failed to adapt to the changing landscape of the industry. Their lack of proper market research led to a failure to recognize the impact of digital streaming on their business. They failed to anticipate the rapid growth of streaming services such as Netflix and didn't invest in the necessary technology to compete in the streaming market. Had they conducted thorough market research, Blockbuster could have stayed abreast of changing market trends and customer preferences, thereby enabling them to remain relevant and ahead of their competitors.

For product marketers, market research is a powerful tool to collect data, analyze it, and convert it into valuable insights, which we can then utilize to make well-informed decisions. Market research is extremely critical for product marketers for several reasons. Firstly, it helps you gain a comprehensive understanding of the market, including the needs and preferences of potential customers, current trends, and competitor offerings. By having this knowledge, product marketers can develop more effective marketing and sales strategies to attract and retain customers. Secondly, market research enables you to identify new opportunities for growth and innovation. By analyzing market data, you can uncover gaps in the market and develop new products or services to fill these gaps, which can lead to increased revenue and market share. Thirdly, market research helps you to evaluate the potential risks associated with launching a new product or service. Let's explore in-depth why market research is an essential tool for product marketers.

Why market research?

Market research serves as a vital tool in the arsenal of product marketers, enabling us to maintain our companies' competitiveness and stay well-informed about customer needs and market trends. By gaining deep insights into our target audience and the broader market landscape, we can craft effective strategies that drive growth and success. As professionals in this field, it's our responsibility to keep our companies updated on evolving market trends and consumer preferences. The following are some key areas that product marketers can delve deep into with the help of market research:

- **Market insights**: Adopting a market research approach enables businesses to identify potential gaps in the market that can be capitalized on. Keeping a finger on the pulse of the latest market trends, including shifts in customer behavior, preferences, and demand, can provide valuable insights to adjust product offerings and marketing strategies accordingly.

Furthermore, customer insights that go beyond basic knowledge of their needs and demographics are essential to build customer loyalty. Through conducting market research, businesses can gain a comprehensive understanding of their various customer segments, create products that meet their specific needs, and develop messaging that resonates with them.

- **Product-market fit**: Achieving a strong product-market fit is essential for the success of any product launch. Through market research, product marketers can gain valuable insights into their target audience's pain points and benefits. This information can then be used to inform the product roadmap and prioritize features that align with the customer's jobs to be done. Market research can also help identify the unique benefits that customers seek in a product or service, which can be leveraged to craft targeted messaging that resonates with them. By effectively highlighting a product's unique value proposition, marketers can increase the chances of product adoption and customer loyalty.

- **Market size and segmentation**: Market research plays a crucial role in helping product marketers identify profitable markets to target and adjust product features and messaging to meet the specific needs of each market. By conducting thorough research, companies can gain insights into the market size and potential, allowing them to identify the most promising customer segments. This enables them to tailor their marketing efforts and product offerings to meet unique market demands, increasing the chances of success and maximizing revenue potential. Additionally, market research empowers companies to assess the growth potential of their products within identified target markets, by providing insights to answer critical questions about consumer suitability and product feature desirability.

- **Competitive landscape analysis**: Conducting competitive analysis is an integral part of market research that empowers product marketers to gain a comprehensive understanding of their main competitors. By performing a competitive analysis, marketers can pinpoint the strengths and weaknesses of their rivals, while also closely monitoring their pricing, promotion, and product development strategies.

Armed with this information, marketers can leverage their product's unique selling points to stand out from the competition, identify areas for innovation, and develop targeted marketing campaigns that resonate with customers. By staying vigilant about the competitive landscape, product marketers can stay ahead of the curve and make informed decisions about a product's roadmap and positioning within the market.

- **Pricing strategy**: Market research plays a pivotal role in helping product marketers determine the optimal pricing strategy for their products. By analyzing several factors, such as a customer's willingness to pay, competitor pricing, and market trends, marketers can set prices that maximize revenue and profitability. In order to set an effective pricing strategy, product marketers must first understand the value that their product provides to customers.

Through market research, they can gain insights into how much customers are willing to pay for the benefits that the product offers. This information can then be used to establish a pricing structure that aligns with customer expectations and maximizes revenue. Moreover, competitive analysis is also a crucial element of pricing strategy development. By evaluating the pricing strategies of competitors, product marketers can identify opportunities to differentiate their products through pricing or set prices that are competitive in the market. Lastly, by keeping a close eye on market trends, product marketers can adjust their pricing strategy to stay relevant and competitive. For example, if the market experiences a shift in demand or supply, product marketers can respond accordingly by adjusting their prices to ensure maximum profitability.

This exploration of market research's multifaceted role in product marketing naturally leads us to crucially consider when it comes into play within the **go-to-market (GTM)** life cycle.

The role of market research across the GTM life cycle

Market research plays a critical role in informing and improving decision-making throughout the GTM life cycle. To ensure a successful GTM launch, it's essential to make sure, as a product marketer, that you are involved in market research early in the product development life cycle. It's important to understand where market research fits into the GTM life cycle and which stages require its integration, from business case justification to launch and post-launch adoption.

However, before embarking on market research, it's crucial to identify the pain point you're trying to address, ideally before building anything. To get started with market research, you should first determine your specific research needs and prioritize the most valuable information. By doing so, you can obtain actionable insights that will inform your decision-making and help you achieve a successful GTM launch.

In my experience, these are the phases where I applied market research to the GTM life cycle:

1. **The exploration/business case justification phase:** Market research can be a valuable tool in this phase, helping businesses identify and evaluate new market opportunities and determine the feasibility of a new product or service:

    I. **Market sizing and total addressable market (TAM) analysis,** where market research can help identify potential customers and determine the maximum potential revenue opportunity for a product in a specific market.

    II. **Market trends analysis,** where market research can give an insight into the current state of the market, including factors such as customer preferences, emerging technologies, and competitive offerings. This information can be used to identify key trends and patterns that may impact the market in the future.

III. **A usage and attitude (U&A) study,** where market research can be used to better understand your market at a deeper level and who is buying what, from where, and how often, in addition to use cases.

IV. **Competitive intelligence,** where market research helps gather information on competitors' product offerings, marketing strategies, and market share.

2. **The pre-launch phase:** Market research plays a critical role in the pre-launch phase, particularly during product development. Here are the ways market research fits into different phases of the pre-launch stage:

   I. **Persona development:** Through market research, you can gather insights into the demographics, psychographics, and pain points of your potential customers, allowing you to create accurate and effective buyer personas.

   II. **Idea screening:** Through market research, you can gather insights such as market demand and the competitive landscape to assess the potential of new product or service ideas.

   III. **Feature prioritization:** By conducting surveys or focus groups, you can identify which features are most important to customers, helping you to inform the product roadmap and enable the product team to allocate development efforts more effectively.

   IV. **Concept testing:** Market research can be used to evaluate the idea of your product or service. This is a great way to gauge consumers' interest and receptiveness, identify potential issues, and address them before the product launch.

   V. **User Experience (UX) research:** By conducting usability tests and analyzing feedback, you can help improve a product's UX and make it more appealing to the target audience.

   VI. **Price optimization:** Market research can help determine the optimal pricing strategy for your product. Through pricing research, you can gather data on customer perceptions of value, willingness to pay, and competitor pricing. This can help your company set the right competitive price, appealing to the target audience and generating profit.

3. **The launch phase:** During the launch phase of the GTM process, market research plays a vital role in enhancing the impact of messaging, packaging, and creative elements. Here are the ways that market research fits into different phases of the launch stage:

   I. **Value proposition/message testing:** Market research can be used to test messaging to determine which resonates best with your target audience. This can involve the use of surveys or A/B testing to compare different messaging strategies.

   II. **Campaign creative testing:** By conducting creative testing, you can obtain insights into how well your marketing messages, visuals, and more resonate with your target audience. This feedback can then be used to make any required adjustments and fine-tune your marketing campaigns for greater impact.

III. **Package testing:** By conducting surveys or focus groups, you can gather feedback on all things related to packaging and make necessary changes before the product launch.

4. **The post-launch phase:** After a product has been launched, the post-launch phase becomes crucial to ensure its continued success and growth. Market research can be an essential tool for businesses during this phase, as it allows them to keep track of key performance indicators, monitor market trends and competition, gather customer feedback, and develop future growth strategies. In this regard, market research can help businesses in several ways:

   I. **Brand and product awareness:** By analyzing metrics such as brand awareness, recall, and sentiment, market research can help companies gain a deeper understanding of how their product is perceived by their target audience. This data can then be used to create effective marketing strategies that resonate with the companies' customers and drive brand awareness and product adoption.

   II. **Voice of customer (VoC) and customer experience (CX) research:** Market research enables businesses to collect feedback from customers and monitor their satisfaction levels. This includes conducting VoC research to obtain insights directly from customers, which can be used to enhance the customer experience. We will discuss this in more detail in *Chapter 5*.

   III. **Prioritizing product enhancements:** By collecting input from customers about their requirements and preferences, market research can assist companies in prioritizing product enhancements and the development of new features. This data can be used to establish ongoing product development strategies that guarantee that the product remains relevant for the long term.

   IV. **Thought leadership content:** Utilizing market research or analyzing available data can assist in producing content that showcases expertise and reliability within your industry.

   V. **Ongoing competitive intelligence:** Market research helps you stay informed about competition and the broader market landscape, which is essential in maintaining the competitiveness and relevance of your product in the long term.

It is important to note that PMMs should not be accountable for all aspects of market research. To ensure clear ownership of your research projects, consider creating a **Driver, Approver, Contributor, Informed (DACI)** chart. This chart will help identify who is responsible for each research initiative, and it may make sense for different teams, such as strategy, product, product design, and UX research, to share the workload. The following section will explore the different methods of market research. It's essential to understand the various approaches to data collection and analysis to effectively plan and communicate your research within an organization.

Primary versus secondary research

As a PMM, you will likely have a good understanding of the target customers and the overall business objectives. However, conducting market research and analysis requires specific skills and expertise in data analysis and research methods. This is where your collaboration with analytics and strategy experts comes into play. These experts can provide valuable insights and help you understand the data that is being gathered. They can also help you identify trends and patterns that you may have missed on your own.

Your role in guiding the research is critical. You can help ensure that the research is aligned with the business objectives and that the insights gained from the research are actionable. You can also help communicate the research findings to stakeholders within the company, in a way that is easy to understand and can be used to make informed decisions.

It's often recommended to use multiple research methods, as they can complement each other and provide a more comprehensive understanding of the subject matter. However, with numerous research methods available, it can be challenging to select the most suitable ones for your needs. Without a clear understanding of the types of data and the best ways to collect and process them, you risk making costly mistakes that could hinder the success of your research. Therefore, gaining familiarity with various research methods can significantly enhance your ability to conduct research effectively and achieve your desired outcomes.

There are two types of market research *primary* research and *secondary* research.

Primary research is the original research conducted by an organization to gather data directly from the source. This type of research involves collecting data from surveys, interviews, focus groups, and observations. Primary research provides you with specific and tailored information, which allows you to gather insights that are relevant to your specific needs.

Conversely, secondary research involves analyzing information that has already been gathered and published by other sources. This information can be found in industry reports, government publications, and other publicly available sources. Secondary research provides a broad overview of the market and can be a cost-effective way to gather information, but it may not be tailored to your company's specific needs.

The following diagram illustrates various types of market research, along with examples of each type:

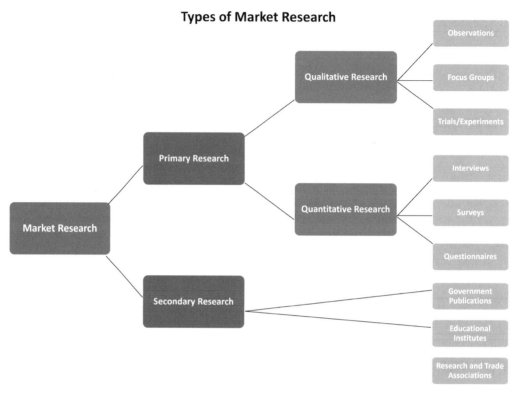

Figure 4.1 Types of market research

Both primary and secondary research have their advantages and disadvantages. Primary research is more expensive and time-consuming, but it provides specific and tailored information. Secondary research is less expensive and quicker, but the information may not be as specific to a company's needs.

Primary market research

One of the most common methods of conducting market research is through *primary research*. This approach involves collecting data directly from customers or external sources on behalf of a company. Essentially, primary research is conducting fieldwork, and it provides several benefits that can give a business a competitive edge.

One key advantage of primary research is its *context-specific* nature, which allows researchers to focus on questions that are tailored to the specific needs and interests of their target audience. By asking questions that haven't been asked before, primary research can uncover new insights that businesses may not have previously considered. These fresh perspectives can be invaluable in helping a company identify new opportunities or refine its approach to better meet customer needs.

Perhaps the most significant benefit of primary research is that it can provide a business with a competitive advantage by providing unique knowledge that is not available to its competitors. By gathering data on their customers' preferences, behaviors, and experiences, businesses can develop a deeper understanding of what their customers want and need. Armed with this knowledge, they can make informed decisions about product development, marketing strategy, and other key areas that can help them stay ahead of the competition.

In the realm of primary research, it is essential to differentiate between two types of information *exploratory* and *specific*.

Exploratory research

This is an approach that focuses on gaining new perspectives and insights about a particular topic (in contrast to specific research, which is geared toward answering specific questions or addressing particular issues). Exploratory research does not aim to provide conclusive results but, rather, to help researchers better understand a topic and identify areas that may require further investigation. Through exploratory research, researchers can assess the feasibility of their research questions, gain insights into relevant variables, and refine their research objectives. This can ultimately help save time and resources by ensuring that subsequent research efforts are focused and informed by a more comprehensive understanding of the topic. As such, the exploratory stage is a valuable tool to map out the direction and next stages of a research project.

Specific research

Unlike exploratory research, which aims to uncover new perspectives on a particular topic, *specific research* (also referred to as descriptive research) is a structured and focused approach that addresses a specific problem or research question identified during the exploratory phase. The goal of specific research is to gather data that defines the attitudes, opinions, or behaviors of individuals or groups related to a particular topic. This type of research often utilizes surveys or questionnaires and yields quantifiable and measurable data. By relying on a structured approach, specific research can help reduce the risk of bias in the research process, leading to more accurate and reliable insights and conclusions. This reliability is essential to make informed decisions based on research findings.

Primary research involves collecting data directly from the source, which can be done using various methods. Some of the most commonly used methods for primary research include the following:

- Interviews: One-on-one conversations between a researcher and a respondent, where the researcher asks questions to gather information about the respondent's opinions, experiences, and attitudes.

- **Focus groups:** Sessions designed to provide a more comprehensive understanding of a specific topic or issue by engaging participants in interactive discussions. Focus groups can be conducted either in person or online, depending on the needs of the research project.
- **Trials/experiments:** Testing a product/feature or marketing campaign with a sample of potential customers.
- **Observations and ethnographies:** Observing individuals or groups in their natural environment to gather data about their behaviors, habits, and interactions.
- **Surveys and questionnaires:** A form of questions distributed to a significant number of participants. Surveys and questionnaires can be conducted online, by mail, or in person.

Quantitative versus qualitative data

Primary research involves collecting data using both *quantitative* and *qualitative* methods. Quantitative research involves the collection of numerical data through structured methods, such as surveys, questionnaires, and experiments. Qualitative research involves the collection of non-numerical data through open-ended interviews, observations, and focus groups.

Both quantitative and qualitative research methods can be used in primary research to collect new data directly from the source. Using a combination of both quantitative and qualitative methods in primary research can provide a more comprehensive understanding of a topic. Each method has its strengths and limitations, and choosing the right one depends on the research questions and objectives. We will now delve into each method in more detail.

Qualitative data

As a product marketer, you hold a crucial responsibility to integrate the voice of the customer into your product marketing strategies. That's why qualitative research is a valuable tool for you to gather customer-based information. Through this method, you're able to gather insights into your customers' behaviors and attitudes, allowing you to gain a better understanding of the context in which they'll use your product. By using open-ended and unstructured techniques to collect data, you're able to uncover nuanced information that may not be easily quantifiable. Of course, qualitative research has its limitations. The sample size is often small, which may make it difficult to generalize findings. Also, because the interpretation of qualitative data is subjective, it can be challenging to analyze and draw conclusions. However, investing time and effort in this type of research can give you a competitive edge. By speaking directly to your customers and gathering their perceptions, you're able to create accurate and detailed personas, identify areas for improvement, and even find new product opportunities.

When it comes to gathering customer insights through qualitative research, *one-to-one interviews* are often the method of choice. The benefits of speaking to customers individually are numerous. Firstly, individuals are more likely to share deeper insights into their experiences and ideas when they have your undivided attention. In a one-to-one interview, there are no competing voices or group dynamics to influence their responses, making their feedback more authentic and reflective of their thoughts. Moreover, one-to-one interviews allow product marketers to adjust their interview style to match a participant's personality, making them feel comfortable and more likely to share honest feedback. This approach is particularly helpful for participants who may not feel comfortable sharing their opinions in a group setting. One-to-one interviews are also useful for B2B companies looking to understand their customers' needs and experiences. In a one-to-one interview, participants can feel more at ease discussing sensitive topics without the worry of their competitors hearing their thoughts.

One-to-one interviews can certainly provide valuable insights for product marketers looking to gather customer feedback. However, *focus groups* offer a unique opportunity to engage participants in collaborative discussions and idea exchanges. Group dynamics can lead to more in-depth conversations, as participants can bounce ideas off of one another and build upon each other's opinions. Focus groups are a valuable tool for product marketers in multiple ways. Firstly, they allow for brainstorming market trends by providing a platform for participants to share their opinions and experiences. This can help product marketers identify emerging trends in the market and adjust their product development or product marketing strategies accordingly. Secondly, focus groups can help test out different concepts before a product or service goes into production, leading to a more successful product launch by identifying potential issues or areas for improvement early on in the development process. This can save time and resources in the long run. Additionally, focus groups can help test messaging for a product or service. Product marketers can use them to obtain feedback on different messaging options, such as taglines, slogans, or product descriptions. This ensures that the messaging resonates with the target audience and effectively communicates the benefits of the product or service.

Another method of qualitative research is ethnographies or customer observations. This method involves observing customers in their natural environment, such as their homes, workplaces, or other settings where they interact with products or services. One of the main benefits of ethnographic research is that it allows product marketers to see firsthand how their customers use and interact with their products or services. This can reveal valuable insights into customer needs, preferences, and pain points that may not be apparent through other research methods. For example, a product marketer observing a customer using a product in their home may notice that the customer struggles with a particular feature or experiences frustration with the product's design, leading to ideas for improvements or new product features. Ethnographies also allow product marketers to gain a more nuanced understanding of their customer's behaviors and cultures within a social context. By observing customers in their natural environment, product marketers can see how they interact with others, the role the product or service plays in their daily lives, and how it fits into their broader cultures and social norms. This can be particularly valuable to develop messaging or marketing campaigns that resonate with customers on a deeper level and speak to their values and beliefs. However, it is important to note that conducting ethnographic research requires a significant investment of time and resources. Product marketers must be willing to immerse themselves in their customers' environments and be patient in observing and documenting their behavior. Additionally, ethical considerations must be taken into account, such as obtaining consent from participants and ensuring their privacy and confidentiality. Despite these challenges, ethnographic research can provide invaluable insights into customer behavior and culture.

Defining the primary research method depends on the research questions and the target audience. For example, if the research question is about understanding customer satisfaction, surveys or interviews may be the most appropriate methods, whereas if the research question is about understanding consumer behavior, observations and ethnographies may be more suitable. Conversely, answering a research question might involve a combination of research methods qualitative and quantitative.

A great example here is the Amazon Research and Experimentation team (also known as the A/B testing team). The A/B testing team at Amazon uses a combination of qualitative and quantitative research methods to test and optimize the performance of various elements of Amazon's website and customer experience. For example, they may conduct usability testing to gather qualitative data on how customers navigate the site and what issues they encounter. They may also use A/B testing to collect quantitative data on the effectiveness of different design elements, such as the placement of buttons or the wording of product descriptions. By combining these different research methods, the A/B testing team is able to gain a more comprehensive understanding of how customers interact with Amazon's website and develop insights that drive continuous improvement of the customer experience. Additionally, their multidisciplinary approach enables them to make data-driven decisions that can help optimize Amazon's conversion rates, customer satisfaction, and overall business performance.

Quantitative data

As a product marketer, your role often involves launching new products for your company. However, launching a new product without understanding your target market and their needs can be risky. Imagine you have a limited budget and time frame to gather insights about your target market. This is where quantitative research comes in as a valuable tool in the research process.

Quantitative research is an approach that involves collecting numerical data to uncover variables, such as attitudes, opinions, behaviors, and trends. It can provide valuable insights that might not be immediately apparent through qualitative research methods. One of the key advantages of quantitative research is that it allows for the collection of large amounts of data in a relatively short amount of time, and at a lower cost than other research methods. By using standardized methods of data collection such as surveys or questionnaires, you can easily distribute them to a large sample size. This can help to produce statistically significant results and increase the generalizability of the findings. Another important advantage of quantitative research is that it provides objective and reliable data. Because the data collected through quantitative research is numerical and can be analyzed using statistical methods, there is less chance of bias or subjective interpretation. This can help to produce more accurate results and increase the credibility of the research findings.

With these insights gathered through quantitative research, you can better understand your target market and their needs. This can inform important decisions, such as messaging, market segmentation, pricing, customer feedback, and prioritizing product features.

Quantitative research is often associated with closed-ended *questionnaires and surveys*, which are popular methods to gather consistent and statistical data. They are affordable, reliable, and efficient ways for small start-ups to do market research that is specific to their target market. Surveys and questionnaires are also quicker and easier for respondents to answer, which means you are likely to receive more responses. Surveys can be conducted in a variety of ways, including the following:

- Over the phone
- Online
- Mail
- Face to face

When Slack, a messaging platform for teams to communicate and collaborate, first launched its product, it conducted a quantitative survey to understand its target market better. The survey included closed-ended questions that asked respondents about their communication preferences, their use of existing tools, and their pain points with those tools. Slack distributed the survey to a sample of their target audience through online ads, social media, and email marketing campaigns. By using a quantitative research method, Slack was able to gain valuable insights into its target audience's preferences and pain points, which helped them to develop a product that solved a real problem and met a genuine need. This, in turn, helped Slack to gain a foothold in a crowded market and establish itself as a major player in the team communication space.

It's worth mentioning that qualitative research provides rich insights and context, guiding early decisions and uncovering nuanced user perspectives. However, it's when coupled with quantitative research that businesses gain the statistical confidence needed for scalable, data-driven decision-making, ensuring a well-rounded research strategy. Now, let's move on to secondary market research.

Secondary market research

Secondary research, also known as *desk-based research*, is a method of gathering information that already exists and has been published by other sources. This information can be obtained from various sources, such as research institutions or market research firms. Secondary research is useful because it can provide a comprehensive and cost-effective way of gathering information about the market. Generally, secondary research serves as a preliminary step prior to primary research. You can acquire secondary data from multiple internal and external sources without any cost. This is why for small businesses with limited budgets, secondary research is often the preferred choice, as it can be obtained more quickly and affordably than primary research.

Secondary market research can be classified into two subcategories *internal* and *external* research. Internal sources can include customer details or sales reports, for example, while external sources are publicly accessible and can be obtained through government websites, industry reports, and so on.

The following are some resources for both internal and external sources to collect secondary data:

- Internal sources:
  - Customer relationship management (CRM): Analyze interactions with customers and identify trends.
  - Customer feedback: Feedback from customers, such as surveys, can be analyzed to identify areas where a company's products or services can be improved.
  - Sales reports: Provide valuable information on products or service performance, revealing which are selling well and which are not. This data can be used to identify market trends.
  - Analytics platforms: Google Analytics and mobile analytics software such as AppsFlyer are examples of tools that can provide valuable insights into users' behaviors, how they interact with your products, what features they use the most, and how often they use them.

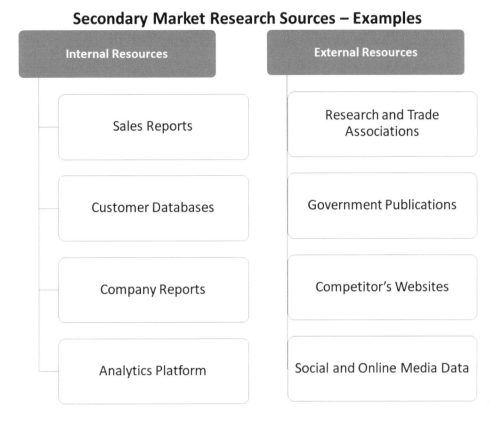

Figure 4.2 Examples of secondary market research sources

- External sources:
  - Government data: Governments publish data on demographics, spending habits, commodity use, and so on that can be accessed through their websites. This enables you to gain insights into consumer behavior and market trends. The US Small Business Administration and the Bureau of Labor Statistics are examples of free government data sources.
  - Market research reports: Market research firms conduct surveys to gather data on consumer behavior and market trends. eMarketer, Gartner, and Statista, and Forrester are popular examples of such firms.
  - Competitor websites and apps: Analyzing competitors' websites and mobile apps can reveal crucial information about your target audience's preferences, which can be used to inform your product roadmap and GTM strategy. You can access this data through their product demos, free trials, and newsletter/blog subscriptions. Later in this chapter, we'll take a deep delve into what competitive analysis involves.

- ° **Social and online media data:** Social media data provides insights into user behavior, including engagement. Product marketers can use this information to identify opportunities to connect with target audiences.

- ° **Academic research:** Academic researchers frequently conduct research on consumer behavior and market and industry trends. **Harvard Business Review (HBR)** is an example of an academic journal that features articles and research on various subjects, such as marketing, strategy, and leadership.

Now that we've discussed the types of market research in detail, we're ready to move on to the next part of the chapter, where we will delve into competitive intelligence.

Competitive intelligence

Competitive intelligence (CI) plays an essential role in product marketing. Keeping a close eye on your competition provides valuable insights into their strategies, strengths, and weaknesses. These insights can then be used to inform your product roadmap to enhance existing products and develop innovative ones, ultimately leading to meeting your customer's needs and providing better customer experiences. CI can provide several benefits, including the following:

- **Identifying your competitive advantage:** By analyzing your competitors' strengths and weaknesses, you can identify opportunities to differentiate yourself from them.

- **Understanding your target market:** Through competitive analysis, you can gain insights into the needs and preferences of your target market. This information can help you develop products and services that meet those needs and stand out from your competitors.

- **Identifying industry trends and gaps in the market:** Monitoring your competitor's activities enables you to identify trends and changes in your industry and adapt your business strategy accordingly.

- **Improving product development:** By analyzing your competitors' products and services, you gain insights into what works and what doesn't. This enables you to improve your products and services and stay competitive.

- **Enhancing customer experience:** Understanding how your competitors interact with their customers allows you to identify areas where you can improve your own customer experience.

It can be overwhelming for you to keep up with every move of your competitors, especially when juggling other responsibilities. As product marketers, we require competitive intelligence tools that can offer real-time coverage, immediate mention alerts, and a dedicated report for competitive analysis. These tools should automate the research process and provide a comprehensive overview of the competitive landscape. Fortunately, there are competitive intelligence tools available that provide the necessary information without sacrificing countless hours of research.

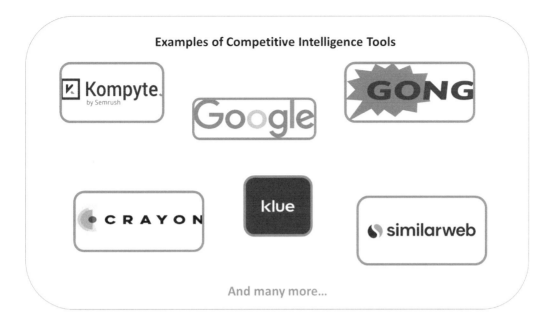

Figure 4.3 Examples of competitive intelligence tools

These competitive tools facilitate the seamless sharing of vital information across teams on a regular basis.

Best practices to execute effective competitor analysis

To conduct a successful competitive analysis, you need to first identify your competitors. Keeping a close watch on them not only provides valuable market insights but also helps you uncover gaps in your own product offerings. By examining the strategies of your competitors, you can gain useful knowledge from their successes and failures and use it to develop a product differentiation strategy that sets you apart from the competition.

It's also important to consider competitors from different industries. These companies may have found unique ways to differentiate themselves that could be applicable to your industry. For example, a technology company might learn from the customer service approach of a luxury hotel chain, or a clothing retailer might find inspiration in the marketing tactics of a popular snack food brand. You may be competing against products or services that are not immediately obvious. For example, a coffee shop may be competing against energy drinks or tea as much as they are against other coffee shops. By broadening your perspective on competition, you can identify new opportunities for innovation, differentiation, and growth.

As mentioned earlier, after conducting research and building a comprehensive profile of your competitors, you'll be ready to put your findings to use. The first step is to categorize your competition into two groups *direct and indirect*. When dividing your competition into direct and indirect categories, it's important to note that direct competitors are companies that offer similar products or services to your own and often target the same customer base as you. Direct competitors are typically the most obvious and immediate threat to your business, as they are vying for the same customers and revenue streams, and they operate in the same geographic location. Conversely, indirect competitors are companies that offer products or services that are not exactly the same as yours but can be seen as substitutes or alternatives to your offerings. Indirect competitors may not be targeting the exact same customer base as you, but they could satisfy the same customer need or solve the same problem, and they still compete for your customer's attention, time, and money.

While it's essential to focus mainly on your direct competitors when comparing your brand, it's important not to overlook indirect competitors entirely. They may present new opportunities or pose potential threats, and they could quickly become direct competitors in the future. Remaining vigilant about both direct and indirect competitors can help you stay informed about changes in the market and adjust your strategy accordingly. By staying proactive and adaptable, you can maintain a competitive edge and continue to meet your customer's evolving needs and preferences.

Competitive Analysis - Checklist

Evaluate competitors product quality	Compare their product features with yours	Analyze your competitors' pricing strategy	Asses their distribution channels	Understand your competitor' target audience	Check how they differentiate their products
Examine customer reviews and ratings to identify common complaints for issues.	Make note of any unique features that differentiate your competitors' product.	Pay attention to discounts or promotions and comparing online pricing with in-store pricing.	Look at your competitors online presence, physical stores, and partnerships with other businesses.	Study their customer needs, you can identify any gaps in the market that you can fill.	This could be through unique features, branding or marketing messages.

Figure 4.4 The key steps to conduct competitive analysis

Conducting research on your competitors is crucial to gain a better understanding of the market and to benchmark your own growth against theirs. You can gather important information, such as their founding date and fundraising rounds, from websites such as Crunchbase or LinkedIn. Surveys and other methods can also be used to gather data on the products and companies that are most commonly used, providing insights into your competitors' market share. While larger companies may invest heavily in competitive research, smaller businesses can still gain valuable insights without spending a significant amount of money. By leveraging available resources and analyzing data, you can stay ahead of the competition and make informed decisions that drive your business forward.

Analyzing your competitors' products can provide valuable insights and help you identify opportunities to improve your own products and gain a competitive edge in the market. Research their products thoroughly by looking at their website, product catalogs, and online reviews to understand what products are distributed, the key features, and the benefits of those products. Also, pay attention to the packaging, branding, and marketing messages used to promote their products.

While it's true that keeping up with competitors by implementing product enhancements and new features can help you maintain a competitive edge and meet evolving customer needs, it's important to avoid getting caught up in a feature war. Instead, focus on your own unique value proposition and strengths. To prevent your product team from becoming a feature factory, it's crucial to prioritize features based on their importance and potential impact on user experience. A clear product roadmap can help you stay focused and deliver high-quality user experiences that provide real value to your customers.

Now, let's delve deeper into the practice of sharing competitive analysis among various teams.

Sharing competitive analysis across teams

It's important to conduct competitive intelligence regularly to stay up to date with your competitors' actions and market trends. The frequency of competitor research can vary, depending on the number of products you're monitoring and your company's stage in the life cycle. However, it's generally advisable to conduct competitive intelligence at least once a month to stay ahead of the competition and make informed business decisions. Additionally, if you're launching a new product or service or enhancing your product or service, it's critical to conduct competitor research to ensure your solutions are competitive and meet the needs of your target audience. Providing different teams with regular competitive analysis and updates is crucial. This allows the sales, marketing, and product teams to stay informed about the ever-changing competitive landscape and make informed decisions about product strategy and development.

It is also important to note that real-time competitive intelligence can be valuable, but it can also be overwhelming and difficult to manage. By providing a structured and consistent approach to competitive analysis, teams can avoid getting lost in the noise and focus on actionable insights and recommendations. Furthermore, documenting and sharing competitive insights and recommendations in a timely manner is essential to effectively inject information from the marketplace into product development. This allows the product development team to act on relevant information quickly and make informed decisions about product features, pricing, and positioning. Every month, I share with my team a newsletter that provides a summary of the latest competitive developments, including changes to competing products, acquisitions, funding, pricing updates, headcount changes among competitors, and any other relevant competitor mentions that I have tracked through a CI tool. This regular update ensures that my team remains informed about important market trends and can make informed decisions based on the latest competitive intelligence.

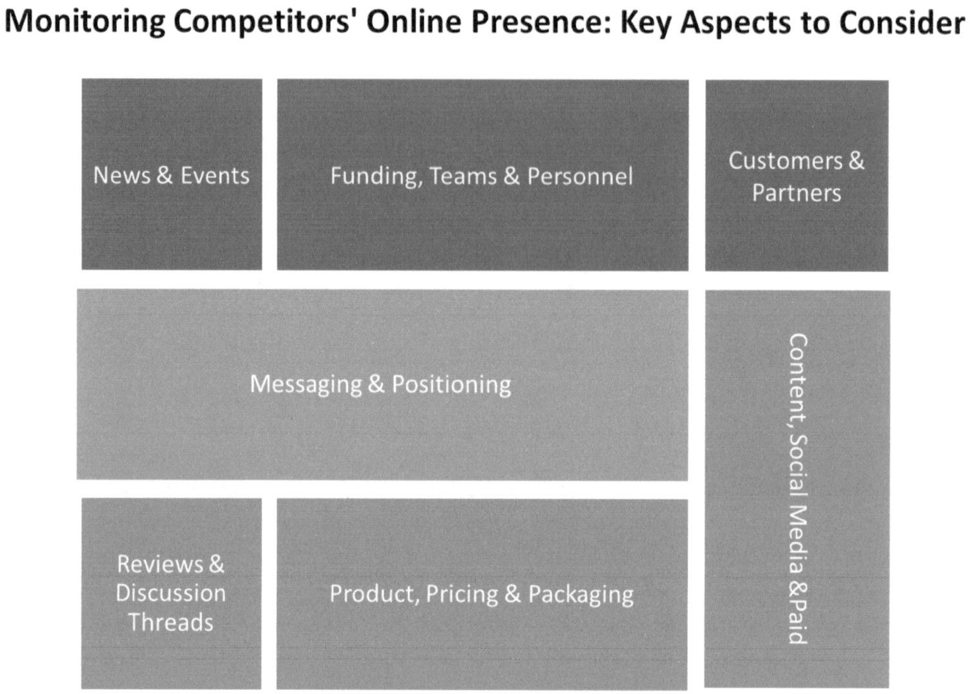

Monitoring Competitors' Online Presence: Key Aspects to Consider

Figure 4.5 The key aspects to consider when monitoring competitors' activities

In my experience, the product development process is very different from marketing and sales. For sales and marketing, I set some goals across the customer journey. Although some of these goals may not be easily quantifiable, they can still serve a valuable purpose in tracking progress. Incorporating competitive differentiation at every stage of the customer journey can help you stand out from your competitors, improve your sales processes, and increase your opportunity to win. From top-of-funnel branding to bottom-of-funnel sales enablement, every touchpoint is an opportunity to showcase your unique value proposition and persuade prospects to choose you over the competition.

At the *top of the funnel*, focus on incorporating competitive differentiation in your primary brand messaging and properties such as websites, marketing campaigns, and social media platforms. This will help prospects become familiar with your unique value proposition and distinguish you from your competitors. To measure your success, you can compare your SEO and web performance against your closest competitors.

In the *middle of the funnel*, use competitive differentiation in your materials, campaigns, and other tactics to engage prospects and educate them about your products or services. This can include case studies, white papers, and other resources that highlight your unique features and benefits. By doing so, you can help prospects understand why your offerings are better than those of your competitors.

Finally, at the *bottom of the funnel*, enable your sales team with battlecards, objection-handling strategies, and rip-and-replace customer stories that emphasize your competitive advantages. This will help your sales team overcome objections and close deals more effectively. You should also regularly update your sales materials to reflect what you've learned from your competitors and how you've differentiated yourself from them. In *Chapter 10*, *Enabling Your Sales Team and Maximizing Effectiveness*, we will delve deeper into equipping sales teams with collaterals that emphasize our competitive advantages.

Competitive analysis is a great insight resource for product managers and product development teams as they work to create a roadmap for their products. Competitive analysis provides insights into the competitive landscape and emerging market trends. It helps in understanding how your products compare to those of its competitors, allowing you to make informed decisions on feature prioritization and product differentiation strategies.

Integrating CI throughout the GTM and product launch plan

By conducting a thorough competitive analysis, companies can gain a better understanding of their competitor's strengths and weaknesses and identify opportunities to develop innovative products or features that meet unmet needs in the market. Furthermore, competitive intelligence can also help companies stay up to date on emerging trends and technologies, providing valuable insights that can inform product development decisions and drive innovation. In this part, we will examine some of the most prevalent forms of competitive analysis that can provide such valuable insights.

Substitute analysis (part of Porter's five forces)

As previously mentioned, it is crucial to take into account competitors that are not just in the same industry but also those that offer similar products or services. This is commonly referred to as keeping an eye open for substitutes. These are products or services that are not in the same category as your product or service but can fulfill the same customer needs or jobs to be done. Customers may consider substitutes when they are looking for alternatives to the product or service offered by your company.

Cloud-based solutions are a great example of substitutes for on-premises (on-prem) solutions, as they offer the same jobs to be done due to their similar functionalities, but they offer the added advantage of being accessed through the cloud instead of requiring local installation on a company's own infrastructure. On-prem software demands businesses to invest in their own IT infrastructure, including hardware, software licenses, and IT staff to support it. During my time at Microsoft, we took significant steps to encourage our customers to shift to cloud-based solutions, such as Azure and Office 365, rather than relying on on-prem software. This strategy helped us to retain our customers, remain competitive, and cement Microsoft's position as an industry leader.

In line with Porter's Five Forces model, the threat of substitutes is a key factor that determines the competitive dynamics of an industry. This threat refers to the extent to which consumers can easily switch to comparable products or services. When there are multiple substitute products or services available, consumers gain more leverage and can choose to purchase from competitors or other industries, thereby reducing the market share of firms in that industry. In industries where substitute products or services are abundant, businesses may encounter more intense competition and may need to either reduce prices or differentiate their products in order to remain competitive.

Monitoring Competitors' Online Presence: Key Aspects to Consider

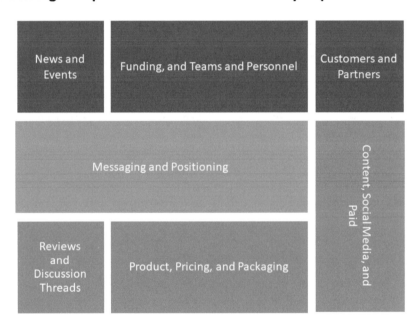

Figure 4.6 The key steps to perform a substitute analysis

By understanding what factors lead customers to choose substitutes, companies can develop innovative solutions that address these factors and better differentiate their products from the substitutes. This can include improving product features, offering better pricing, enhancing the customer experience, or targeting new customer segments.

In addition, substitute analysis can also help companies identify emerging trends and new opportunities for innovation. For example, if a company discovers that customers are using a new technology or product as a substitute, they may choose to explore developing a similar product or partnering with the substitute to offer complementary services. Slack is a widely adopted communication and collaboration platform for teams across various industries. Despite its popularity, the company recognized the potential threat of substitutes, such as email, group chat applications, and video conferencing software, that could pose a risk to its market position. To stay ahead of the competition, Slack's competitive intelligence team conducted comprehensive research on these substitutes to identify areas for improvement and differentiation. They discovered that the lack of integrations with other software applications was a significant pain point for businesses, which prompted Slack to develop an API that allowed third-party applications to integrate with their platform.

This strategic move proved to be a game-changer for Slack, helping the company establish itself as a leader in the team communication and collaboration market. Today, Slack remains one of the most popular and widely used team communication and collaboration platforms available.

SWOT analysis

Competitive intelligence can play a crucial role in shaping a company's product roadmap by providing insights into the strengths and weaknesses of its competitors' products, as well as emerging trends in the marketplace. By analyzing this information, a company can make informed decisions about which features to prioritize, which markets to target, and how to differentiate its products from those of its competitors.

For example, if a company's main competitor releases a new product with advanced features that the company's existing product doesn't have, competitive intelligence can help the company identify whether those features are likely to be in high demand and whether they should be added to the product roadmap. Similarly, if the company's competitors gain traction in a particular market segment, competitive intelligence can help the company decide whether to focus its product development efforts on that segment.

After gathering enough information about your competitors, you can leverage your findings to create a SWOT analysis. This strategic planning and management framework allows you to identify your competitors' strengths, weaknesses, opportunities, and threats. Keep in mind that a SWOT analysis isn't limited to analyzing your competition. It's also an effective tool to evaluate your own company's strengths, weaknesses, opportunities, and threats.

Example of a SWOT Analysis for a Competitor

Strengths

- Established brand with a loyal customer base
- Wide range of product offerings
- Efficient supply chain and logistics network
- Strong online presence and e-commerce capabilities

Weaknesses

- Limited international presence compared to competitors
- Slow to adopt new technologies and innovations
- Higher pricing compared to some competitors
- Some negative customer reviews on product quality

Opportunities

- Expanding into new markets and regions
- Developing new products to capture market share
- Leveraging emerging technologies to improve customer experiences
- Partnerships with other companies in the industry

Threats

- Intense competition from other players in the industry
- Economic downturns impacting consumer spending
- Disruptive technologies that may make traditional offerings obsolete
- Potential supply chain challenges - natural disasters

Figure 4.7 An example of a SWOT analysis for a competitor

There are four areas designated for SWOT analysis:

1. Strengths

2. Weaknesses

3. Opportunities

4. Threats

Strengths

Assessing your strengths is important to determine where your company excels. It provides insights into what you should focus on, identifies potential competitive advantages (or those that could be developed with additional effort), and helps you stay ahead of the competition.

Your strengths may include a range of factors, such as successful product features, strong leadership, sustained growth, positive customer feedback, revenue generation, or effective marketing campaigns. To compile a comprehensive list of strengths, consider what sets your company apart from others in your industry or market. If you're not sure where to start when compiling your strengths list, consider asking yourself these questions:

- What makes our product or service unique?

- What do our customers appreciate most about our product?

- What are some key accomplishments we've achieved as a company?

- What skills or expertise do we have that other companies in our industry may not possess?

By understanding your strengths, you can leverage them to differentiate yourself from competitors, expand your market share, and enhance your overall performance. Therefore, it's crucial to regularly evaluate your strengths and build upon them to remain competitive and achieve long-term success.

When using a SWOT analysis to evaluate your competitor, it's important to remember that your competitors have strengths and that you need to approach their "strengths" section in the same way you did for your own company. By fully understanding their strengths, you can also identify potential threats and weaknesses that your company may face in the future.

Weaknesses

Assessing your weaknesses is important to identify and address what may be holding your company back. If you struggle to identify your company's weaknesses, here are some questions to consider:

- What are the areas where your business underperforms compared to competitors?

- What are the most common customer complaints or pain points?

- What features are missing from your product?
- Are there any internal processes or systems that cause inefficiencies or bottlenecks?
- Are there any skills or expertise that your team lacks?

By asking yourself such questions, you can gain a better understanding of your company's weaknesses and start taking steps to address them. Remember, identifying weaknesses is not about being critical or negative; it's about recognizing areas where you can improve to drive growth and success.

In addition, when analyzing your competitors' weaknesses, you can gather valuable intel by looking at their business model, customer reviews, and press coverage. This can help you identify areas where they may have fallen short, such as lacking robust product features. By calling out these weaknesses in your analysis, you can gain a better understanding of how you can differentiate yourself and gain a competitive advantage.

Opportunities

Opportunities are where you identify external factors that could potentially benefit your business. These opportunities could be in the form of market changes, emerging trends, technological advancements, or any other development that could give your business a competitive advantage.

It's important to keep in mind that opportunities are often tied to external factors such as changes in the market or regulatory landscape. By monitoring these external factors, you can identify opportunities that could help your business grow and thrive.

When building your opportunities list, consider asking yourself the following questions to gain a deeper understanding of your business's potential growth areas:

- Are there any emerging trends or changes in the market that your company can leverage?
- Are there any untapped customer segments/markets that your company can expand into?
- What are the areas where your competitors are weak, and how can your business fill those gaps?
- Are there any new technologies or innovations that your organization can adopt to improve its products/services?

By considering these questions, you can identify opportunities that can help your business grow and succeed. Remember, opportunities are not just about finding new markets or customers but also about finding ways to improve your current operations and solutions.

Threats

Make a comprehensive list of threats that you have discovered through your extensive market research. You need to delve deeper and consider potential changes in the market landscape, economic downturns, technological advancements, rising competitors, and other factors that could negatively impact your organization.

If you're struggling to identify your company's threats, here are some questions to consider:

- Are there any new competitors entering the market or established competitors expanding their offerings?
- Are there any changes in customer behavior or preferences?
- Are there any new technologies or trends that other competitors are applying that could make your products or services obsolete?
- How could your competitor take advantage of your company's weaknesses?

When conducting a SWOT analysis on a competitor in the same industry, it is common to find similar threats for both your own company and your competitor, as you both face similar challenges and risks. However, it's important to keep in mind that indirect competitors may have unique threats that are specific to their business and not applicable to yours. So, while some threats may be identical, it's essential to consider the unique challenges that each competitor faces in the market.

SWOT analysis is a powerful research tool for product marketers, which they can use to identify the strengths and weaknesses of their product relative to competitors. Armed with this information, product marketers can refine their products and messaging to better meet customer needs and stand out in the marketplace. By evaluating opportunities and threats, such as emerging trends and changing customer preferences, product marketers can define the direction of their products and tailor their messaging accordingly to capitalize on opportunities. SWOT analysis can also help product marketers better understand customers' needs and preferences, enabling them to refine both their product and marketing strategies to better meet customer wants. Ultimately, SWOT analysis empowers product marketers to make more informed decisions about their product strategy and marketing messaging, leading to more successful product launches and revenue growth.

Win/loss analysis

Win/loss analysis is a great approach to evaluate and gain insights into why you were successful in winning a deal and, conversely, why you lost a deal to a competitor. These insights can be invaluable to help identify the strengths and weaknesses of your product or service, as well as the sales approach. This information can then be used to make strategic improvements to the sales process, marketing messaging, and product development efforts.

Win/loss analysis entails examining both successful and unsuccessful sales deals to determine the underlying factors that influence the outcome. Typically, this involves soliciting feedback from customers, the sales team, and other stakeholders who are involved in the sales process. The objective of win/loss analysis is to detect recurring patterns and trends in customer behavior, preferences, and decision-making, while also pinpointing areas in which sales teams can improve. By gathering insights through this analysis, you can refine your sales enablement program to better align with the needs and wants of your target audience.

For example, a win/loss analysis might reveal that customers consistently choose a competitor over your product due to a particular feature that your product or service is lacking. Armed with this insight, you could work with the product team to improve that feature and make it a key selling point for future sales efforts. Alternatively, the analysis might reveal that your sales team consistently loses deals due to a lack of product knowledge or poor communication skills. In this case, investing in training to enable your sales team could help improve their performance and increase the chances of winning future deals.

Beyond identifying areas for improvement, a well-designed win/loss program can also inform your product roadmap and aid in prioritizing feature development. Instead of solely comparing features, it's crucial to understand why your competitors succeed or struggle. By conducting a win/loss analysis, you can gain an inside look into the decision-making process of key stakeholders and the factors that influenced their choices. This provides valuable insights into the decision-making process of both customers and competitors. By collecting feedback directly from decision-makers, you can gain a deeper understanding of the factors that influenced their decision to choose your product or a competitor's product. An effective win/loss program can help identify the features and capabilities that are most important to your customers. By using this feedback to inform the product roadmap, you can prioritize the development of new features and improvements to existing features, ultimately leading to more innovative, competitive, and customer-focused products.

HubSpot, a marketing, sales, and customer service software company, is a classic example of a company that improved its product thanks to a win/loss analysis. HubSpot used win/loss analysis to understand why some customers were choosing their product while others were not. Through this analysis, they discovered that while customers loved the software's marketing and sales features, they struggled with the complexity of the customer service tools. To address this issue, HubSpot simplified its customer service tools, making them easier for customers to use and understand. The company also provided additional training and support resources to help customers get the most out of the tools. As a result of these improvements, HubSpot's customer retention rates improved significantly, and the company saw an increase in customer satisfaction and loyalty. HubSpot's win/loss analysis allowed them to identify areas for improvement and make changes that directly impacted their customers' experiences with their product.

Win/loss program has been shown to have a significant impact on win rates. By making strategic improvements based on the insights gained from the analysis, you can help your company increase its chances of winning future deals. Win/loss analysis is particularly important in the B2B context, where the sales process is often more complex and involves longer sales cycles, higher-value deals, and multiple decision-makers. In these situations, it is critical to understand why deals are won or lost, as this can help refine sales strategies, optimize the sales process, and improve overall performance. However, win/loss analysis can also be valuable in the B2C context, particularly for companies that sell high-value products or services. For example, a company that sells luxury goods or high-end services may find that win/loss analysis is essential to understanding the factors that influence customer decision-making and identifying opportunities to improve the customer experience.

PMMs are the ones who are well-suited to conduct win/loss interviews. This is because they have a unique perspective on the business, as they're typically involved in various aspects of product development, marketing, and sales processes. PMMs have a deep understanding of a product and its value proposition, as well as the competitive landscape and the target market. They also have insights into the sales team's challenges and the customer's pain points.

PMMs can leverage this broad perspective to ask insightful questions during win/loss interviews and analyze the results in a meaningful way. They can identify patterns and trends in customer feedback, as well as areas where the sales team could improve their performance. They can then use this information to inform product strategy, marketing messaging, sales enablement, and other key business decisions.

Conducting a win/loss analysis

Conducting a win/loss analysis is not just about understanding why sales opportunities were won or lost, but also about gathering information that can be used to inform broader business decisions. It's important to understand the needs and priorities of other internal stakeholders, such as product development teams, marketing teams, and senior leadership, to ensure that the win/loss analysis provides insights that are relevant and actionable and can be used to drive business outcomes.

By aligning a win/loss analysis with an organization's overall needs, you can maximize the value of the insights gained from the analysis. For example, if the product development team is interested in learning about the need for specific features, the win/loss analysis can focus on these areas to inform future product development efforts. Similarly, if the marketing team launched a new campaign for a new feature, and they want to evaluate the effectiveness of this campaign to drive awareness and generate interest, the win/loss analysis can clearly provide insights to help inform the marketing strategy.

Another important thing to consider when conducting a win/loss analysis is when a win/loss interview should take place. It's essential to gather feedback while the customer's experience is still fresh in their mind, as this can lead to more accurate and detailed insights. The best time to conduct win/loss interviews is typically within the first four weeks of when a product or service was bought or declined. This allows the customer to recall their experience with the product or service in detail.

To ensure you get the most value from a win/loss analysis, it's essential to be prepared for the interview process. This means understanding the goals of the analysis, identifying key areas of inquiry, and planning how to gather the most relevant and insightful feedback from the interviewee. Being well-prepared for the interview enables you to ask the right questions, actively listen to the interviewee's responses, and gain a deeper understanding of their decision-making process. Knowing basic information about the person being interviewed, such as their job title, their involvement, and the deal outcome, is very important. Additionally, any notes left by the sales team can provide helpful context and guide the direction of the interview.

As mentioned previously, planning out the key topics and questions to ask in a win/loss interview is crucial because it can help ensure that the conversation covers the most relevant and important areas. However, it's also important to be flexible and open to following the conversation where it naturally leads. Sometimes, unexpected insights and perspectives can arise in the course of a conversation, and being open to exploring those can lead to valuable insights that might have been missed if the interview was too structured. So, while having a framework of key topics and questions is helpful, it's also important to be adaptable and flexible during the interview. Depending on the aspects you want to investigate, you may find the following questions helpful as samples:

- What has influenced you to purchase/not purchase our product?
- Which specific problems were you trying to solve with our product?
- Did you check product reviews and ratings before making the purchase? How did they impact your decision to make the purchase?
- Were you the only one in the decision-making process? If not, who else has been involved? What was their role in the process?
- How do you think we can improve our product?
- What do you think about our pricing? Did you compare it with other quotes in the market?
- Which other solutions (players) in the market did you explore? What were the reasons behind choosing/not choosing those solutions?
- Is there any other feedback or comments you would like to provide us?

After conducting win/loss interviews, it is necessary to examine the data for recurring patterns. Once the trends are identified, the next critical step is to integrate these observations into your business strategy. Ensure that you gather the right insights from the right people within your company, and update your battlecards accordingly. Similarly, update your marketing personas to create campaigns based on the most comprehensive and up-to-date information available. Pass on any relevant product feedback to your product development team. They can use it to make informed decisions when working on future updates. If there are significant wins, it may be wise to consider pursuing case studies. Alternatively, if the sales team lacks product knowledge, you'll need to build a sales enablement program to train them on your product. When multiple losses are due to competitor pricing, it may be necessary to review your pricing strategy. Gathering data on competitors through SWOT analysis could also be useful.

In *Chapter 10*, *Enabling Your Sales Team and Maximizing Effectiveness*, we will delve deeply into the win/loss program that is relevant to sales enablement.

Competitive pricing intelligence

By adopting a competitive pricing intelligence approach, organizations are able to effectively track the pricing and performance of competitors within their respective markets, thus enabling them to make informed pricing decisions based on reliable and up-to-date information. There are several important steps to take in order to improve your pricing intelligence strategy:

- **Define your pricing objectives**: What do you want to achieve through your pricing strategy? This might include increasing revenues or improving customer loyalty.

- **Gather data**: To optimize your pricing strategy, it's crucial to learn about your competitors' pricing strategies.

- **Analyze the data**: Analyzing the data you collected can help you identify patterns and trends that can inform your pricing strategy. For example, you may notice that your competitor offers discounts on certain features or a freemium version of its product to attract new customers; if so, you can adjust your prices to match your competitor's or offer discounts on certain features to attract more customers.

- **Set your pricing strategy**: Based on your objectives and data analysis, set your pricing strategy; you can adjust your prices or offer discounts.

- **Monitor and adjust**: Use pricing automation tools to continuously adjust your prices in real-time and optimize your pricing strategy.

Competitive pricing intelligence can serve as a crucial catalyst for innovation, offering valuable insights into how customer preferences can be influenced by both your own pricing strategy and that of your competitors. For instance, if you discover that customers are willing to pay more for specific product enhancements, this presents an excellent opportunity to introduce new features that meet their needs while simultaneously boosting your revenue.

GoToMeeting was a web conferencing and online meeting software that allowed businesses to conduct virtual meetings and webinars. However, the company failed to anticipate the potential threat of other web conferencing software providers, such as Zoom and Cisco Webex, which offered similar services at competitive prices. GoToMeeting continued to focus on its existing business model and did not invest enough in developing new features, pricing strategies, or partnerships that could help it compete effectively. As a result, the company's market share declined sharply, and it struggled to retain customers. In 2016, GoToMeeting's parent company, Citrix, announced that it would spin off GoToMeeting and merge it with LogMeIn's products, forming a new company called "GoTo."

If GoToMeeting had invested in developing a competitive pricing strategy or innovative features that could differentiate itself from the competition, it may have been able to retain its market share and remain a leading player in the web conferencing and online meeting software market.

Summary

This chapter has taken us on a journey through the diverse realms of market research. We've explored the various data collection methods available and how they seamlessly integrate into different phases of the GTM life cycle. From shaping pricing strategies to honing in on the perfect product-market fit and strategic segmentation, market research has proven to be an indispensable tool for informed decision-making. Despite the resource-intensive nature of market research, its continuous execution is paramount to staying attuned to evolving industry trends.

The latter part of this chapter delved into competitive intelligence, illuminating its pivotal role within the broader landscape of market research. We emphasized the necessity of regularly reassessing the competitive landscape and the importance of crafting comprehensive competitor profiles. In addition to direct competitors, we underscored the significance of monitoring indirect ones. We uncovered key analytical approaches, such as the regular updating of battlecards, quick SWOT analysis of emerging competitors, staying abreast of competitor news, and conducting win/loss analyses of closed opportunities. These tools empower us to make informed decisions in an ever-evolving competitive landscape.

Our upcoming chapter will shift our attention toward customer research and delve into the intricacies of establishing an impactful VoC program within your organization.

Customer Research – Creating an Effective Voice for Customer Programs

5

In our previous chapter, we explored the vast landscape of market research, delving into its data collection and analysis techniques to gain a comprehensive understanding of the competitive landscape and overall markets in which your company operates. However, now, we will shift our focus to customer research, a crucial process that enables you to gather and analyze data about your customers' needs, behaviors, and motivations. By understanding your customers in this way, you can develop, promote, and enhance products that provide them with a seamless, personalized experience that caters to their unique needs.

Customer research has transcended its role as a mere tool for product marketers; it has become an invaluable source of data-driven insights that not only shape our marketing efforts but also steer the entire trajectory of our companies. With technology enabling easier access to data, relying on gut feelings and salespeople's intuition for understanding customers is now an outdated approach. Modern product marketers use a blend of quantitative and qualitative data from multiple sources to form a complete picture of their customer's behavior. Furthermore, with the advent of remote interviewing capabilities, product marketers have an unparalleled opportunity to cross-check their quantitative data against qualitative insights, thereby gaining an in-depth understanding of their customers. By leveraging these insights, product marketers can help improve the overall customer experience and boost customer satisfaction.

In this section, we will delve into the world of customer research and outline strategies for creating an effective **Voice of Customer (VoC)** program. Throughout the discussion, we will dig into key questions such as the following:

- How can customer research inform the product roadmap?
- How can an effective VoC program be developed to create differentiation?
- How can you measure the return on investment (ROI) of your VoC program?

Understanding customer research for effective decision-making

In today's customer-centric business landscape, conducting customer research is a crucial tool for achieving business success. It offers valuable insights into customers' needs and behaviors, enabling businesses to develop effective customer experiences that align with their needs and preferences. Customer research typically aims to answer questions such as the following:

- What factors influence customer satisfaction and loyalty?

- How do customers perceive the quality of a product or service?

- What are the factors that play a significant role in shaping customers' purchasing behavior and decision-making processes?

- What are the top channels for connecting and engaging with customers?

- What are the emerging developments and changes in the market that can influence customer attitudes and behaviors?

An in-depth grasp of customers holds immense significance for the growth of any thriving business. Essential to achieving this understanding is the practice of customer research, which serves as a linchpin. It involves a meticulous process of gathering and analyzing data regarding the diverse needs, preferences, and behaviors exhibited by your customers. Employing an array of methods such as thoughtfully constructed surveys, enlightening interviews, and keen observations, customer research delves profoundly into customer attitudes and actions concerning a particular product or service.

Customer research acts as a guiding light in the complex maze of consumer behaviors, shedding light on hidden patterns, untapped desires, and emerging trends. It goes beyond the surface level, delving into the core motivations and aspirations that drive customer decision-making.

Furthermore, customer research is not a one-time endeavor but a continuous and iterative process that allows you to stay in sync with your customers' ever-changing preferences and needs. By regularly engaging in customer research, you can help your company craft seamless customer experiences, staying ahead of the curve and remaining responsive to the evolving demands of their customer base.

Zoom, the widely recognized video conferencing platform, is a great example of a company that harnessed the power of customer research to achieve remarkable growth. During its early stages, Zoom's visionary founder and CEO, Eric Yuan, diligently engaged in extensive customer research endeavors to pinpoint the pain points and shortcomings of existing video conferencing solutions. By conducting thorough customer surveys and interviews, Eric Yuan uncovered significant pain points among users. These included dissatisfaction with the video and audio quality, complex setup and joining processes, and the high costs associated with existing video conferencing solutions. Armed with this valuable insight, Yuan and his team set out to develop a video conferencing platform that addressed these challenges head-on. The result of their efforts was Zoom, a game-changing solution that swiftly gained traction due to its exceptional video and audio quality, user-friendly interface, and affordable pricing options. By enhancing the customer experience and continuously improving its products, Zoom has propelled its remarkable growth to become a leader in the competitive video conferencing industry.

Differentiating between market research, customer research, and user research

Customer research and market research play vital roles in enabling product marketers to gain profound insights into their target audience and make informed marketing decisions. During the initial phases of product development, market research becomes instrumental in providing a holistic understanding of the market landscape. It involves meticulous investigations into the needs, preferences, and expectations of potential customers, while also revealing invaluable insights regarding market readiness, size, and competitive dynamics.

In contrast, customer research takes a more focused approach, building upon the foundation of market research. It delves deeper into the specific needs and preferences of the intended customer base. This process involves analyzing, categorizing, and evaluating the data and insights gathered from broader market exploration, leading to a more nuanced understanding of customers. By blending the insights from both market research and customer research, you can gain a holistic perspective that enables them to make informed decisions and enhance customer experience.

Simultaneously, it might be useful to consider the definition and distinction of user research. User research focuses on a specific group of individuals, known as users, who interact with a product or a specific component of it. By understanding users' needs, behaviors, and expectations, product designers and developers can create products that prioritize user-centricity. While both user research and customer research strive to comprehend the needs and preferences of people who use or may use a product or service, they differ in certain ways:

- Scope: User research focuses specifically on the needs and behaviors of people who use a product or service, while customer research looks at a broader range of people who may or may not use the product or service.

- Timing: User research is typically conducted during the design and development process of a product or service, while customer research can be conducted at any point in the customer journey, including before and after a purchase.

- Methods: User research often uses more qualitative methods, such as interviews, observations, and usability testing, while customer research may use both qualitative and quantitative methods, such as surveys and data analysis.

- Goals: User research aims to inform design decisions and improve the user experience, while customer research may have broader business goals, such as identifying market trends, understanding customer segments, and improving customer loyalty.

User research and customer research have some differences, but both are crucial for helping businesses create products and services that meet the needs of their users and customers. In this section, we'll focus on the importance of customer research.

Types of customer research

Customer research can take many forms, but two of the main types are *primary* and *secondary* research. To effectively gather and analyze customer data, it's also important to understand the distinction between *quantitative* and *qualitative* data. Knowing which type of data is most relevant to your project goals can help you collect the right information and draw meaningful insights from your research.

As mentioned in the previous chapter, primary research refers to data collected directly by an organization from its customers. This can be done through various research methods, such as surveys, focus groups, or analytics. The advantage of primary research is that it allows you to obtain the data that is most relevant to your specific needs. Additionally, because you are directly involved in the data collection process, you have a better understanding of what data has been collected and can more easily collate that information into meaningful insights. Secondary research involves using data collected from external sources, such as research groups, to gain insights about customers. Unlike primary research, you have less control over the data collection process, but using secondary research can be cost-effective. Primary research provides a more tailored and specific understanding of customer behaviors, whereas secondary research can help you broaden your knowledge and identify industry trends. Therefore, a combination of both primary and secondary research can provide a more comprehensive view of customers and their needs. In my experience, primary research is the most effective method for gaining insights into your customers. This includes monitoring their digital behavior, conducting focus groups and customer advisory boards, and immersing yourself in their natural environments. Additional tactics such as conducting win/loss interviews, interviewing your customer-facing teams, and visiting clients on-site can also provide valuable information.

In addition, when planning a research project, it's important to consider which type of data will be most helpful in achieving the project's goals. Qualitative data is obtained directly from users and can provide valuable insights into their behaviors, opinions, and needs. Common methods of collecting qualitative data include in-depth interviews, focus groups, usability testing, and field studies. Qualitative data is particularly useful for designers because it allows them to understand not only what users do but also why they do it. By gaining a deeper understanding of users' motivations and perspectives, designers can develop solutions that more effectively address their needs and preferences. Quantitative data typically involves measurements of numerical values, such as how much, how many, and how frequently. Common methods for collecting quantitative data include surveys, metrics, and user tests. This type of data can provide statistical insights into user behaviors and preferences, allowing designers to identify trends, patterns, and correlations. However, quantitative data alone may not provide a complete understanding of user needs and motivations. Therefore, a combination of qualitative and quantitative data can provide a more comprehensive picture of users and their experiences. Before selecting a customer research approach, consider posing these questions:

• What is the most crucial information we require about our customers?

• Do we possess a comprehensive understanding of our target audience?

- Does our product solve a real-life concern for people? Do we have supporting evidence?
- Is our product the best solution for our customers?

Once you have determined the research goal and identified the knowledge gap, you can proceed to select the appropriate research method, that is, primary or secondary customer research.

Primary customer research

This category encompasses any research that is directed toward your target audience. Examples of such research may include the following:

- **Customer surveys**: Surveys are a commonly used research method that involves posing a set of specific questions to customers. They can be conducted in various formats, including online questionnaires, phone calls, or email inquiries. Remember that the effectiveness of a survey is dependent on the quality of its questions. Be certain that the questions you ask are designed to elicit the most relevant and useful data about your customers. Here are some practices to follow:
  - To get as much insights as you can from customers, ask open-ended questions
  - Add consistent rating scales
  - Ask short questions to prevent overwhelming participants
- **Focus groups**: Focus groups are a widely recognized and favored research methodology that can efficiently reveal significant insights within a brief duration. Typically, a small group of individuals, usually of eight or fewer members, gather together to discuss products, challenges, preferences, and engagement possibilities. A moderator or a representative from the organization conducts the focus group. The moderator presents a set of predetermined questions or themes to the group for discussion. Focus groups offer several advantages, including the following:
  - Revealing information about critical issues and pain points
  - Enhancing comprehension of what your users want from a solution
  - Uncovering spontaneous responses that may not have been uncovered otherwise
  - Providing valuable insights into how users perceive your product

    Despite their benefits, focus groups also pose certain challenges. In a group setting, dominant voices may influence others to conform to the consensus instead of expressing their genuine opinions. To address this, it is essential to create a safe space where all members can comfortably share their thoughts. Encourage diverse and differing viewpoints to be expressed.
- **Analytics**: Real data is invaluable when it comes to understanding your customers. While people may express certain behaviors, their actions may contradict their words. Analytics, such as those available through product dashboards or other data collection methods, can

provide extensive insights into customer behavior. By leveraging such data, you can streamline your business, eliminate areas of friction, and enhance the overall customer experience. Metrics such as heat maps, amount of time spent, click tracking, and session counts can all contribute to a comprehensive understanding of your customers' behaviors and product engagement.

- **Customer interviews**: Interviewing customers directly is a simple yet effective way to uncover their views, wants, and needs. Through one-on-one conversations, either with a team member or a neutral party, you can gain new insights that might have otherwise gone unnoticed. While this method may not yield quantitative data, it can provide valuable qualitative insights into your customers' thoughts and perceptions of your products. If you're conducting customer interviews, it's important to follow some best practices to ensure that the insights gathered are valuable and relevant:

    ◦ Prepare a list of questions in advance to ensure that the interview stays focused and on-topic.

    ◦ Actively listen to the interviewee, asking follow-up questions and clarifying points as needed.

    ◦ Keep the interview conversational and allow for open-ended questions to encourage detailed responses.

    ◦ To gain unbiased and accurate insights from customer research, it's important to challenge your assumptions and avoid bringing any preconceptions to the table. Instead, encourage customers to share their honest thoughts and feelings.

Secondary customer research

This category encompasses any data that is collected by external sources. Examples of such research may include the following:

- **Industry reports and publications**: Reports and publications from reputable industry sources can provide valuable insights into market trends, consumer behavior, and competitor analysis

- **Government statistics**: Publicly available government data, such as census data or employment statistics, can provide demographic information about your target audience

- **Social media analytics**: Analyzing social media activity and engagement can provide insights into how customers perceive your brand, as well as their interests and behaviors

- **Customer reviews**: Reviews on sites such as Yelp or Amazon can provide valuable feedback about your product or service, as well as insight into customer preferences and pain points

- **Online forums and discussion boards**: Monitoring online forums related to your industry can help you stay informed about what customers think and feel

- **Market research firms**: Hiring a market research firm to conduct surveys or focus groups on your behalf can provide additional insights into customer preferences and behavior

When it comes to conducting customer research, a well-defined set of goals and a carefully selected research method are crucial. Once you have established these foundations, you are poised to embark on your customer research journey. In this context, *Figure 5.1* serves as a great resource, presenting a comprehensive and systematic step-by-step guide that will empower you to conduct customer research effectively.

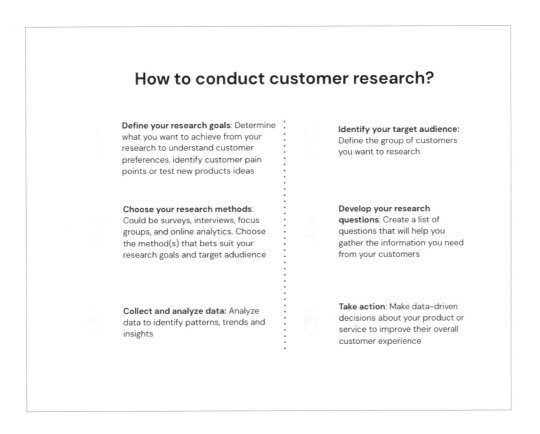

Figure 5.1 – Steps for conducting customer research

As depicted in the preceding figure, the customer research process begins with defining research goals and selecting appropriate methods. It then progresses to the critical final stages, involving the analysis of data to gain insights into customer needs and make informed decisions. Although this may seem straightforward, it is important to acknowledge the complexities that arise in practice. In the coming part, we will explore strategies to effectively overcome these challenges and maximize the utilization of customer insights in making well-informed decisions.

The challenge of using customer insights effectively

Effective use of customer insights is crucial for product marketers to succeed in meeting customer needs and driving business growth. However, it requires careful planning, collaboration, and adaptability to stay ahead of evolving customer preferences and achieve business objectives. Product marketers face unique challenges when it comes to effectively leveraging customer insights for business success.

One of the primary hurdles is developing a deep understanding of customers' needs and preferences. This entails gathering and analyzing customer data, including feedback and behavior, to gain valuable insights into the factors influencing customer satisfaction and purchase decisions. Refer to *Figure 5.2* for a visual representation of the steps for tracking customer needs.

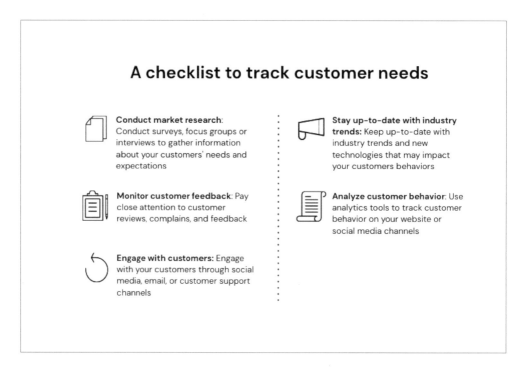

Figure 5.2 – Steps for identifying customers needs

Another challenge lies in translating these insights into actionable plans that address customer needs. For example, product marketers need to closely collaborate with product development teams to ensure new products and features align with customer preferences. Effective communication of customer insights across teams is also vital to deliver a superior customer experience. Additionally, product marketers must strike a balance between customer needs and business goals, such as revenue growth and profitability. This demands careful analysis and decision-making to ensure that the new products align with both customer needs and business objectives. Staying up to date with changing customer preferences and behavior is equally important to remain competitive. In fast-moving industries, customer preferences can shift rapidly, and product marketers must adjust their strategies accordingly to stay ahead of the competition.

To overcome these challenges, product marketers must prioritize customer insights and invest in tools and processes to effectively collect and analyze customer data. Close collaboration with product development, marketing, sales, and customer service teams is crucial to integrating customer insights into all aspects of the business. Furthermore, product marketers must remain agile and adaptable to keep pace with evolving customer preferences and market trends.

Guiding product roadmaps and fostering innovation through customer research

In today's fast-paced and highly competitive market, businesses are recognizing the increasing importance of customer research. It offers an opportunity to gain profound insights into customer's pain points and behaviors, serving as a catalyst for identifying untapped possibilities for innovation. Customer research plays a pivotal role in unveiling unmet needs, enabling businesses to bridge market gaps with tailored solutions. By understanding the specific challenges customers face, companies can create products or services that alleviate those difficulties, enhancing customer experiences.

Furthermore, customer research provides invaluable insights into customer behavior, allowing businesses to optimize their existing offerings or develop new ones that better align with customer needs. By staying attuned to emerging trends and shifts in customer preferences, businesses can proactively develop innovative solutions to meet future needs, whether it's addressing environmental concerns or adapting to evolving demands. This ongoing research empowers businesses to remain agile and customer-centric in a rapidly changing landscape.

Understanding customer needs is crucial for creating a successful product roadmap. By conducting customer research, businesses gain valuable insights that inform every stage of product development, from concept to launch. These insights act as a compass, guiding decision-making and ensuring that the product resonates with the target market. By aligning the product roadmap with customer insights, businesses can confidently navigate the competitive landscape and deliver solutions that truly meet the needs and expectations of their customers. This customer-centric approach not only drives innovation but also enhances customer satisfaction and fosters long-term relationships with the target audience. Here are some ways that customer research can help you create a customer-centric product roadmap:

- **Uncovers customer needs and pain points**: Customer research provides insights into the needs, preferences, and pain points of your target audience. By analyzing customer feedback, surveys, and support requests, you can identify common issues and prioritize solutions that address your customers' most pressing problems.

- **Monitors customer behavior and usage:** Customer research helps you understand how customers use your product and what features they value the most. By analyzing usage data, conducting user testing, and gathering feedback, you can improve the user experience and optimize the product's features and functionality.

- **Prioritizes product features and improvements:** With customer research, you can prioritize which features and improvements to focus on based on customer feedback and demand. By creating a feature backlog and scoring each item based on its impact and effort, you can ensure that your product roadmap aligns with your customers' needs and expectations.

- **Identifies new market opportunities:** Discover new markets or use cases for your product. By analyzing customer feedback, competitor analysis, and market trends, you can identify untapped opportunities and prioritize new features or product lines that meet customer needs.

- **Tests and refines product concepts:** Validate product concepts and prototypes before investing in development. By conducting user testing, gathering feedback, and iterating on designs, you can reduce the risk of launching a product that doesn't meet your customers' expectations.

A great example of a company that effectively employs customer research to shape its product roadmap and drive innovation is **Intercom.** Founded in 2011, Intercom has become widely recognized as a customer messaging platform that facilitates personalized and efficient communication between businesses and their customers. A vital factor contributing to Intercom's success is its steadfast dedication to customer research and profound comprehension of user needs. The company proactively interacts with its customers, employing diverse approaches such as gathering feedback, conducting user interviews, and analyzing user behavior. This active engagement allows Intercom to continually improve its product and introduce cutting-edge features that effectively meet the evolving demands of its B2B customers. Through the utilization of customer research, Intercom adeptly identifies pain points and uses those insights to make informed decisions regarding its product roadmap. For example, upon discovering that customers were facing challenges with lead qualification, Intercom responded by integrating chatbots and automation tools to enhance lead management capabilities. Moreover, Intercom places great emphasis on regular usability testing to ensure an intuitive user experience, thereby enabling it to prioritize feature development based on iterative feedback. This customer-research-driven approach has not only enhanced the quality of their existing offerings but has also resulted in the introduction of new features such as chatbots, product tours, and self-service support, collectively delivering a comprehensive customer engagement platform.

Having recognized the value of customer research in gaining a deeper understanding of customers, let us now delve into the practical application of this knowledge. We will explore various programs and strategies that can be implemented to prioritize customer needs and elevate the overall customer experience.

Enhancing customer understanding through effective VoC programs

In the current business landscape, there is growing recognition in the tech industry of the value of implementing VoC programs as part of a broader effort to prioritize customer needs and enhance the customer experience. While customer success and support teams focus on driving product usage and solving issues, VoC programs centralize customer feedback to better understand their needs, wants, expectations, and challenges with your products. VoC is a key component of customer experience that focuses on creating programs that offer visibility to customer and prospect feedback across the organization, allowing every team to make informed decisions. Despite the obvious benefits of these programs, organizations are still working to establish the framework and identify the technology needed to make them possible.

Although technology has made significant progress, including advancements in big data, AI-powered analytics, and generative AI, tech businesses still face significant challenges in collecting and distributing customer feedback across multiple platforms. This is because customer feedback comes from various sources and requires advanced technology to aggregate and analyze effectively. The diversity and unstructured nature of customer feedback further complicate the process of extracting valuable insights. Additionally, integrating feedback across multiple systems can be a complex and time-consuming task. However, collecting and analyzing customer feedback is a crucial aspect of running a successful tech business. Businesses can gather valuable insights from online review sites, customer service platforms such as **Zendesk** and **Salesforce,** and other sources to identify customer trends and prioritize areas for improvement. By centralizing and integrating this feedback, Tech businesses can gain a comprehensive understanding of customer needs and preferences, enabling them to make informed decisions that enhance the customer experience and drive business growth.

Implementing a VoC program can assist businesses in leveraging existing data to gain valuable insights into customer needs and wants. By collecting and analyzing customer feedback, companies can address important questions, such as identifying essential features that may be missing from their product roadmap, determining whether their pricing model is impacting sales, assessing the need for additional customer training or self-help resources, and evaluating the effectiveness of their latest marketing campaign in engaging customers. Such insights can enable businesses to make informed decisions and enhance customer satisfaction, ultimately resulting in improved business performance.

What exactly does VoC mean?

VoC is a term used to describe the process of collecting and analyzing feedback from customers about their experiences with a product or service. It is a method for gathering insights and understanding customer needs and expectations, which can be used to inform product development, marketing, sales, and customer service decisions. VoC typically involves identifying and using internal and external customer feedback channels to gather feedback from customers. The goal is to capture their perceptions and opinions about the product or service, as well as identify areas for improvement and potential opportunities for innovation. Product marketing teams often utilize the insights obtained through VoC to develop customer personas, journey maps, and additional resources, which aid in comprehending their target audience more effectively. This information can also be used to inform product roadmaps, prioritize feature development, and optimize the customer experience. VoC programs are valuable for any organization that wants to stay customer-focused and competitive in the market. By listening to the voices of their customers, companies can improve their products and services and build stronger relationships with their customers.

It's important to note that customer research and VoC are related in that both involve gathering information from customers to better understand their needs and preferences. However, they differ in terms of their scope and focus. Customer research is a broader term that refers to any type of research conducted on customers or potential customers. On the other hand, VoC is a specific type of customer research that focuses specifically on capturing and analyzing the feedback, opinions, and sentiments of customers about a product or service. It is a method for gathering insights and understanding customer needs and expectations, which can be used to inform product development, marketing, and customer service decisions. Both customer research and VoC are important tools for building customer-centric products and services and improving the customer experience.

Many companies have built successful VoC programs. One great example is **Airbnb**, the popular vacation rental platform. Airbnb's VoC program is built on several key pillars. The program provides customers with multiple feedback channels, such as in-app ratings and reviews, surveys, and customer support interactions. Real-time monitoring tools are also used to track customer feedback and quickly identify and address any issues. To ensure a consistent and effective customer experience, Airbnb fosters cross-functional collaboration across the organization. Finally, Airbnb uses data analytics tools to extract actionable insights from customer feedback, which are used to inform business decisions.

Airbnb's VoC program has had a significant impact on improving the customer experience by addressing pain points and implementing features and policies that align with customer preferences. This has led to increased customer loyalty and satisfaction, which in turn has driven Airbnb's growth. Through the program, Airbnb has been able to leverage customer feedback to identify areas in which customers may be experiencing issues or encountering challenges. For instance, by analyzing multiple reports on a specific property, Airbnb can collaborate with the host to streamline the check-in process and provide detailed instructions to enhance the experience. Furthermore, the VoC program has enabled Airbnb to align its policies and features with customer preferences, identifying opportunities to introduce new features or adjust policies to better serve customer needs. By addressing customer preferences, such as offering more flexible cancellation policies, Airbnb can further enhance customer satisfaction and foster loyalty.

Airbnb's VoC program has been instrumental in driving the company's business growth. By addressing customer pain points and aligning its features and policies with customer preferences, Airbnb has been able to improve the customer experience and increase customer satisfaction. This has led to positive word-of-mouth from satisfied customers, which in turn has helped attract new customers and retain existing ones. By prioritizing the VoC, Airbnb has created a virtuous cycle of customer loyalty, repeat bookings, and revenue growth.

Product marketers play an essential role in bringing the voice of the customer into the business. This involves a comprehensive process that begins with gathering and capturing customer insights and transforming them into actionable insights. The next step is to disseminate the data to the relevant departments within the organization, ensuring each recipient knows what actions are expected of them in return for accessing the information.

As a product marketer, you will be interested in understanding your customers' needs, preferences, and opinions about your products or services. This feedback can come from various sources such as surveys, customer interviews, social media monitoring, website analytics, and so on. To manage this feedback effectively, one great approach is to create a centralized knowledge hub for customer insights. This hub can serve as a repository of all the feedback gathered from different sources, making it easy to access and analyze. By having a centralized knowledge hub, you can make sure that all the relevant teams within your organization have access to the same information and insights, leading to a shared understanding of customer needs. The knowledge hub can contain various types of feedback, including customer interviews, social listening trends, feature requests, **Net Promoter Score (NPS)** or **Customer Satisfaction (CSAT)** scores, product usage data, and so on. By collecting all this information in one place, you can identify patterns and trends that can help you improve your products or services. Moreover, a centralized knowledge hub can help you transform customer feedback into actionable insights. You can use the insights gained from the hub to inform product development decisions, marketing strategies, and customer service improvements. This approach can help you better understand your customers' needs, leading to more successful products and happier customers.

In some cases, product marketers may not be involved in certain processes, especially in product marketing organizations that are still growing to match the size of larger product and/or sales teams. For instance, in the product roadmap development process, it's important to ensure that the VoC is heard, even if product marketers aren't directly involved. To do this, it's helpful for product marketers to proactively identify gaps in the current process and offer assistance. By providing intelligence at the right time, such as just before road mapping sessions, product marketers can help guide decision-making and provide valuable input to the process.

Building an effective VoC program

Obtaining the VOC doesn't have to be expensive. It just needs to be a programmatic effort. Customer insights can be gleaned from a wide range of sources, including monitoring digital behavior such as campaign responses, website tracking, and social media, as well as conducting customer focus groups, user group meetings, win/loss interviews, feedback surveys, and more. Even your customer support teams can provide valuable information.

The key to a successful VoC initiative is to systematically analyze all of these data sources and strategically transform them into actionable insights for the business. By doing so, you can gain a deeper understanding of your customers' needs and preferences, and use that knowledge to improve products or services, enhance your customer experience, and ultimately drive growth to your company.

Here are the key steps to build an effective VoC program:

- Gaining buy-in across different departments
- Identifying customer feedback channels
- Analyzing common issues
- Using feedback analysis to prioritize strategic actions
- Monitoring the impact

To provide a more comprehensive breakdown of these steps mentioned earlier, let's elaborate on them further.

Gaining buy-in across different departments

To establish a successful VoC program, it's crucial to get buy-in from your entire organization. It's not enough to simply gather and analyze customer feedback – you must also take action based on the insights you gain. This requires alignment on both the vision and the practice of your VoC program. You need to understand what you hope to achieve collectively and how you'll put what you've learned into practice.

One effective way to gain support from different departments within your company is to demonstrate the immediate value to their area. Connect your VoC goals with core business objectives and demonstrate how they can help each department achieve its specific goals. A great VoC program should involve cross-functional collaboration and have a positive impact on a variety of business goals. As you develop your program, it's important to identify your objectives, measure progress, and consider how VoC can contribute to achieving those objectives. Here are a few areas to consider:

- **Sales**: Having access to critical information is essential for informing successful customer acquisition and maximizing cross-selling and upselling opportunities with existing customers. This empowers frontline sales teams to meet and exceed their goals. Some key questions to consider include the following:
  - Can pricing be a reason for potential customers to turn away?
  - Are there any significant features absent from the product roadmap that could lead to more sales?

- **Customer support:** To gain a deeper understanding of customer issues and improve the support experience, it's important to identify gaps in the support process and evaluate the channels through which customers are expressing their issues. Some key questions to consider include the following:

  - Are support teams adequately trained? Are they equipped to handle a variety of issues, or do they need additional training to improve their skills?

  - Do hold times meet customer expectations? Are customers waiting too long to speak with a support representative, leading to frustration and dissatisfaction?

  - Are technical documentation and resources enabling customers to self-serve? Do customers have access to the information they need to troubleshoot issues on their own, or are they forced to rely on support?

    By answering these questions, you can identify areas where the support process may be falling short and develop strategies to address those gaps. This can lead to faster resolution times, higher customer satisfaction, and reduced churn. In addition to evaluating the support process itself, it's important to understand the channels through which customers are expressing their issues. This could include phone, email, chat, social media, or other channels. By understanding where customers are expressing their issues, you can ensure that your support team is available and responsive across all channels, improving the overall customer experience.

- **Product management:** Gathering feedback from users is crucial to identify missing features, capabilities, and pricing models that may affect the product experience. For instance, if the platform's stability has been an issue, this may have led to decreased customer retention. Evaluating customer expectations for a simpler user experience at a more affordable price point is also important. By understanding how customer needs have evolved, product strategy can be adjusted accordingly to better align with their expectations.

- **Customer success team:** Your customer success team plays a critical role in helping customers achieve their goals and ensuring their ongoing success with your product or service. As they work closely with customers, they have a unique perspective on what's working well and where there may be room for improvement. Because of this close relationship with customers, your success team is well-positioned to provide valuable feedback to your organization. They can share insights about the following:

  - Features or services that customers are using most frequently and finding most valuable

  - Pain points or areas of frustration that are preventing customers from achieving their goals

  - Opportunities for upselling or expansion based on customer needs and usage patterns

    By leveraging this feedback from your success team, you can make informed decisions about how to improve your product or service and enhance the overall customer experience. This can help you build stronger relationships with your customers, improve retention and reduce churn, and drive revenue growth over time.

To ensure that your organization is fully committed to improving the customer experience, it's important to identify individuals who can champion the VoC program in key areas of your business. These champions can be from departments such as customer support, customer success, sales, demand generation, or product management/product marketing. They can serve as advocates for the VoC program and promote a customer-centric culture throughout the organization. Collaborating with these champions can help you address customer feedback more effectively, pinpoint areas for improvement, and drive growth and success for your business. Additionally, it's vital to provide opportunities for stakeholders to hear directly from customers by participating in interviews, focus groups, or even monitoring chats and support calls. This approach can help stakeholders gain a deeper understanding of the customer's needs and pain points. Another effective strategy is to create case studies that showcase customer experiences, which can be used in marketing materials and distributed internally to help personalize your customers for those who may not have direct customer-facing roles. To facilitate the sharing of customer insights, consider creating a centralized knowledge hub that brings together various data sources, such as interviews, NPS or CSAT scores, feature requests, social listening trends, website behaviors, and product usage. By making this information easily accessible, you can help stakeholders better understand the customer's perspective and enhance the overall customer experience.

Identifying customer feedback channels

To develop a successful voice of the customer program, it is crucial to determine the different channels using which customers share their feedback. This encompasses both *public* and *internal* channels where customers are likely to express their opinions.

Some examples of public channels include the following:

- Online review platforms such as G2, Capterra, or Trustpilot
- Social media networks such as Facebook or LinkedIn groups
- Customer communities and forums like Reddit or GitHub
- Email listservs

By identifying these channels, you can collect and analyze customer feedback to improve your product or service. Some examples of internal channels include the following:

- Customer support tickets such as customer inquiries, issues, or requests submitted via a customer support system
- CRM Notes from sales and success calls that involve customer interactions with sales and success teams

- Emails and phone calls that involve direct communication between customers and relevant business representatives

- Collaboration and chat tools, which are internal communication tools such as Slack or Microsoft Teams that can be used to share customer feedback and insights

- NPS, CSAT, and win/loss surveys, which are used to gather feedback and insights on customer satisfaction, loyalty, and preferences, as well as reasons why customers choose or don't choose a product or service

Product marketers have various techniques at their disposal to collect customer feedback and improve products. These include conducting face-to-face interviews with individual customers to gain insight into their experiences, administering surveys to gather feedback on particular product features or overall user experience, creating digital communities for customers to share feedback and ideas, providing feature request forms on your company website, organizing virtual feedback sessions and focus groups, establishing user groups composed of power users, monitoring online forums to gauge customer sentiment and identify issues, and performing market research to discern broader trends and consumer preferences. By utilizing these strategies, product marketers can pinpoint areas for improvement and make informed decisions based on data to enhance their products.

As mentioned earlier, there are multiple avenues for gathering customer feedback and input regarding your products. Among these options, one effective approach is the establishment of a **customer advisory board (CAB)**. Typically composed of a small group of customers who represent the broader customer base and have a genuine interest in your company's products or services, a CAB offers regular meetings to discuss various subjects related to the company's strategic direction, emerging market trends, and proposed product features. The primary purpose of a CAB is to provide a platform where customers can openly express their opinions, share insights and ideas, and provide feedback that significantly contributes to the company's product development and strategic decision-making processes. When selecting CAB members, it is crucial to consider factors such as their product experience and industry knowledge. By establishing a CAB, you can tap into the valuable perspectives of your customers, fostering a collaborative environment that shapes your products and strategies to better align with their needs and expectations.

Product marketing is an ideal owner of CABs due to its unique position at the intersection of various teams, including product, engineering, sales, marketing, customer success, and more. This cross-functional role allows us to effectively connect the dots between these teams and ensure that the customer's voice is heard throughout the product development process, as well as during the optimization of the customer experience. For product marketers, CAB is one way to gain insights into customers' experiences and opinions. Product marketers can use such insights to develop **market requirement documents (MRDs)**, which can influence product roadmaps. In addition, by tapping into the insights gained from CABs, product marketers can build a range of marketing collaterals and materials such as use cases, narratives, messaging, and case studies that resonate with the target audience. Another essential aspect of CABs is *customer advocacy*. By identifying and cultivating customer advocates, product marketers can turn satisfied customers into evangelists who can help promote the product/service to other potential customers. Customer advocates can provide valuable resources such as customer stories/testimonials and references for other prospects and help customers become champions within their organizations.

Establishing a CAB program requires prioritizing transparency as a critical factor. It is vital to openly share your product roadmap with customers, even if it's still in the early stages of development. By providing customers with early-stage concepts and prototypes and actively seeking their feedback, you can integrate their input into the development process and create a product that caters to their specific needs. Additionally, fostering a two-way relationship with your customers is essential. Take the time to understand their expectations and customize your approach accordingly. Demonstrating that you value their insights by offering exclusive access to new features or products further emphasizes their importance. By nurturing customer advocates, you can transform satisfied customers into ambassadors who play a crucial role in promoting your product to potential customers. Remember, the primary objective of a CAB is to actively listen to your customers and gain valuable insights into their pain points and needs. Give them a platform to share their experiences and opinions without interruption or judgment, ensuring that they feel genuinely heard and valued. Integrating the insights derived from a CAB into your product development roadmap is vital to aligning your offerings with customer expectations and needs. This approach fosters an ongoing dialogue with the advisory board, enabling you to remain responsive to evolving customer preferences and requirements. Keep in mind that this process is continuous rather than a one-time event. Consistently collect and analyze advisory board feedback, incorporate it into your plans, and adapt to market changes to stay relevant and meet customer expectations. While it demands constant attention and effort, this approach can lead to increased customer satisfaction, loyalty, and retention.

After acquiring customer feedback, the subsequent crucial step is to establish a robust system for the collection and analysis of that feedback. If you lack a tool that automatically consolidates feedback from various channels, it is important to assign specific responsibilities for each channel and establish a regular schedule for data collection. This could involve creating a weekly or monthly plan for extracting data from each channel and assigning a team member or department to oversee the data collection process. By establishing a transparent process for feedback collection and analysis, you ensure that your VoC program is methodical and effective in identifying customer needs. You can incorporate various details, such as deal size, use case, competitors, and so on, and determine a suitable location to store the data, which could be as simple as starting with a Google Sheet to avoid getting caught up in complex technological decisions. Additionally, it is crucial not to let technology-related choices hinder your progress.

Analyzing common issues

After you begin gathering feedback, you can begin to recognize recurrent issues and link them with performance metrics such as sales and retention. By categorizing the feedback into key issues, it becomes easier to link the feedback to specific business initiatives and take targeted actions to address those issues. For example, if multiple customers complain about high pricing, you can link that feedback to the pricing strategy, and consider adjusting it to improve customer satisfaction and retention. Similarly, if several customers report issues with the product, you can link that feedback to the product development process and take action to improve its quality. This approach will help your team identify ownership and take the necessary actions to address the issues.

Using feedback analysis to prioritize strategic actions

To make the most of a VoC program, we must analyze and prioritize the feedback we receive to drive improvements and enhance customer satisfaction and loyalty. This may involve identifying priority areas such as pricing, support, or new features based on the feedback analysis. However, internal company politics can make it challenging to implement these initiatives. Establishing a consistent forum and schedule for feedback discussions is crucial. This can take the form of a dedicated meeting, incorporating it into an existing planning meeting, or even creating a Slack channel. The key is to ensure that everyone knows when and where to expect the discussions and that they make a commitment to attend and participate. The goal of the meetings is to prioritize actions based on common issues and assign ownership. Regularly reviewing the feedback and taking action can help us meet customer needs, stay ahead of market trends, and stay competitive.

Monitoring the impact

In order to ensure long-term support and buy-in for a voice of the customer program, it is important to establish a process that tracks feedback and maps it to changes made within the organization. This involves identifying **key performance indicators (KPIs)** that will be measured in order to evaluate the effectiveness of the program. For example, if customer feedback suggests a trend related to pricing, the organization may develop actions to update pricing metrics or packaging strategies. The program would then track feedback received after the changes are made, as well as the impact on sales revenue. If the feedback becomes more positive and sales impact increases, this indicates that the strategies are effective. If the impact does not improve, it may be time to try a different approach.

Essential principles for a successful VoC program

Simply collecting customer feedback is not enough to improve your business. You also need the right technology to analyze and act upon that feedback. VoC tools can help companies by providing real-time visibility into feedback trends and progress to actions. This enables all stakeholders to access the necessary information and make informed decisions, leading to reduced customer churn. *Figure 5.3* a wide range of VoC tools, organized into different categories based on their types and functions:

Voice of the Customer (VOC) Tools

Feedback management platforms

Consolidate customer feedback into a centralized database, allowing for easier analysis and tracking of customer sentiment over time.

Sentiment analysis software

Analyze text data and identify the sentiment or emotional tone behind it.

Customer journey mapping tools

Help to understand the customer journey, from initial awareness to post-purchase support, and to identify opportunities to improve the overall customer experience.

Customer surveys

Survey tools can be used to create and distribute surveys and analyze the responses.

Online review monitoring tools

Allow companies to monitor and track customer reviews on third-party websites such as Yelp, G2, Facebook, etc..

Live chat software

Help gather feedback and identify customer issues while they're happening.

Social media listening tools

Can identify patterns and trends in customer feedback and provide insights into agent performance.

Voice analytics tools

Help gather feedback and identify customer issues while they're happening.

Figure 5.3 – VoC tools

By utilizing the appropriate technology, such as implementing a feedback tracker, you can scale up your VoC program to gain real-time insights into feedback trends, empowering all stakeholders to make smarter decisions and improve customer experiences.

Consistency and accessibility are crucial for a robust VOC program, as it has the potential to identify customer priorities before they turn into significant challenges. A well-established VOC program can help businesses stay ahead of the curve and provide better customer experiences by being attentive to their evolving needs. The key principles to ensure an effective and successful VoC program are as follows:

- **Engaging with customers on their preferred channels:** In the current era of digitalization, customers use diverse communication channels such as email, social media, and web platforms. An effective VoC program is equipped with tools that enable organizations to conduct real-time surveys across all channels. This streamlined process allows customers to conveniently provide their feedback, which in turn provides valuable insights to organizations about how customers view their products and services. By integrating customer feedback across all touchpoints, organizations can enhance customer satisfaction, engagement, and loyalty.

- **Leveraging insights to foster stronger connections with customers:** Creating deep connections with customers and building lifelong relationships that foster loyalty and advocacy requires a comprehensive understanding of their perceptions, needs, and preferences. To achieve this, organizations can utilize a strong VoC program that employs advanced tools such as AI analysis and customer satisfaction metrics such as NPS. These metrics allow for ongoing monitoring of customer perceptions, enabling organizations to stay informed about their evolving needs. By analyzing and visualizing direct feedback in an easy-to-understand way, organizations can tailor their future interactions with customers. This not only makes it easier for sales, marketing, and customer service teams to adjust their daily interactions and decisions but also helps them to better align with what matters most to their customers.

- **Enabling cross-functional data integration:** Breaking down data silos and creating a customer-centric culture is essential for businesses looking to deliver impactful and authentic customer experiences. VoC programs can achieve this by integrating data across departments and empowering teams with the right information at the right time. By sharing insights from direct feedback, you can create comprehensive customer profiles that combine both attitudinal and behavioral data. These profiles can be accessed directly from the VoC platform, allowing teams to gain a complete understanding of your customers and respond appropriately.

- **Responding quickly to customer feedback:** Providing prompt responses to customer feedback is essential for a successful VoC program. Organizations can achieve this by integrating data from various applications and leveraging real-time notifications, improving response times, and addressing customer concerns effectively. Closing the feedback loop is also critical to enhancing the customer experience, and VoCs can help organizations meet this expectation by setting triggers that immediately alert them to changes in customer satisfaction levels, allowing them to deliver excellent customer experiences seamlessly.

By building and implementing a well-designed VoC program, we can enhance the overall customer experience, boost customer satisfaction, and foster long-term loyalty. With this in mind, let's now delve into the next section where we will explore effective strategies for translating the valuable insights gained from the VoC program into actionable plans.

VoC program to create differentiation

As **Product Marketing Managers (PMMs)**, our primary objective is to develop a differentiated product that addresses the unique needs of our customers and stands out in the marketplace. To achieve this goal, the VoC program can serve as a valuable tool for us. Our responsibility includes converting the VoC program's insights into actionable plans. This involves a comprehensive approach that begins with recognizing trends and common patterns in the feedback we receive from our customers. We then analyze and present this information in an easy-to-understand format to acquire a profound comprehension of our customer's pain points and preferences. Once we have a clear understanding of the VoC insights, we integrate them into our product marketing process. By aligning our marketing efforts with our customers' needs and desires, our goal is to improve their overall experience with our products. Furthermore, we utilize VoC insights to identify areas for improvement and innovation and create differentiation in the market.

Turning customer insights into action

By tapping into the invaluable insights obtained directly from our customers, we gain the ability to make informed decisions and implement carefully customized strategies that deeply resonate with our target audience. Through the seamless integration of continuous customer feedback into our product marketing strategies, we not only proactively address their ever-evolving needs but also anticipate emerging market trends, ensuring we maintain a steadfast competitive advantage. We can turn customer insights into action at different aspects of the product marketing process:

- Product/feature development
- Go-to-market (GTM) strategy
- Product launch

Let's explore each in further detail.

Product/feature development

During many of my previous roles, we held quarterly prioritization meetings that involved various stakeholders, such as customer success, sales, and customer service teams, in addition to the product manager and product marketing manager. Together, we mapped out the next product roadmap while assessing the importance of each feature to our customers. Furthermore, we maintained an online forum where customers could submit feature requests, and we prioritized the most urgent and important requests for our roadmap. This approach helped us establish a scalable and effective product feedback strategy. As a product marketer, this enabled me to actively engage in the product development process from its earliest stages and collaborate closely with the product team to incorporate the voice of the customer at every step, including idea validation, testing, and planning.

Adopting a customer-first approach during the product development process can be a key differentiator in a crowded market. By actively listening to customer insights and feedback and identifying gaps in the market, product development teams can create products and features that fulfill unmet needs and align with user preferences. This not only helps in developing innovative solutions but also enables the creation of a personalized customer experience. The information gathered about customer preferences, behaviors, and feedback can be leveraged to tailor interactions with customers, leading to a more positive customer experience. When customers feel that their needs and preferences are understood and catered to, it enhances their satisfaction and loyalty.

GTM strategy

When developing a GTM strategy, it's crucial to make the customer the top priority. This means placing the customer at the forefront of every step in the GTM strategy, from identifying the target market and defining customer personas to selecting the most effective channels for reaching them. It's essential to consider what will provide the best customer experience and maintain customer-centricity throughout the entire GTM strategy. For example, to accurately identify customer segments and personas, we can leverage VoC programs. By thoroughly analyzing customer behaviors, demographics, and relevant characteristics, we can precisely identify distinct customer segments. Moreover, by carefully examining the data we collect, we can create detailed customer personas that capture their individual needs, motivations, and preferences. Armed with this invaluable information, we gain profound insights that empower us to refine our marketing and sales strategies, tailoring them to meet the distinct and specific needs of our customers.

When it comes to messaging, utilizing the VoC becomes essential in effectively communicating the value of our products or services. We go beyond just talking about features and benefits and strive to truly grasp and express the value that customers look for when choosing our offering. By seamlessly incorporating VoC insights into our messaging strategy, we can convey how our product or service meets those desires, delivering unmatched value to our customers.

Product launch

It's crucial to set clear expectations with current customers when introducing a new product or feature. This can involve communicating the launch date, included features, and any potential changes to pricing or service levels transparently. By doing so, customers are more likely to feel valued and engaged and may be more receptive to trying out the new product or feature upon release. Implementing a closed beta test within the current customer base is an excellent way to foster stronger relationships with customers. This exclusive access to the new product or feature can create excitement and anticipation around the launch, generating positive word-of-mouth marketing among the customer community. The closed beta also provides invaluable insights into customer experiences, identifying pain points and areas of friction in the customer journey. By analyzing this feedback, improvements can be made to the onboarding process, user interface, or customer support services, improving the overall customer experience and increasing satisfaction.

Developing and refining a customer journey map is an important step in this process, as it allows you to visualize the customer experience from start to finish and identify areas where improvements can be made. This can include things such as optimizing the onboarding process, simplifying the user interface, or providing better customer support. Finally, the feedback and insights gathered during the closed beta can also inform a content strategy that addresses common questions or concerns customers may have about the product. By anticipating these issues and providing helpful resources and information, you can improve the overall customer experience and increase engagement and adoption of the new product or feature.

As product marketers, it's essential that we facilitate the closing of the feedback loop with customers by collaborating with sales and customer success teams. It's critical to keep customers informed when their feedback is acted upon, and the new feature or product is launched. Sales and customer success teams can revert to customers, thank them for their feedback, and update them on the launch. Closing the feedback loop with customers is crucial as it makes them feel involved in the process and that their feedback matters. It's also essential to communicate with customers about how their feedback is being used and keep them updated on any changes or updates to the product resulting from their feedback. Doing this builds trust and loyalty among customers and can even lead to additional insights and ideas for future product development.

To improve your product and marketing strategies and ensure their continued relevance to your target audience, it's crucial to continuously monitor the feedback obtained through VoC channels. Additionally, understanding whether customers upsell or downgrade after a feature or product launch is essential to measure the impact of customer feedback.

These considerations take us to the final part of this chapter, which delves deeply into measuring the impact of VoC programs.

Boosting ROI with a VoC program

Integrating a VoC program into your company strategy can play a pivotal role in driving revenue growth and improving the overall customer experience. By tapping into the valuable insights gathered from customer feedback, you gain a deeper understanding of their preferences, expectations, and interactions with your products or services. This priceless knowledge empowers you to identify areas for enhancement and customize your offerings to better align with customer needs. By implementing data-driven improvements, you effectively enhance customer satisfaction, nurture loyalty, and foster advocacy, ultimately resulting in increased customer retention and higher spending. Your VoC program can also help you identify areas where you may be falling short of customer expectations, allowing you to proactively address those issues and prevent customer churn. By doing so, you can improve your overall customer experience, which can have a positive impact on your company's revenue performance.

To accurately determine the ROI for your voice of the customer program, it is essential to first evaluate the vital customer feedback metrics that demand our attention. By prioritizing and comprehending these metrics, we can analyze and interpret customer feedback data more efficiently. This, in turn, will lead to better decision-making and ultimately result in a more robust ROI.

What are VoC metrics?

VoC data is a valuable resource for customer-centric companies seeking to identify pain points in the customer journey, understand business challenges, assess marketing campaign effectiveness, and develop strategies that improve customer satisfaction and loyalty. However, some businesses struggle to leverage VoC metrics effectively, hindering their ability to align priorities and goals with those of their customers, leading to lower-than-expected ROI. By optimizing the use of VoC metrics, companies can gain a deeper understanding of their customers and tailor their approach to better meet their needs, ultimately leading to higher customer satisfaction, loyalty, and revenue growth. Let's go over the top VoC metrics:

- NPS: The NPS metric is a widely used metric for measuring customer loyalty and satisfaction. It is based on a simple question asked to customers: "How likely are you to recommend our company to a friend or colleague?" The response options range from 0 (not likely at all) to 10 (extremely likely). After customers provide their response, they are classified into one of the three groups:

  - Promoters: Customers who rate a company with a score of 9 or 10. They are the most satisfied and loyal customers who are highly likely to recommend the company to others.

  - Passives: Customers who give a rating of 7 or 8. Although they are satisfied with the company, they may not necessarily be loyal or enthusiastic about it.

- **Detractors**: Customers who give a rating between 0-6. They are the least satisfied customers who are more likely to share negative feedback and may even discourage others from using the company.

  To calculate the NPS, you need to subtract the percentage of detractors from the percentage of promoters. The formula is *NPS = % Promoters – % Detractors*. The resulting score can range from -100 to +100. A higher score indicates a higher level of customer satisfaction and loyalty, while a negative score indicates that your company has more detractors than promoters.

- **CSAT**: Surveys are commonly employed to gauge the level of contentment of customers with a specific product or service they have received. These surveys are usually conducted by requesting customers to rate their satisfaction with a particular interaction, such as a purchase, a customer service call, or a website experience. The survey questions may take different forms, such as using a scale of 1-5 or offering a range of answers from "very satisfied" to "very dissatisfied." Following data collection, the responses are analyzed to determine the percentage of customers who expressed satisfaction with their experience. CSAT metrics can be useful for businesses to monitor the effectiveness of their offerings and identify areas where improvements can be made. Low CSAT scores can indicate that customers are not happy with certain aspects of the product or service, such as pricing, quality, or customer service. Conversely, high CSAT scores can indicate that the product or service is meeting or surpassing customer expectations, enabling it to identify its strengths.

- **Customer Effort Score (CES)**: This is a metric used to measure the ease and friendliness of a customer's experience when interacting with your company or using its products or services. It focuses on the effort required by the customer to achieve a desired outcome or resolve an issue. The survey typically asks customers to rate how much effort they had to expend on a scale of 1-5, with 1 being "very easy" and 5 being "very difficult." The CES survey question could vary depending on the nature of the task being evaluated. For instance, a customer might be asked to rate how easy it was to resolve an issue with customer support, or how easy it was to navigate a company's website to find the desired information. You can use CES metrics to identify the areas where they can simplify the customer experience and reduce customer effort. The goal is to create a seamless and effortless experience for customers, which can improve customer satisfaction and retention. By collecting CES data regularly and analyzing it, you can identify trends in customer effort and take action to improve the customer experience. This can involve streamlining processes, providing more helpful resources, or improving customer support services, among other initiatives.

- **Customer churn rate**: A metric that measures the fraction of customers who terminate their usage of your company's products over a given period of time. To calculate the churn rate, you must first determine the number of customers they had at the beginning of a given period and then subtract the number of customers you have at the end of that period. The result is the number of customers lost during that time. The next step is to divide the number of customers lost by the number of customers at the beginning of the period, and then multiply the result by 100 to get the percentage of churn. For example, if a company had 500 customers at the beginning of the month and lost 50 customers during the month, the churn rate would be 10% for that month. A high churn rate can indicate that customers are dissatisfied with a company's products or services, customer support, or other aspects of the customer experience. To reduce churn, you can analyze customer feedback and identify the reasons why customers are leaving. This can help make improvements to your company's products or services, address customer complaints and concerns, and ultimately improve customer retention. Reducing churn is important because it is typically more expensive to acquire new customers than to retain existing ones.

- Customer Lifetime Value (CLTV): This is a crucial metric that gauges the total revenue a customer is anticipated to generate for your company during their tenure as your customer. By determining the CLTV, you can evaluate the long-term profitability of your customer base and identify the most valuable customers. To compute the CLTV, you must first calculate the average value of a customer's transaction or purchase, and then multiply that by the expected average number of purchases or transactions they will make over the course of their lifetime as your customer. This calculation considers factors such as customer retention rates, the average duration of the customer relationship, and the customer's spending habits. For instance, if a customer's average purchase is $300, and they are expected to make five purchases, their CLTV would be $1,500. Armed with the CLTV of your customer base, you can make informed decisions about marketing, customer acquisition, and retention. For example, you may opt to implement marketing campaigns with a higher Cost Per Acquisition (CPA) targeted at customers who are likely to have a high CLTV.

- Customer Loyalty Index (CLI): This is an effective tool that assesses customers' loyalty toward a product or brand. It is calculated by analyzing the responses to a set of questions aimed at gauging customers' loyalty behaviors, such as their willingness to recommend the product/brand to others, the probability of making repeat purchases, and their overall satisfaction with the brand. The CLI takes into account various aspects of customer loyalty, including their emotional attachment to the brand, satisfaction with the product or service, and overall perception of the brand. By averaging the scores across these different dimensions, the CLI provides a comprehensive assessment of customer loyalty. Businesses can utilize the CLI to pinpoint ways to improve customer retention and advocacy. It can also be utilized to track changes in customer loyalty over time and to evaluate their performance against competitors in the industry.

How to measure the ROI of your VoC program?

Earlier, we explored the impact of VoC programs on revenue. In this section, we will delve into the steps involved in calculating the ROI of your VoC program:

1. Calculate retention metrics: One of the most important indicators of whether your product meets customer expectations is customer churn. This is why it's crucial to calculate retention metrics at this stage. These metrics provide valuable insights that can help you

understand why customers are churning and determine the direction you need to take based on their feedback. By analyzing retention metrics such as the **Annual Recurring Revenue (ARR)** and **Monthly Recurring Revenue (MRR)** retention rates, you can gain a better understanding of how your product and GTM decisions are impacting your company and your customers:

I. **ARR** is a key metric for measuring the yearly value of your subscriber base, including all recurring elements such as account upgrades, downgrades, and churn. ARR is an important metric that reflects your company's top-line revenue, making it a useful tool for measuring **year-over-year (YoY)** growth.

ARR = [MRR at the beginning of the month + MRR gained from new and upgrading customers for the month - MRR lost from downgrading and churned customers for the month] * 12 months

II. The **MRR** retention rate is a metric that takes into account the recurring revenue generated by your existing customers, including any cancellations. It measures how well your company is retaining revenue from its customers. It provides valuable insights into the effectiveness of your customer retention strategies and can help you identify areas for improvement to retain more customers and increase revenue.

MRR = [Monthly MRR at the beginning of the month - MRR lost from downgrading and churned customers for the month] / Monthly MRR at the beginning of the month

2. **Calculate the percentage of positive feedback:** To determine the percentage of positive feedback, you can analyze the feedback you've received (you can use different sources such as NPS/CSAT surveys and so on) and classify it based on whether it's positive, negative, or neutral. Then, calculate the total number of positive feedback responses and divide it by the total number of feedback responses you've received. This will give you the percentage of positive feedback and provide insights into how well your product or service is meeting your customers' expectations.

Percentage positive feedback = Total positive customer feedback / Total customer feedback

3. **Calculate the happy customer retention multiplier:** After calculating the percentage of positive feedback, it's important to analyze how it impacts customer retention. By comparing the retention rates of customers who provided positive feedback versus those who gave negative or neutral feedback, you can gain valuable insights into the revenue impact of creating more satisfied customers through your VoC program. This analysis can help you identify areas of improvement in your product or service and develop strategies to increase customer retention and revenue.

Happy customer retention multiplier = the MRR retention rate of customers who gave positive feedback / the MRR retention rate of customers who gave negative or neutral feedback

4. **Leveraging the ROI of your VoC program to increase overall revenue:** To increase overall revenue, it is reasonable to expect that VoC efforts will lead to an increase in the number of customers providing positive feedback, as well as an increase in the overall percentage of positive customer feedback.

By undertaking the process of measuring the ROI of your VoC program, you can unlock a wealth of valuable insights pertaining to the financial benefits and overall effectiveness of your program. Calculating the ROI allows you to quantitatively assess the impact of your VoC initiatives on your company's bottom line and gauge the value they bring in terms of increased revenue and improved customer satisfaction.

Summary

In today's customer-centric business environment, VoC programs have become essential for businesses seeking to gather and consolidate customer feedback. These programs provide a means to collect valuable insights into customers' experiences by soliciting feedback on their needs, desires, expectations, and issues related to a product or service. By leveraging VoC programs, businesses can cultivate a customer-focused culture, empowering all teams to make informed decisions based on the feedback received from customers and prospects. Moreover, customer research and VoC programs are invaluable tools that provide us with a comprehensive understanding of our customers, offering deep insights into their behaviors and motivations.

This wealth of data gathered from customer research serves as a robust foundation for crafting the right products and shaping your product roadmap. In the upcoming chapter, we will explore the intricacies of the product roadmap, investigating how the data gathered from customer research empowers you, as a product marketer, to dynamically reshape the roadmap, ensuring its continued relevance and influence in guiding product development and strategic decision-making.

Influencing the Product Roadmap 6

In the role of inbound product marketer, we hold a critical position in shaping the direction of our company's products. Our main goal is to ensure that the products not only satisfy the present needs of our customers but also adapt to meet their evolving demands. To achieve this, it is essential to have a thorough grasp of the product's future trajectory, and this is where the product roadmap becomes crucial. Drawing upon our extensive knowledge of the market, customers, and competitors, we have the ability to exert influence over the product roadmap.

The product roadmap serves as a **strategic compass** for all teams – product, sales, marketing, and so on – delineating the goals, initiatives, and milestones that steer the product's development and evolution. It acts as a guiding framework, aligning the product's trajectory with market dynamics, customer insights, and business objectives. Through active involvement in crafting and maintaining the product roadmap, we have the power to influence the prioritization of features, enhancements, and updates. This collaborative endeavor entails close collaboration with product managers, engineers, and other stakeholders, ensuring the roadmap reflects a shared vision and effectively addresses customer needs. By acquiring a clear comprehension of the product roadmap, we can proficiently communicate its future direction to internal teams, external stakeholders, and customers, fostering confidence in the product's long-term viability and instilling trust in our customers.

Our active involvement in the product roadmap process as inbound product marketers ensures that our company's products remain relevant, competitive, and attuned to the evolving needs of our customers. By steering the product's direction, we play a crucial role in driving its success and forging strong connections with our target audience.

In this chapter, we'll explore what a product roadmap is, why it's important, and how we can use it to drive growth for our products and company. We'll discuss several topics, including the following:

- The role of product marketing in the product roadmap
- Strategies to influence the product roadmap
- Recommended frameworks to prioritize features

What is a product roadmap?

A product roadmap acts as a vital strategic guide, charting the course for a product's vision, direction, and goals within a specific timeframe. It offers a visual representation of the planned features, enhancements, and strategic initiatives, effectively showcasing the evolution of the product. Beyond its visual aspect, the roadmap plays a crucial role in aligning the development team, stakeholders, and customers, fostering a shared understanding of the product's future direction, and ensuring everyone is on the same page.

A range of tools are available to facilitate the creation and management of product roadmaps, each offering unique advantages. Aha! stands out for its comprehensive features and strategic planning capabilities, while Jira's advanced roadmaps excel in agile project management and integration with development workflows. **Airtable** provides a flexible and collaborative platform for roadmaps, and Monday.com offers an intuitive interface and extensive collaboration features. When choosing a tool, it's important to consider factors such as usability, integration capabilities, visualization options, team collaboration, and pricing. Conducting a thorough evaluation of each tool's strengths and weaknesses will help you select the one that best suits your organization's specific requirements. The tool of choice is secondary as compared to finding the right tool that fits within the respective team's workflow. A well-designed product roadmap includes the following elements:

- **Timeline:** The product roadmap establishes a specific timeframe, whether it's a quarter, six months, or a customized duration, to provide clarity on the roadmap's scope based on the unique requirements of the product and business.

- **Goals and objectives:** By outlining the overall purpose and objectives of the product, the roadmap communicates the strategic goals it aims to achieve and demonstrates its alignment with the broader business strategy.

- **Initiatives and features:** The roadmap identifies and highlights significant initiatives, projects, or features that are planned for development and delivery within the specified timeframe. It offers a high-level overview of the planned milestones and deliverables.

- **Prioritization:** Within the product roadmap, stakeholders gain valuable insights into the relative importance and order of execution assigned to different initiatives or features. This prioritization process empowers stakeholders by providing a clear understanding of which elements carry greater significance and will be given higher priority during implementation.

- **Dependencies:** The product roadmap brings attention to the interconnections and dependencies among different initiatives or features. By shedding light on these relationships, stakeholders can understand the potential impact on the overall timeline if certain dependencies are not fulfilled. This awareness enables proactive management of dependencies to ensure smooth progress and timely delivery.

- **Value:** A well-crafted product roadmap transcends a mere listing of deliverables. It offers a compelling rationale for each initiative or feature, effectively elucidating their significance and how they directly address customer needs or contribute to overall business value. By providing this rationale, stakeholders gain a comprehensive understanding of the purpose and impact of the planned work, fostering informed decision-making and ensuring alignment with strategic objectives.

- **Alignment:** The product roadmap plays a pivotal role as a powerful communication tool, promoting alignment among various stakeholders, including internal teams, executives, customers, and partners. It fosters effective collaboration, enabling seamless teamwork toward shared objectives. By setting clear expectations, the roadmap ensures a common understanding of the product's direction among all involved parties. It also facilitates efficient resource allocation and priority management, leading to enhanced productivity and successful outcomes.

It is important to recognize that product roadmaps are adaptable and responsive to new information, market dynamics, and customer feedback. They are designed to evolve in line with the changing needs and goals of the product and business. Regular review, updates, and refinement are essential to ensure ongoing alignment with emerging requirements, guaranteeing that the roadmap remains a relevant and effective guide for product development and strategic decision-making. Let's explore the pivotal role of product marketing in the product roadmap.

The role of product marketing in the roadmap

For efficient execution of the roadmap, the active involvement of product marketers is vital throughout the planning process. From the initial stages of ideation, we bring valuable insights, questioning assumptions and ensuring a market and customer-centric approach. We leverage past outcomes, identify product gaps, and analyze competitive functionality to shape the roadmap with a strategic perspective. Moreover, as PMMs, we go beyond a feature list by crafting a narrative that adds context and storytelling, enabling effective communication with customers and enhancing their understanding of the roadmap's value proposition.

To ensure effective roadmap execution, regular check-ins such as quarterly roadmap review meetings should encompass various aspects, including progress updates, process changes, decision timelines, KPI reviews, pipeline discussions, and communication updates to different teams. It is crucial to share roadmap updates internally and maintain a centralized source of truth, such as an internal wiki page, to ensure the roadmap is followed and updated consistently. In addition, conducting roadmap presentations to different teams serves as a valuable practice to provide insights, gather feedback, and ensure alignment with the roadmap. This fosters collaboration, enhances understanding, and ensures that all teams are working toward the shared goals outlined in the roadmap. Product marketers serve as a crucial link between diverse teams and the product itself, facilitating effective collaboration and enabling valuable contributions to sales enablement efforts. We achieve this by crafting informative materials and presentations that provide in-depth context about product features. This empowers sales teams to engage with prospects and customers in a confident and informed manner. By equipping sales teams with the essential knowledge and resources they need, we significantly enhance sales effectiveness and contribute to overall customer satisfaction.

Measuring the success of a product and informing future roadmap decisions can be achieved by tracking metrics such as win rates, customer satisfaction, and product adoption. These metrics provide valuable insights into the impact of the product and help refine the roadmap based on real-world performance and customer feedback.

Now, let's delve into possible approaches to shape and impact the product roadmap effectively.

Implementing strategies to influence the product roadmap

Product marketers serve as vital catalysts in shaping the product roadmap, playing integral roles as valued contributors and passionate advocates. Equipped with our profound knowledge of the market and deep customer insights, we collaborate closely with stakeholders to ensure the roadmap accurately captures market demands, fuels innovation, and aligns seamlessly with organizational objectives. Actively engaging with customer success managers, sales teams, executives, and diverse cross-functional departments, product marketers actively seek out a broad range of perspectives to inform and enrich the roadmap's evolution. Drawing on our expertise in market trends and thorough competitive analysis, we skillfully prioritize features that directly address customer needs, cultivate unique market differentiation, and firmly support the overarching product strategy.

Collaboration between product marketers and product management is a vital component of an effective roadmap strategy and communication. By working closely together, product marketers can align priorities, gain a deep understanding of market needs, and advocate for customer-centric features. It is essential to strike a balance in this collaboration, respecting the expertise and responsibilities of the product management team while leveraging the insights and feedback provided by product marketers. Product marketers play a crucial role in collaborating with product management to infuse valuable market insights and customer feedback into the decision-making process. This collaborative partnership ensures that the company's strategic direction is reflected in the roadmap. By closely working together, product marketers and product managers can define clear goals and objectives for the roadmap and effectively communicate them to all teams and stakeholders involved. Effective collaboration between product marketers and product management involves gaining a comprehensive understanding of the strengths and weaknesses of the product management team. This understanding enables product marketers to provide valuable support and guidance and bridge any existing expertise gaps. By fostering a strong and collaborative partnership, the effectiveness of the roadmap strategy and communication is significantly enhanced. This collaborative approach ensures that the roadmap is aligned with the company's goals and enables the delivery of impactful solutions to meet customer needs. By leveraging the respective strengths of product marketers and product management and fostering a collaborative environment, the roadmap can be shaped to deliver customer-centric solutions.

As product marketers, we have the opportunity to assist product managers with the prioritization of product features. With our deep understanding of the product and its target audience, we are in a prime position to provide valuable insights. Particularly when faced with a wide range of potential features, especially if the number exceeds 10, we can employ an effective internal prioritization framework known as the **RICE model**. This framework enables us to evaluate and rank features based on crucial factors, such as their potential **reach, impact, confidence** in problem-solving, and **effort** required from the engineering team. By leveraging the RICE model, we contribute to well-informed decision-making, ensuring that resources are allocated to the most impactful and feasible features.

The RICE method presents a systematic approach to prioritizing features while emphasizing the significance of customer engagement and flexibility in successfully executing the roadmap and delivering value to both the business and its customers. Developed by Sean McBride during his tenure as a product manager at Intercom, the RICE method revolves around employing a scoring system for effective prioritization. McBride suggests four factors to evaluate each feature or project: reach (the estimated number of people impacted within a specific timeframe), impact (the magnitude of influence on each individual, categorized as Massive = 3x, High = 2x, Medium = 1x, Low = 0.5x, and Minimal = 0.25x), confidence (the level of certainty in estimates, rated as High = 100%, Medium = 80%, Low = 50%), and effort (the estimated time required in person-months, using whole numbers with a minimum of half a month). By assessing these factors for each feature, the RICE score can be calculated using a simple formula:

RICE Score = [Reach X Impact X Confidence] / Effort

The score that emerges from this evaluation gauges the "collective impact achieved relative to the effort invested" – precisely the aspect we strive to maximize. By methodically assessing features or projects according to their reach, impact, confidence, and effort, we are empowered to make informed decisions that prioritize endeavors with the utmost potential to propel business success and meet customer satisfaction.

Project name	Reach	Impact	Confidence	Effort	RICE score
Project 1	450	3	100%	2	675
Project 2	2,000	1	80%	4	400
Project 3	800	2	50%	1	800

Figure 6.1 – RICE scoring example

Source: https://www.intercom.com/blog/rice-simple-prioritization-for-product-managers/

In parallel, if we are dealing with a limited set of 10 or fewer features that require testing, I highly recommend utilizing the **Kano method**. Kano employs a classification framework that organizes features into four distinct categories, determined by the varying customer reactions to the level of functionality they provide. With this approach, we ask a set of three questions for each feature: whether users would like to have the feature, whether they don't want it, and how important it is to them. This allows us to analyze the responses and visually plot them to determine whether the features would be appealing to our target audience, enhance performance, are considered "must-be," or whether they might actually be detractors. This approach proves invaluable in identifying which features should not be prioritized, or at least not developed immediately, saving countless hours in production. By leveraging the Kano method, PMMs can effectively influence feature development and subsequently shape the product roadmap.

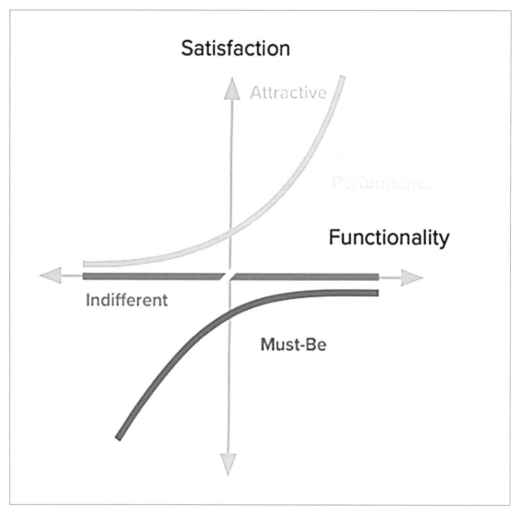

Figure 6.2 – Kano model: The four categories of features.

Source: https://foldingburritos.com/blog/kano-model/

To make informed decisions and prioritize features effectively, the **RAPID** (which stands for **Recommend, Agree, Perform, Input, Decide**) framework is highly recommended. This framework facilitates decision-making and trade-offs by actively involving key stakeholders, gathering their input, and reaching a consensus on priorities. Its collaborative nature ensures that decisions are made with a comprehensive understanding of various perspectives and considerations. Let's consider an example where product marketers collaborate with a product development team tasked with designing a new mobile application. As a team, they acknowledge the need to determine the most important features for the initial release and choose to utilize the RAPID framework. First, each team member independently recommends features based on their expertise and understanding of user needs and market trends. This step encourages the exploration of diverse perspectives and allows for individual analysis. Next, the team comes together to engage in discussions and compare their recommendations. Through open dialogue and active listening, the goal is to reach a collective agreement on the priority of the features. Once a general agreement is reached, the team proceeds to conduct further analysis and evaluation of the recommended features. As product marketers, we may conduct user surveys, market research, and technical assessments to gain a more comprehensive understanding of the benefits and costs associated with each feature. The aim is to acquire meaningful insights that inform the decision-making process. During the input phase, PMMs actively seek feedback from key stakeholders, such as customers, product managers, and executives. Finally, armed with the gathered information and stakeholder input, the PMMs, along with the product development team, evaluate trade-offs and collectively make the final decision on feature prioritization.

As mentioned earlier, PMMs can actively engage customers through surveys and beta programs to gather feedback on specific features. This feedback serves as a valuable validation of roadmap decisions, ensuring that the chosen initiatives align with customer needs and expectations. By involving customers in the roadmap process, product marketers can create a sense of ownership and foster stronger customer relationships. It is important to allocate some space in the roadmap for unexpected tasks and ad hoc requests that may arise. This flexibility allows for adjustments and adaptations to accommodate changing market conditions, emerging opportunities, or unforeseen challenges. By anticipating and accommodating these unexpected activities, product marketers can navigate changes while staying focused on the overall objectives of the roadmap.

In addition to internal communication, establishing effective channels to share the roadmap externally is a vital component of roadmap communication. Product marketers can leverage various methods, such as webinars, customer communication platforms, and other engagement tools to disseminate the roadmap to customers. By proactively sharing the roadmap with customers, product marketers can foster stronger relationships, demonstrate transparency, and actively involve customers in the product's evolution. This open approach not only builds trust but also ensures that customer needs are aligned with the product's direction.

In the external communication of the roadmap, product marketers can contribute by crafting compelling narratives that vividly illustrate the vision and strategic direction of the roadmap. By telling a captivating story, product marketers help stakeholders understand and envision the future plans for the product in a more meaningful way. This storytelling approach enhances comprehension and generates excitement about the product's trajectory, effectively engaging customers and other external stakeholders.

Let's delve deeper into the strategies for effectively communicating the product roadmap both internally and externally.

Communicating the product roadmap

Effectively communicating the product roadmap to customers and prospects is crucial. This can be achieved by establishing dedicated channels for sharing the roadmap with customers and engaging them through various avenues, such as webinars, user groups, and beta programs. By involving customers in these activities, PMMs generate excitement, foster relationships, and gather valuable feedback prior to the official launch of features. This customer-centric approach not only builds customer loyalty but also ensures that the product roadmap aligns with customer needs and expectations, ultimately driving product success.

The success story of Twilio – a renowned cloud communications platform offering a range of tools and services for businesses to effectively connect with their customers through diverse communication channels such as voice, messaging, video, and email – serves as a prime example of the profound influence a product marketing team can exert on molding a company's product roadmap. Through their in-depth understanding of customer needs, market trends, and industry dynamics, the product marketing team at Twilio has played a pivotal role in expanding the platform's capabilities for omnichannel communication. By carefully analyzing customer feedback, conducting thorough market research, and staying abreast of industry trends, they championed the development of key features such as multi-channel messaging orchestration, intelligent routing, and chatbot integrations. These enhancements have empowered businesses to deliver personalized and contextually relevant communication experiences to their customers.

Moreover, the product marketers at Twilio recognized the critical role of analytics and reporting in evaluating the effectiveness of communication strategies. Working closely with product management and engineering teams, they prioritized the incorporation of robust analytics capabilities within the Twilio platform. This resulted in the introduction of features such as real-time analytics dashboards, detailed reporting, and performance metrics, enabling businesses to track, optimize, and make data-driven decisions to enhance their customer engagement strategies.

Through their deep market insights, customer-centric approach, and collaborative efforts with cross-functional teams, the product marketing team at Twilio has successfully influenced the product roadmap to address the evolving needs of businesses and deliver innovative solutions in the realm of cloud communications.

Sharing the product roadmap with customers is a strategic imperative in today's highly competitive business landscape, offering a range of benefits that go beyond mere communication. It builds trust, nurtures customer relationships, and drives business growth by creating a collaborative environment where customers actively contribute to the evolution of the product. An excellent illustration of a company that regularly shares its product roadmap every quarter is Dell Boomi. They provide a comprehensive overview of recent achievements and upcoming enhancements for the Dell Boomi platform (*for a concrete example, you can visit the following link:* https://community.boomi.com/s/article/Everything-You-Want-to-Know-About-the-Boomi-Product-Roadmap-Q3-2022).

Sharing the roadmap is essential for several reasons, which are as follows:

- **Fostering trust and strengthening relationships**: Openly sharing the roadmap cultivates trust and confidence in your company, reinforcing customer relationships.

- **Providing insight and managing expectations**: The roadmap offers customers valuable insight into your product's future, enabling them to align their strategies and manage their expectations accordingly.

- **Gathering customer feedback and collaboration**: Sharing the roadmap invites customer feedback and collaboration, making customers feel valued and empowering them to shape the product's direction.

- **Competitive differentiation**: The product roadmap differentiates your company by showcasing its vision, innovation, and commitment to improvement. Aligning future plans with customer needs sets you apart as a forward-thinking solution provider.

- **Enhancing sales and upselling opportunities**: Sharing the roadmap strategically benefits sales by providing valuable talking points and reasons for prospects to choose your product. It demonstrates a commitment to development and future value, facilitating deal closures and upselling opportunities.

- **Strengthening customer engagement and loyalty**: Regularly sharing the roadmap keeps customers engaged and demonstrates your commitment to delivering value and innovation. This fosters loyalty and advocacy, as customers feel invested in the product's success.

Sharing the product roadmap demonstrates your company's dedication to customer-centricity, as it highlights the alignment of your goals with their needs and aspirations. This practice fosters a strong and mutually beneficial relationship, where customers feel valued and actively engaged in the product development process. In the upcoming section, we will delve into effective strategies for transparently communicating the product roadmap to both existing customers and potential prospects, empowering them to be part of the journey.

Effectively communicating the product roadmap and vision

To effectively communicate the product roadmap to customers and prospects, product marketers can employ a variety of channels and strategies. One recommended approach is to host a public-facing product roadmap event once a year, supplemented by smaller updates 1-3 times per quarter based on new information. During these events, a slide deck with a demo can be presented, providing an overview of the roadmap. However, instead of making the slide deck widely available, it can be shared exclusively in 1:1 meetings between a salesperson or customer success manager and the customers or prospects. This personalized approach allows for a tailored discussion, addressing specific customer needs and concerns. It is crucial to set clear expectations during these meetings, informing customers that priorities and plans may change. This helps manage customer expectations and ensures they understand that the roadmap is subject to adjustments based on evolving market conditions and customer feedback. When presenting the roadmap, it is advisable to maintain a relatively high-level overview of the roadmap categories rather than diving into granular details. This approach provides flexibility and adaptability as the product team continues to gather insights and refine their priorities.

To effectively communicate the roadmap and ensure widespread understanding, a combination of strategies can be employed. In addition to dedicated roadmap events and one-on-one meetings, it is valuable to leverage various communication channels, such as webinars, a dedicated web page, blog posts, and videos. When engaging with the sales team and customers, it is essential to emphasize the dynamic nature of the roadmap and its potential for change. Webinars offer the advantage of reaching a larger audience, enabling controlled messaging, and establishing the company as an industry expert. These sessions provide an opportunity to educate the sales team on the latest updates and equip them with compelling messaging to effectively engage with prospects and customers. A dedicated web page on the company's website serves as a centralized hub for roadmap information. This web page can be regularly updated with relevant details, milestones, and progress updates. Additionally, informative blog posts and engaging videos tailored to the target audience's preferences can be published to keep customers well-informed and involved in the company's journey.

In addition to these online channels, product marketers can leverage other avenues, such as press articles, analyst presentations, email communications, physical events, and user groups, to disseminate the product roadmap. Collaborating closely with the sales and customer success teams to showcase the roadmap to customers on an individual basis, providing personalized insights and addressing their specific needs, can significantly enhance the customer experience. Furthermore, hosting webinars that invite broader engagement and interaction with prospects and customers can foster a sense of inclusivity and collaboration.

Effectively communicating the product roadmap and vision requires positioning the company as a **trusted partner** and advisor for customers. This can be achieved by actively supporting and providing context for the roadmap decisions, advocating for transparency and accessibility to the roadmap, and emphasizing the value that the roadmap brings to the overall product strategy. It is important to recognize that the product roadmap and strategy are highly impactful topics within the organization, involving various cross-functional teams with their unique perspectives and interests. As product marketers, it is crucial to influence the roadmap and collaborate on its strategy and communication without overstepping boundaries.

One way to effectively communicate the product roadmap is by crafting a compelling narrative around it. This narrative should highlight the problem-solving capabilities and the value that the roadmap brings to customers and the market. By weaving a coherent story that aligns with the company's vision, product marketers can engage stakeholders and inspire them to support and contribute to the roadmap's success. Sales enablement is another key aspect of roadmap communication. Providing comprehensive training to the sales team ensures that they are equipped with the necessary knowledge and messaging to effectively communicate the roadmap's value proposition to customers. This includes understanding the roadmap's strategic direction, key features, and anticipated customer benefits. Sales enablement materials such as presentations, sales decks, and FAQs can further empower the sales team to have meaningful conversations and address customer inquiries related to the roadmap.

Customer feedback is indeed invaluable when it comes to shaping and refining the roadmap. Product marketers should actively engage with customers, seeking their input and involving them in beta programs or early access opportunities. One effective way to gather customer feedback is through surveys, interviews, and focus groups. These interactions provide valuable insights into customer preferences, pain points, and desired features or improvements. By actively listening to customers and involving them in the roadmap process, product marketers can build a strong sense of partnership and co-creation. In addition to direct customer engagement, product marketers can leverage user analytics and data to gather insights. Analyzing user behavior, usage patterns, and feedback can provide valuable information on how customers are interacting with the product and what areas may require attention or enhancement.

It is important to maintain open lines of communication with customers throughout the roadmap journey. Regularly updating customers on the progress and status of their feedback and involving them in the decision-making process fosters a sense of ownership and investment.

Product marketers play a crucial role in roadmap communication by positioning themselves as partners and advocates for the product roadmap. They can achieve this by providing context, advocating for transparency, and emphasizing the value of the roadmap to various stakeholders within the organization. While product marketers undeniably play a pivotal role in communicating roadmaps, it's important to acknowledge that there exist businesses, or individuals within the realm of product marketing, that maintain the perspective that sharing a product roadmap externally, that is, with customers, competitors, or the public, might pose certain challenges and potential downsides. From their standpoint, this sharing can sometimes be perceived as a distraction due to several reasons:

- **Competitive concerns**: Sharing a roadmap can potentially expose a company's strategic plans to competitors, giving them insights into future developments. This could lead to a competitor adjusting their own strategies in response, potentially undermining the company's competitive advantage.

- **Managing expectations:** External parties, including customers, investors, or even the media, may interpret the roadmap as a firm commitment. If unexpected changes occur or deadlines aren't met, it can lead to disappointment or skepticism.

- **Market shifts:** The business landscape is dynamic, and unforeseen shifts can alter the relevance or feasibility of certain roadmap items. This might necessitate frequent adjustments, leading to potential confusion among external stakeholders.

- **Focus on execution:** Some argue that excessive external communication about future plans could divert attention from effectively executing the present initiatives that directly address customer needs and concerns.

- **Resource allocation:** Sharing a roadmap could potentially result in customers focusing on future features and solutions rather than utilizing existing offerings. This might skew resource allocation decisions and impact the product's overall growth trajectory.

While these concerns are valid, it's important to note that the decision to share a product roadmap externally depends on various factors, including the industry, company culture, and customer expectations. Many companies find value in transparent communication, building trust with customers, and leveraging their roadmap to engage the market effectively.

Summary

In this chapter, we have explored the significant role that product marketers play in shaping the product roadmap and guiding product directions. Our journey began with a clear definition of what a product roadmap entails. We then dove into the crucial internal and external contributions product marketers make to the roadmap. To effectively influence the product roadmap, we discussed various frameworks and strategies that we, as product marketers, can employ. By applying these strategies, we can effectively collaborate with product managers, taking a systematic and data-driven approach to feature prioritization. This ensures that the product roadmap maximizes its impact and delivers value, ultimately leading to successful product development and customer satisfaction.

In the upcoming chapter, we will take a deep dive into the realm of segmentation and personas, exploring proven methodologies and best practices that will help us leverage customer research to build them effectively.

Customer Segmentation and Personas 7

Today's consumers are more fragmented than ever, and in order to truly connect with them and uncover their buying patterns, you need to deeply understand who they are, what their needs are, and what motivates their buying behavior. That's where segmentation and personas come in – they're like your trusty compass and map, helping you navigate the complex terrain of your target market.

The process of segmentation involves dividing a larger market into smaller, more manageable groups based on customers' shared characteristics, behaviors, or desires. This approach provides a deeper understanding of customers' specific preferences or interests, enabling you to tailor your marketing efforts and allocate your resources effectively.

And personas? Well, they're like the colorful characters that populate the world of your market. They're fictional representations of your ideal customers – complete with names, personalities, and even hobbies. By creating detailed personas, you can get a deeper understanding of your customers' wants and needs and understand the jobs to be done (JTBD) to tailor your product marketing strategies accordingly.

This chapter will explore the ways in which segmentation and personas can revolutionize your understanding of your customers, influence your product development and marketing tactics, and set the stage for customized customer experiences. As we delve into this topic, we will address critical points, such as the following:

- What is segmentation and how can we improve customer segmentation?
- How can personas be used effectively to enhance your marketing efforts?
- How can JTBD improve your product development process and make it more relevant to each customer segment?

To start, let's delve into the topic of customer segmentation.

Segmentation – How to improve customer segmentation

Before delving into customer segmentation, it's important to understand the difference between market and customer segmentation. Market segmentation involves dividing a larger market into smaller groups of customers who share similar needs or characteristics. A market segment refers to a subset of customers within a larger target market who possess common characteristics or behavior patterns that distinguish them from other customers. In other words, a market segment is a group of customers or businesses that share similar needs, preferences, or interests, and who are likely to respond in a similar way to marketing messages and promotions. Market segmentation is a crucial tool that helps businesses gain a comprehensive understanding of their target audience as a whole, with the ultimate goal of gaining insights into the overall market and its segments. This allows companies to connect with and create targeted and effective marketing strategies for each group of potential customers in various ways, such as product awareness, designing new products that cater to specific market needs, or enhancing existing products by introducing new features.

Zoom, for example, is a popular video conferencing software that offers a range of features for personal and business use. To target their market effectively, Zoom uses market segmentation. They segment their market by size of business, industry, and type of use. For example, they target small businesses with up to 50 employees, as well as larger businesses with more than 1,000 employees. They also target specific industries, such as healthcare and education, and offer features tailored to those industries, including integration with **learning management systems** (**LMSs**) such as **Blackboard** and **Canvas** for educational institutions. Additionally, they segment their market by the type of use, such as virtual events, webinars, and online classes. This allows them to create targeted marketing campaigns and product offerings to meet the specific needs of each segment.

In contrast, customer segmentation involves dividing a company's existing customer base into smaller groups based on similar characteristics, such as demographics, purchase behavior, or retention. It's a process of grouping customers into meaningful buckets to avoid using a generic *one-size-fits-all* approach and instead create customized strategies that cater to the specific needs of each customer group. Customer segmentation is the right tool to validate or discredit earlier hypotheses about consumers and needs in the market. This enables companies to make more informed decisions about their marketing strategies, messaging, and product development. By providing objective data, companies can refine their understanding of their customers and tailor their strategies accordingly. Additionally, customer segmentation analysis can uncover opportunities among segments that have been underserved or overlooked. By identifying customer groups with unmet needs, your company can develop new products or services tailored to those segments, ultimately expanding your customer base and driving revenue growth.

It's true that commissioning and activating a deep segmentation study can be a major investment for a business, but it can also be a valuable tool for driving growth and success. A comprehensive segmentation study not only provides a crystal-clear comprehension of the market and its customers but also acts as a unifying force for the entire organization. It helps to align stakeholders and promote teamwork toward shared goals, much like a conductor leads an orchestra to create a harmonious symphony.

This study involves the division of a market or customer base into sub-groups based on specific characteristics, such as demographics, behaviors, or attitudes. In particular, a deep segmentation study can inform product-market fit with various sub-segments of the market. By understanding the unique needs, preferences, and behaviors of different customer groups, businesses can tailor their offerings to better meet customer needs and preferences. This leads to higher customer satisfaction and, ultimately, greater revenue growth. Additionally, a deep segmentation study can guide future **total addressable market (TAM)** expansions. By identifying new and underserved customer groups, businesses can expand their market reach and tap into new revenue streams.

Spotify is a good example of a company that uses customer segmentation to identify groups of customers with different music preferences, listening habits, and willingness to pay for its premium service. Spotify divides its customers into three main segments:

- Free users who listen to music with ads
- Premium subscribers who pay a monthly fee to access ad-free music and additional features such as offline listening and higher audio quality
- Family subscribers who pay a higher monthly fee to share the premium service with up to six family members

Spotify also uses data analytics and machine learning to personalize the music recommendations and playlists for each customer based on their listening history, location, and other factors. This allows Spotify to tailor its marketing campaigns and product offerings to each segment and improve the overall customer experience.

Now that we have clarified the distinction between market segmentation and customer segmentation, let's delve deeper into customer segmentation.

Understanding why segmenting your customer base is critical

Analyzing customer data is a crucial step toward developing a comprehensive understanding of your customers and gaining valuable insights that can help you allocate your resources more effectively and focus on the most profitable customer segments.

Customer segmentation is a powerful tool that enables businesses to create user profiles and group customers based on similarities, allowing for a tailored experience at each touchpoint of the customer journey. This approach provides businesses with valuable insights to create targeted marketing campaigns and advertisements that resonate with specific customer segments, reaching them through their preferred channels and platforms. By customizing content to meet the unique needs and challenges of each group, businesses can increase customer engagement and satisfaction. With more effective targeting, businesses can improve their marketing **return on investment (ROI)** by focusing on those customers most likely to make a purchase, delivering the right marketing messages at the right time in their journey.

In addition, customer segmentation is instrumental in optimizing new product development. By gaining insights into the diverse needs and preferences of various customer segments, businesses can develop products that better align with the desires of their target customers. This can lead to a significant boost in customer loyalty and satisfaction.

Moreover, segmentation is a powerful tool for improving customer relationship management, allowing companies to tailor communication strategies and customer service and customer support efforts to better meet the needs and preferences of different customer segments. By doing so, companies can provide a more personalized and satisfactory customer experience. Next, let's explore the various types of customer segmentation in detail.

Navigating the types of customer segmentation

As you start to develop your customer segmentation strategy, it's essential to consider the various types of segmentation models available and the different variables that can be used. There is no one-size-fits-all approach when it comes to customer segmentation, as different companies may require different models based on their specific needs and goals. Effective customer segmentation can provide valuable insights into your customers' preferences and behaviors, helping you identify new opportunities for product and service development and optimize your marketing and sales strategies. To achieve this, you can utilize various types of customer segmentation models that best fit your needs and goals. The following are some common forms of customer segmentation mainly for a B2B company:

- **Post hoc:** This is a segmentation method that seeks to identify consumer groups that are significant for various marketing purposes. Unlike other segmentation methods, it does not involve predefining target groups. Instead, it aims to discover relatively homogenous and distinct groups. To achieve this, companies can gather data from different sources, including consumer surveys, customer transaction records, market research, and competitor analysis. By using *cluster* analysis, a statistical technique, the datasets can be analyzed to classify consumers into different segments. The resulting segments can be defined and profiled based on various criteria, such as consumer attitudes, behavior, and demographics. Data can be sourced from different databases, including consumer surveys and customer records, or by combining attitudinal data with factual data from customer transaction databases.

  HubSpot, a software company specializing in marketing and sales, employed the post hoc segmentation technique to pinpoint customer groups that are most inclined to use specific features of its platform. By using this method, HubSpot discovered that customers who utilize the email marketing tool are also more likely to use its blog platform. With this information, HubSpot developed targeted email campaigns aimed at promoting its blog platform to customers who had not yet used it.

- **Behavioral:** This involves grouping customers based on their actions when interacting with a product or service. The purpose of this segmentation approach is to gain a more comprehensive understanding of how customers use a product or service and to determine what benefits they are seeking.

Drift, a conversational marketing platform, is a great example of a company effectively implementing behavioral segmentation. Drift allows businesses to engage with website visitors in real-time through chatbots and targeted messaging. Drift uses behavioral segmentation to identify visitors who are more likely to convert into customers based on their behavior on the website, such as the pages they visit, the actions they take, and the time spent on the site. Drift then delivers personalized messages and recommendations to these visitors to nudge them toward a conversion. For example, if a visitor spends a significant amount of time on the pricing page, Drift can trigger a chatbot message that offers a discount or a demo of the product. This approach has helped Drift increase its **conversion rates (CVRs)** and improve the overall customer experience on its platform.

- **Geographic**: This is a customer segmentation strategy that divides a customer base into distinct geographic units based on various factors, such as location, climate, and culture. This approach aims to identify similarities and differences among customers in different locations and adjust marketing strategies accordingly.

- **Firmographic**: Categorizes customers into groups based on the specific characteristics of their business. These characteristics can include factors such as company size, industry, location, revenue, and other relevant attributes.

Sisense, a provider of business intelligence and analytics software, employs firmographic segmentation to target particular industries and company sizes. Sisense's software is ideal for companies with complex data needs, making it a suitable solution for industries such as finance, healthcare, and e-commerce where data analysis is crucial. They offer different product packages based on the size of the company, catering to small businesses as well as large enterprises. Through the use of firmographic segmentation, Sisense customizes its marketing messages and product offerings to the unique requirements and challenges of different industries and company sizes, enhancing the effectiveness of its marketing campaigns.

- **Needs-based**: This approach involves grouping customers based on their specific needs and desires, such as financial, emotional, and physical. To successfully execute this segmentation approach, it's crucial to gather qualitative and quantitative data that will enable you to develop a comprehensive understanding of your customers' requirements.

Salesforce uses needs-based segmentation to categorize customers according to the specific business challenges they seek to overcome. This approach enables Salesforce to develop targeted marketing campaigns and customized product packages that address the unique needs of each customer segment. For example, Salesforce tailors its marketing automation solutions to customers who prioritize enhancing their marketing efforts, while offering a variety of features and packages to help improve sales processes, customer service, and more. By leveraging needs-based segmentation, Salesforce gains a deeper understanding of its customer's needs and pain points, enabling it to provide solutions that are most relevant to their business objectives.

- **Value-based:** Value-based segmentation is a type of audience segmentation that involves grouping customers based on the financial value they provide to your business. This is achieved by analyzing customer data to determine which groups generate the highest lifetime value. With this information, you can direct your marketing efforts toward the most profitable customer segments and optimize their ROI.

  Value-based segmentation is a crucial process for businesses seeking to maximize their marketing effectiveness. By understanding which customer groups are most cost-effective to target, retain, and convert, companies can prioritize their marketing resources and allocate their budget more efficiently.

  Salesloft is a sales engagement platform that uses value-based segmentation to target customers who prioritize sales efficiency and productivity. The company divides its customer base into different categories based on their sales cycle complexity, sales team size, and overall revenue. Salesloft offers different product packages and features that cater to each customer segment's specific needs and challenges, such as email tracking, cadence management, and analytics. By using value-based segmentation, Salesloft is able to create tailored solutions that help its customers achieve their sales goals more efficiently and effectively.

To ensure the effectiveness of your customer segmentation strategy, it's essential to evaluate your objectives and select a suitable segmentation approach that aligns with them. For example, say you're a winter gear company that focuses on selling products to people in colder regions. In that case, you could use geographic segmentation to target customers living in those areas. Conversely, if your aim is to persuade your existing clients to upgrade to a premium software version, you might prefer using firmographic segmentation to target large organizations with more workers who may require advanced features. While choosing the segmentation model is an important part of the customer segmentation process, it is not the only step. Let's take a closer look at the entire customer segmentation process.

Mastering the customer segmentation process

The customer segmentation process can involve four steps:

1. Gathering data
2. Pattern identification
3. Performance analysis
4. Prioritizing segments

Let us explore these in a bit more detail:

- **Gathering data:** Creating an effective customer segmentation strategy requires a reliable and accurate dataset. The process begins by analyzing existing customers to gather as much information as possible. This involves collecting relevant data from multiple sources, such as customer profiles, purchase history, demographic information, geographic location, and any other data points that can provide valuable insights into customer characteristics. To create a comprehensive dataset for customer segmentation, it is crucial to combine all available data on customers' demographics, geography, psychographics, and behavior. This includes incorporating any additional account or business data you may have, such as win/loss interviews, customer surveys, or engagement scores such as NPS. By consolidating these diverse data sources, you can obtain a holistic view of your customer base. A recommended approach is to create a spreadsheet that includes data for all current customers, as well as past customers, including those who have churned or were on a free trial. The master dataset should encompass all the relevant data points necessary for customer segmentation. In order to enhance the accuracy and completeness of the dataset, I recommend leveraging external tools and resources to supplement your existing data. Once the master dataset is compiled, the next step is to sort the data to identify patterns.

- **Pattern identification:** To identify patterns, sort relevant data by volume, including demographics, geography, and account information. This helps identify three to five customer groups representing a significant portion of your customer base. These groups can form the basis for a hypothesis, which will be validated in subsequent stages. Thoroughly analyze the sorted data to discover patterns and similarities among customers. Look for common characteristics or behaviors that define distinct groups. These identified groups should have clear defining features, enabling easy identification and meaningful implications for targeting these groups.

- **Performance analysis:** To confirm the accuracy of your customer segment hypothesis and assess the effectiveness of your selected customer groups, we will conduct a thorough analysis of the entire customer life cycle. In order to validate this, we will evaluate five key performance indicators – CVR, **average revenue per unit** (ARPU), retention rate, churn rate, and **customer lifetime value** (CLTV). After obtaining the customer metrics, you can integrate the data into your segment hypothesis spreadsheet. This will provide you with a comprehensive perspective of the performance of each customer segment. By contrasting and evaluating the metrics of each segment with one another and with those of the average customer, you can identify which segments are the most valuable and those that may be less valuable.

- **Prioritizing segments:** Once you have identified your largest groups of customers by volume and then validated their performance, it's time to prioritize your segments. Moving forward, take into consideration the following aspects when evaluating each segment:

  - **Customer value:** When prioritizing segments, it's crucial to consider the customer value by assessing the average and median CLTV within each segment. A higher CLTV indicates a higher level of customer quality and potential value.

  - **Segment size:** When prioritizing segments, it's essential to consider the market representation of each segment and select those that offer a substantial market size to capture, aligning with your revenue and growth objectives. Allocate your sales and marketing efforts and budget toward segments that exhibit both high quality and sufficient size.

- ◦ **Growth potential:** When prioritizing segments, it is crucial to evaluate their potential for future growth by examining market trends, demographic shifts, and upcoming regulatory changes. Analyze how external factors can influence the growth trajectory of each segment. For instance, if there is a surge in the demand for sustainable and eco-friendly products, it may indicate a growing market for renewable energy solutions, prompting you to prioritize segments related to clean technology and green energy.

Effective customer segmentation is a continuous process that entails regular optimization of your existing customer segments. To keep your segments up to date, you can utilize various data sources, including win-loss interviews and customer surveys. By gaining further insights into the customers belonging to each segment, you can enhance your understanding of what motivates this group, what your products' benefits are, and what tactics and strategies are most effective in converting and retaining them.

As we've learned, creating customer segments is mainly a quantitative process that aims to optimize a company's operations and business model. This typically involves combining external prospect surveys with internal data on customer interactions to identify attributes that are associated with specific customer behaviors and outcomes. Key factors for segmentation can include purchasing behaviors, customer barriers to entry, demographics, and identifying jobs that customers are trying to accomplish. It's worth noting that companies often use multiple segmentation approaches to guide various business decisions, such as using retention segmentation to identify high-risk attrition segments and market segmentation to prioritize the most promising potential customers. By identifying and understanding the characteristics and behaviors of your ideal customers, you can target prospects who are most likely to become valuable, loyal customers.

As mentioned earlier, when defining customer segments, it's important to consider the specific goals and objectives of the business. The methodology used to create segments should align with the overall strategy and be tailored to meet the business's specific needs. Investing heavily in the upfront phase of segment definition can help ensure that the methodology used is effective and aligned with the organization's needs. This phase typically involves gathering requirements from all internal stakeholders, including marketing, sales, customer service, and product teams, to understand their needs and goals. By involving all relevant parties, the business can ensure that the segmentation is comprehensive and considers all necessary factors.

In addition, getting buy-in on the methodology from all stakeholders is crucial to ensure a smooth and successful implementation. This means communicating the methodology clearly and addressing any concerns or questions that stakeholders may have. By ensuring that all stakeholders are on board, you can create a shared understanding of how the segmentation will be used and its expected impact, which can help promote adoption and success.

Crafting your ideal customer profile

It's important to clarify the concept of the **ideal customer profile** (**ICP**) and its distinction from customer segmentation. An ICP is a comprehensive description of the ideal customer for a business, including firmographic and behavioral traits that define this customer. On the other hand, customer segmentation involves grouping customers based on shared characteristics, usually to identify their needs, preferences, and motivations and to develop targeted marketing and sales strategies for specific segments.

An ICP provides you with a clear and detailed description of the type of company that is most likely to have a genuine interest in your products or services and to become a loyal and valuable customer over time. In addition, an ICP helps you identify the target audience who are more likely to provide positive referrals to others, further expanding your customer base. The ICP is derived from a list of essential criteria and features, such as company size, location, growth rate, situational factors, and decision-making factors, which are most relevant to your company. The customer profile does not focus on individual customer characteristics. Instead, it looks at the shared characteristics and attributes of a group of customers with comparable behaviors.

Ideal Customer Profile – Example

Factors	Description
Segment Sub-Industries Company Size Location Budget	B2B enterprise SaaS Tech companies: Fintech, MarTech, and so on. 1,000+ Global $80K- $300K per year
Decision-Making Factors	CEO and CTO are primary decision makers
Business Goals	• Increase productivity • Improve team collaboration • Enhance remote work capabilities
Pain Points	• Difficulty in managing projects • Siloed information • Inefficient communication
Attributes	• Innovative • Customer-centric

Figure 7.1 – ICP framework – example

The identification of an ICP offers numerous benefits, allowing you to allocate your time, budget, and marketing resources more effectively. The ICP enables you to tailor your messaging and product positioning to better align with your target audience's needs and preferences and validate product-market fit. By narrowing down the target audience, you can identify the most promising leads, which enables you to increase engagement and CVRs, reduce **customer acquisition costs (CACs)**, and increase CLTV. Building customer loyalty is also a key benefit, as you can leverage the feedback and referrals of happy customers to attract new clients.

Customer segmentation is useful for dividing customers into smaller groups based on shared characteristics, but an ICP provides a detailed description of the ideal company that a business wants to target with their products or services. While an ICP may not provide a complete view of customer identities, personas can help provide more comprehensive insights. Personas involve developing fictional characters that represent the ideal customer within each segment, using market research, customer data, and other insights to gain a better understanding of their behaviors, goals, challenges, and preferences. Both customer segmentation and personas involve breaking down a larger target audience into smaller groups, but personas go further by providing a more detailed and personalized view of the target customer.

Incorporating customer segmentation and personas into your strategy allows for tailored marketing and sales efforts for each group, ultimately improving overall performance. By creating products, services, and marketing campaigns that better align with your customer's needs, you can enhance customer satisfaction and loyalty and consequently drive growth. So, let's dive deeper into what personas are and how they can be used effectively to gain a better understanding of customers and create products and experiences that truly resonate with them.

Understanding your personas in detail

Developing personas is a fundamental aspect of any thriving product marketing strategy. Regardless of whether you're developing a sales pitch, launching a new product, or creating a case study, personas should always influence your approach.

Well-developed personas encompass demographic information and behavioral patterns, providing critical insights to guide marketing strategies, product development, and **user experience (UX)** design. With well-crafted personas, product marketers can tailor their messaging to each audience segment, resulting in improved customer engagement. Additionally, personas can help product teams maintain a customer-centric approach throughout the product development process, ensuring that the final product aligns with customer preferences and expectations. Moreover, personas can provide benefits to customer service and support teams by providing a clear understanding of customers' motivations and challenges, enabling personalized and relevant solutions to customer issues, resulting in an enhanced customer experience.

Personas are not just any old fictional characters – they are created with a specific purpose in mind. By conducting thorough market research and analyzing customer data, you can identify common attributes and characteristics of your target audience. These insights are then used to craft personas that represent the ideal customer within each segment. It's important to note that relying on internal assumptions alone is insufficient when creating accurate and effective personas. To achieve this, it's necessary to validate your assumptions by gathering insights from real customers and to regularly update them as you learn and evolve. Nonetheless, when you put in the effort to refine its personas, the rewards can be substantial.

To create a detailed and accurate persona for your target audience, it is essential to have a deep understanding of their demographics, psychographics, motivations, and pain points. This means you need to know who your customer is, what they want and need, and what challenges they face. Effective personas should take into account the obstacles that prevent your target customer from achieving their goals and the problems they are trying to solve. In addition, an effective persona includes information about how your product or service can help your target customer solve their problems. This means identifying the specific features or benefits of your product that are most relevant to their needs. By including these elements in your persona, you can create a more accurate and detailed representation of your target audience.

Navigating persona types – user, buyer, and more

Product marketers can utilize various persona types to gain deeper insights into their customers. While user and buyer personas are widely adopted, negative personas can help identify people who are not a good fit for a product or service. In B2B companies, decision-maker personas are essential in pinpointing individuals with the authority to make purchase decisions. Additionally, there are many other types of personas that can be customized to fit specific situations. In the upcoming section of this chapter, we will delve into user and buyer personas, with a particular emphasis on B2B buyer personas.

User personas

A user persona is an imaginary character that embodies a specific group of potential users for a product or service. It is developed through analyzing user data and provides a window into typical user behaviors, motivations, and challenges. Gaining insight into user needs and expectations enables product designers and marketers to create products and services that are more focused on the user. Let's take a look at a user B2B persona.

Claudia

Age
33 years

Education
MBA

Location
United States

Social Network

Industry
Tech, Travel

Company Size
1,000-5,000

Income
$75K-$85K

Reports to
Performance Marketing Manager

Bio

Claudia reports to the Performance Marketing Manager and is responsible for managing the company's pay-per-click advertising campaigns. She works closely with the marketing team to develop effective strategies that drive traffic and revenue growth for the company.

Role in the Buying process

Influencer

Contact Preferences

Email

Motivators
- Measurable
- Speed
- User-friendly
- Familiarity

Personality
- Detail-oriented
- Data-driven
- Target-oriented
- Collaborative
- Strategic

Job Responsibilities
- Keeping up with PPC trends and best practices to enhance campaign performance
- Managing campaign budgets and ensuring efficient allocation of resources
- Reporting and sharing insights with stakeholders on campaign performance and progress toward KPIs
- Collaborating with cross-functional teams to align campaign objectives and maximize results
- Developing and executing PPC strategies that drive traffic, conversions, and revenue growth
- Analyzing campaign data to identify areas for optimization and making data-driven decisions

Quotes

"I've used various tools and software to manage our PPC campaigns, but none of them have been able to fully meet our needs or save us time."

"We need a partner who can offer fresh insights to help us hit our ROI while delivering enough qualified leads."

Jobs to be done

Ensure campaigns achieve high ROI, and be confident in meeting daily lead delivery targets to the sales team.

Challenges
- Meeting aggressive performance targets set by the Performance Marketing Manager
- Meeting daily delivery targets of qualified leads to sales teams

Tech and Media Consumption
- Google AdWords, Bing, FB ads, and DoubleClick
- Google analytics, AppsFlyer, and Marketo
- Google Sheets and Microsoft Excel
- Podcasts, webinars, events, Google and FB blogs, and academies
- Slack and Asana

Messaging

When talking to Claudia, emphasize our product's ability to improve campaign performance, drive ROI, and save time through embedded features. As a highly motivated individual focused on delivering quality leads to the sales team, Claudia needs a reliable partner to help her achieve her goals. Let us be that partner and provide the support she needs to succeed.

" Effortlessly maximize campaign performance and deliver high-quality leads with our bid management tools."

Figure 7.2 – B2B user persona example continued

Crafting a user persona is an essential step in the product development process, as it allows the product team to gain a deeper understanding of their users and their unique requirements. Rather than designing for a vague and generalized user base, a user persona creates a more precise and realistic representation of the target user group. This enables the product team to make informed decisions on product design and UX, ensuring that the end product meets the needs and preferences of its intended users.

Throughout the product development process, user personas play a critical role as a source of inspiration, guidance, and empathy. During the ideation stage, personas inspire teams to generate new and innovative ideas that align with the needs of their target audience. As the design and development phases commence, personas become invaluable assets for creating user interfaces, features, and functionalities that are tailored to the unique needs of different user groups.

By gathering data and insights on what a user thinks, feels, says, and does, product teams can create effective *empathy maps* that help them better understand and empathize with their users. This understanding enables teams to identify pain points and opportunities for improvement in the UX, which can then guide the development of new features and enhancements to existing ones. As a result, user personas and empathy maps work together to ensure that the user's needs and goals remain at the forefront of the product development process, from ideation to launch and beyond.

Moreover, user personas are frequently utilized to establish *user journeys* that offer a graphical depiction of the user's interaction with a product or service. These journeys highlight both the positive and negative aspects of the UX, allowing product teams to gain a comprehensive understanding of their users and identify opportunities for enhancement. This information can be leveraged to prioritize areas requiring urgent attention and enhance the overall UX.

While user personas focus on understanding the needs and preferences of potential users of a product or service, buyer personas provide insights into the motivations and decision-making processes of the individuals or groups who are responsible for making purchasing decisions. Next, let's delve into buyer personas in more detail.

Buyer personas

A buyer persona is a carefully crafted representation of a business's ideal customer, created using data gathered through market research. The primary objective of a buyer persona is to identify the customers who are most likely to make a purchase of a product or service. By using this tool, you can gain a comprehensive understanding of your customers' unique needs, behaviors, motivations, and preferences. This information can then be utilized to tailor marketing and sales strategies that are specifically designed to attract and retain these customers. Effective use of buyer personas enables you to increase engagement and CVRs by delivering messaging, content, and advertising campaigns that resonate with your target audience, ultimately leading to an increased customer base and sustainable growth.

It's important to note that there is a key distinction between a user persona and a buyer persona in their respective roles in the purchasing process. A buyer persona is a representation of the ideal customer who is most likely to make a purchase of a product or service. This persona focuses on the buying behavior of the customer, such as their decision-making process, budget, and purchasing preferences. In contrast, a user persona is a representation of the ideal customer who will use the product or service after it is purchased. This persona focuses on the user's needs, goals, and behaviors related to the product or service.

While these personas have different focuses, there can be some overlap between them. In some cases, the buyer might also be the primary user of the product or service. For example, a small business owner who purchases accounting software for their company may also be the primary user of the software. In this case, it's important to consider both the buyer and user personas during research and development to ensure that the product or service meets the needs and expectations of both parties.

How to create a buyer persona?

Buyer personas can be a valuable asset for B2B companies looking to segment their customer base and gain a better understanding of their target audience. By identifying individuals with both the desire and decision-making power to become customers, buyer personas can provide a comprehensive view of the ideal customer. The number of buyer personas required for each segment will vary depending on factors such as product complexity, target audience diversity, and marketing campaign goals. However, it's generally recommended to have 3-5 well-researched and detailed buyer personas. B2B companies targeting multiple industries or verticals should aim to create a unique buyer persona for each one to ensure targeted messaging. However, having too many buyer personas can dilute the messaging and decrease effectiveness, so it's important to prioritize quality over quantity.

Creating buyer personas involves a combination of quantitative and qualitative research methods. Quantitative research involves analyzing any available data on your customer base, such as demographic information, purchasing habits, online behaviors, and pain points. This data can provide insights into common patterns and trends among your customers. Qualitative research, on the other hand, involves conducting interviews with both existing and prospective customers to gain deeper insights into their behavior, preferences, pain points, and motivations. This can be done through one-on-one interviews, focus groups, or surveys. Sales and customer-facing teams can also provide valuable insights into your customer's needs and behavior. However, it's essential to interview some existing and prospective customers, if possible, to get a complete understanding of your target audience. Creating personas can be done in five steps:

1. Defining your goals and research questions
2. Gathering data
3. Identifying patterns and themes
4. Creating persona profiles
5. Validating your personas

Let's explore the process of developing buyer personas in greater detail.

Defining your goals and research questions: Defining your goals and research questions is the first step in creating a buyer persona because it sets the foundation for the entire process. This step involves determining what you want to achieve from your research and what questions you need to answer to get there.

To get started, think about the specific goals and objectives you have for your buyer persona research. For example, do you want to better understand your customers' pain points and challenges? Do you want to gain insights into their decision-making process? Or do you want to identify the specific features and benefits that are most important to them?

Once you have a clear idea of your goals and objectives, you can start to develop research questions that will help you achieve them. These questions should be focused on gathering information about your customers' needs, behaviors, and preferences, as well as their demographics and psychographics. Some examples of research questions might include the following:

- What are our customers' biggest pain points and challenges?
- What factors influence our customers' purchasing decisions?
- What specific features and benefits are most important to our customers?
- What are our customers' demographics and psychographics (for example, age, gender, income, interests, values, attitudes, and so on)?
- What is their role in the buying process?

The first step of defining goals and research questions when creating buyer personas is important to ensure that the research is focused and relevant. Additionally, it's important to consider that personas shouldn't be created in a product marketing vacuum. They should be created with input and buy-in from other teams, such as sales, customer success, product, marketing, and engineering, who will all benefit from a deep understanding of the target audience. By involving these teams in the persona creation process, you can ensure that the personas are comprehensive and accurate representations of the ideal customer. The cross-functional collaboration can also foster a shared understanding of the target audience across different teams and help align the overall business strategy.

Gathering data: The second step in creating buyer personas is to gather data from various sources (internal and external) to gain a complete understanding of your target audience. This data can come from a variety of sources, such as customer interviews, customer surveys, online analytics, and sales data.

To gain a comprehensive understanding of your target audience and develop accurate buyer personas, it's essential to gather data from multiple sources. One valuable source is customer interviews, which can provide insights into the needs, behaviors, and preferences of your target audience. You can conduct these interviews in person, over the phone, or via email. Surveys can also be used to gather data and can be conducted online or in person. In addition, online analytics can help you understand how customers interact with your digital assets, including your website and social media pages. Sales data is another important source of insights, providing information on customers' purchasing behaviors, motivations, and preferred pricing models. By analyzing closed won and lost opportunities, you can gain insights into your buyers and champions, as well as understand why you lost customers. It's also crucial to talk to churned customers and probe deeper into their motivations for buying and what jobs they were trying to get done. This can provide valuable insights beyond feature requests and help you understand how your product fell short.

Identify patterns and themes: Once you've collected data from multiple sources, the next step is to analyze it for patterns and themes. This means looking for commonalities, trends, and insights that can help you create accurate and meaningful representations of your target audience. By examining the data from sources such as customer interviews, surveys, online analytics, and sales records, you can identify patterns and themes related to your audience's pain points, needs, and motivations. For example, you may discover that a particular group of customers values convenience and is willing to pay a premium for products or services that offer it. Or you may find that customers in a certain age range have specific preferences for the design and functionality of a product.

Identifying these patterns and themes is essential for creating effective buyer personas. It ensures that the personas are based on real data and insights, rather than assumptions or guesswork, leading to more accurate and useful representations of your target audience.

Identifying these patterns and themes is crucial for creating accurate and effective buyer personas. It helps ensure that the personas are based on real data and insights, rather than assumptions or guesswork.

Creating your persona profiles: Once you have identified patterns and themes from the data you've collected, it's time to create detailed persona profiles that accurately represent your ideal customers. These profiles should be based on real data and insights, and include information about their demographics, behaviors, motivations, challenges, and more.

To create your persona profiles, start by giving each persona a name and a photo to make them feel more tangible. Then, use the data you've collected to flesh out their profiles. This can include basic demographic information such as age, gender, job title, education level, income, and location. However, it's also important to dig deeper and consider additional details that can inform your understanding of their behavior and preferences. This can include insights about the specific tools they are using, their online habits and social media usage, and their product affinity.

Creating a buyer persona is like building a roadmap that guides you to an individual. The goal is to include relevant details in the persona profiles that your teams can utilize. The more detailed and specific the persona profiles, the better the understanding of your target audience. This ensures a comprehensive understanding of your audience, enabling your teams to develop more effective strategies that meet their needs and preferences.

Job Title
CMO

Age
40 years

Education
MBA

Social Network

Reports to
CEO

Team Size
25

Organization Size
1,001-5,000 employees

Industry
Technology

Revenue
$150-200M

Bio

Sarah is responsible for developing and executing marketing strategies that drive revenue growth. With the ultimate goal of delivering value to customers, Sarah is always on the lookout for innovative ways to engage with them and build long-lasting relationships.

Preferred Method of Communication

Email, phone, and face to face

Challenges

- Increased competition in the market
- Balancing short-term results with long-term strategy
- Ensuring marketing efforts align with overall business goals and objectives

Motivations

- Driving business success and growth
- Being innovative and ahead of competition
- Building a strong brand reputation
- Being recognized as a leader in the industry

Job Responsibilities

- Setting marketing strategies and goals for the organization
- Managing and directing the marketing team and their daily activities
- Maintaining relationships with key stakeholders, including customers, partners, and vendors
- Analyzing market trends and data to identify opportunities for growth and innovation
- Managing the marketing budget and allocating resources effectively

Role in The Buying Process

Sarah's responsibilities include the supervision of significant and frequent purchases made by the company. Although she may not participate in the primary research phase, she holds the ultimate authority in decision-making and must authorize all expenses before transactions are completed.

Goals & Objectives

- Increase brand awareness
- Drive lead generation and revenue growth
- Increase customer engagement and loyalty
- Improve ROI on marketing investments
- Keep up to date on merging marketing trends and technologies

Accomplish the Deal

If we can demonstrate that our product is capable of delivering measurable benefits such as lead generation, customer acquisition, and revenue growth, we will have a compelling value proposition that can pave the way to a successful business partnership.

Validators

- Case studies
- Colleagues' testimonials
- Gartner recommendations

Why Won't Sara Buy

With a discerning eye for return on investment (ROI), she rarely approves expenses that don't meet the company's standards.

Figure 7.3 – B2B buyer persona – example

Validating your personas: To ensure that your buyer personas are accurate representations of your target audience, it's important to validate them through various means. These may include the following:

- **Conducting interviews:** Schedule interviews with your existing customers to discuss their challenges and motivations. This will help you to ensure that your personas accurately reflect the attitudes and behaviors of your target audience.

- **Analyzing behavior**: Analyze customer behavior data, such as website traffic and sales data, to see whether it matches the behaviors and patterns you have identified in your personas.

- **Testing messaging**: Use your personas to create targeted messaging and test it with your target audience to see whether it resonates with them.

It is important to regularly review customer feedback and adjust your personas as needed based on the feedback you receive.

Harnessing the power of personas – how to use them effectively

Personas can be used in various touchpoints across your organization. The specific touchpoints will depend on the structure of your organization and the goals you have set. Therefore, it is essential to collaborate with the stakeholders involved in the process to understand where your personas can add value to their activities and objectives.

For example, personas can be used to inform the development of product or feature launch assets, such as onboarding flows and product demos. When creating onboarding flows, personas can help you understand what information and guidance each segment is most likely to need. You can tailor the flow to their specific use cases, providing them with the information and guidance that will help them achieve their goals with your product or feature. Similarly, when creating product demos or other types of educational content, personas can help you ensure that the content is relevant, engaging, and tailored to the specific use cases of each segment.

Other areas where personas can be used include marketing campaigns, customer service interactions, product development, and sales strategies. By leveraging personas in these touchpoints, you can ensure that your efforts are customer centric. For example, by utilizing personas, you can effectively bridge the gap between a customer's position in the buying funnel and the appropriate content required to guide them toward a successful purchase. Through the creation of persona-driven content tailored to the individual needs of each persona, you can deliver a more personalized experience, resulting in higher engagement rates.

One company that effectively utilizes personas to tailor their content to their target audience is HubSpot. They have identified several key personas, including Marketing Mary, Sales Sam, Owner Ollie, and IT Ian, and have created content that speaks directly to each persona's unique needs. For Marketing Mary, they develop content that revolves around generating leads and driving traffic to her website. They provide blog posts on topics such as **search engine optimization (SEO)** and social media marketing, as well as lead generation tools such as landing pages and calls to action. For Sales Sam, HubSpot creates content that helps him close deals and streamline his sales process. They offer resources such as email templates, sales playbooks, and lead-scoring tools that aid Sam in prioritizing leads and focusing on the most promising opportunities. For Owner Ollie, HubSpot develops content that speaks to his broader business goals, such as improving customer retention and increasing revenue. They offer resources such as business case studies and ROI calculators that demonstrate the impact of HubSpot's software on the bottom line. Finally, for IT Ian, HubSpot creates content that addresses the technical aspects of their software, including integrations with other systems and data privacy and security features. They provide resources such as technical documentation, product webinars, and live support from their technical team.

By tailoring its content to each persona's unique motivations and pain points, HubSpot is able to attract and engage a wide range of customers across different industries and roles.

Personas should inform the various functions of product marketing using the following points:

- Product development
- Creating targeted messaging and positioning
- Tailoring sales enablement collateral
- Pricing strategy

Now, let's examine these in more detail:

- **Product development:** When creating a product roadmap, product marketers can use buyer personas to inform the development process. By gaining an understanding of the requirements, challenges, and aspirations of distinct buyer personas, product marketers can prioritize features and functionality that align with the target audience's requirements. For example, if a company is developing a new software application, they may create a persona representing a small business owner who wants to streamline their operations. By incorporating insights from this persona, the company can prioritize features such as easy-to-use interfaces, automation of repetitive tasks, and integrations with other business tools.

  Additionally, product marketers can use personas to validate product ideas by testing them with members of the target audience. This can help identify gaps or areas where the product can be improved to better meet the needs of the target audience.

- **Creating targeted messaging and positioning:** When developing messaging and positioning for a product, a profound understanding of the target audience is critical. Personas offer valuable insights into the needs and desires of the audience, enabling product marketers to craft messaging that truly connects with them.

  By using personas to create targeted messaging and positioning, product marketers will be able to differentiate their product from competitors and attract the attention of the target audience. For example, if a persona for a software product is a small business owner who struggles with managing their finances, the messaging and positioning can focus on how the product can help them save time and simplify their accounting processes. By speaking directly to the pain points of this persona, the messaging and positioning can be more effective in capturing their interest and ultimately converting them into customers.

- **Tailoring sales enablement collateral:** This is a vital part of persona-based selling and can help sales teams have more effective conversations with prospects. One effective way to do this is by creating customized battle cards and sales scripts using persona insights. Battle cards should provide sales reps with key talking points, objections to overcome, and other useful information that will help them engage with each prospect more effectively. Sales scripts should include messaging points that speak directly to the needs and pain points of each persona, as well as questions to ask that will help uncover specific challenges and goals. It's also essential to train sales teams on how to use these materials effectively. This involves ensuring that sales reps understand the persona insights, the key messaging points, and the questions to ask so that they can have more impactful conversations with prospects.

  For example, a company may create different versions of a sales pitch for a new product launch that is tailored to each persona. Each version of the sales pitch may have unique content, language, and messaging that specifically addresses the pain points and challenges of the targeted persona. Additionally, creating case studies or customer success stories that are tailored to specific personas is another way to effectively tailor sales enablement collateral. For instance, a B2B company may have different case studies for various industries or verticals they serve, showcasing how their product or service has helped companies in those particular industries overcome specific challenges.

  Using buyer personas to tailor sales enablement collateral is an effective strategy that can lead to more successful conversations and ultimately more sales. It allows sales reps to speak directly to the unique requirements, pain points, and goals of each persona, making it easier to build rapport and trust with potential customers.

- **Pricing strategy:** Leveraging buyer personas to inform your pricing strategy can provide invaluable insights that can help you make more informed decisions. By understanding what each persona values the most about your product or service, you can determine a price that accurately reflects that value. For instance, if one persona highly values convenience and time-saving features, they may be willing to pay a premium price for a product that delivers on those attributes. In addition, personas can help you evaluate different pricing models and determine which one is most appropriate for each segment. For instance, if one persona is more likely to make repeat purchases, a subscription-based pricing model may be more effective for that segment.

Personas help to bring segmentation and targeting to life by identifying the driving factors behind a buyer's behavior. However, personas have their limitations, as they may not fully answer the question of what particular task or problem a customer aims to accomplish or solve by using the product. While personas offer valuable insights into customers' pain points, they don't necessarily provide a clear picture of the job that customers hired the product to do.

Product marketers can gain a deeper understanding of the customer's needs and motivations by integrating this information with their persona work. This can lead to the creation of more impactful messaging and positioning that speaks to the customer's specific job or goal. Now we'll delve into the JBTD principle.

Creating effective personas with the JBTD framework

The JTBD framework is a game-changing approach to product development that involves gaining a deep understanding of the specific jobs customers need to accomplish and the decision-making process guiding their product selection. By designing products tailored to meet these exact needs, JTBD can significantly increase the chances of product selection. By identifying JTBD, you can craft messaging, positioning, and features that truly resonate with customer needs, resulting in more relevant and compelling products.

The JTBD framework represents a departure from product-centric development frameworks in that it emphasizes the customer's perspective. Yet, it distinguishes itself by going beyond understanding the customer's needs and aims to probe their underlying motivations for purchasing. According to entrepreneur and author Guerric de Ternay (https://guerric.co.uk/jobs-to-be-done-examples/), the JTBD framework *"helps understand what causes people to buy a specific product"* and it can be used in two ways: firstly, to gain insights into the needs and desires of customers within a particular market, and secondly, to develop a customer experience that resonates with those needs and desires, leading to increased satisfaction and loyalty.

While task analysis and use cases primarily focus on how a product can handle users' typical activities, the JTBD approach shifts the focus to desired outcomes and questions whether these activities are the best way to achieve the outcomes users truly seek. Unlike feature-centric design, the JTBD framework prompts product managers and UX teams to consider whether the product enables users to complete the job easily and happily they hired it for and provides a superior outcome to existing solutions. The JTBD framework is exemplified in *Figure 7.4*, which effectively captures both the emotional and functional criteria of JTBD.

JTBD: Functional and Emotional Success Criteria – Example

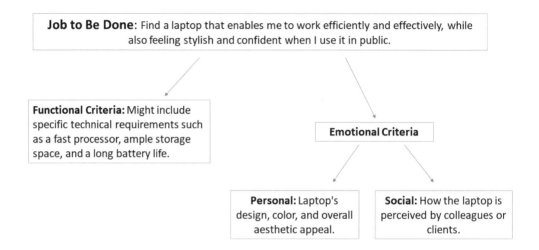

Figure 7.4 – JTBD: Functional and emotional criteria example

The JTBD framework does not impose a specific format or output for a job-to-be-done definition, but it is commonly articulated as a sentence format that describes what users need to do and includes contextual details. Furthermore, a comprehensive JTBD description must incorporate both the functional success criteria, which outline the clear objectives for job accomplishment, and the emotional success criteria, which encompass the user's personal and social considerations, including their perception by others.

JTBD versus personas

Personas and JTBD are both highly valuable methodologies employed in user-centered design to achieve a thorough comprehension of users' needs, motivations, and behaviors. While each approach has its own specific focus, they are not mutually exclusive but can be seamlessly integrated to amplify the effectiveness of the design process.

Personas serve as imaginative portrayals of diverse user types, meticulously constructed through extensive research and data analysis. They delve deep into the traits, behaviors, and motivations of individuals utilizing a product or service. The creation of personas equips teams with a clearer understanding of their target users, thereby enabling them to design products that precisely cater to their unique requirements. On the other hand, JTBD emphasizes comprehending the tasks or challenges that customers aim to accomplish or overcome when utilizing a product or service. Rather than fixating on personal attributes, JTBD revolves around the desired outcomes that customers strive to achieve. This approach empowers teams to pinpoint areas for enhancement and devise product solutions that effectively address the problems encountered by customers.

A well-executed use of personas also takes into account the specific goals that users need to accomplish when using the product. These goals align with the information gathered from the JTBD framework, which focuses on the practical and emotional requirements users have when performing a particular task or job. To maximize their effectiveness, personas and JTBD can be used together, complementing one another. By incorporating JTBD insights into personas, the understanding of user goals is enhanced, resulting in a more comprehensive view of the user and informing design decisions. Likewise, personas provide context to the JTBD framework, enabling a deeper understanding of user behaviors and motivations.

Ultimately, the choice to employ JTBD, personas, or both depends on the specific needs of the organization and the objectives of the project.

Summary

Throughout this engaging chapter, we embarked on a remarkable journey of exploration into the world of segmentation, personas, and JTBD. In doing so, we uncovered their profound potential to unravel the intricacies of our customers, shape our product development and marketing strategies, and create truly exceptional experiences. Our quest has been enlightening, as we delved into the different facets of customer segmentation, gaining a solid understanding of the essential steps of the process. With meticulous attention, we explored diverse personas and recognized their invaluable role in elevating product marketing across various functions. Moreover, our encounter with JTBD provided us with valuable insights to enhance our product development process. With this foundation, we will now transition to the next part of the book. In the upcoming chapters, we will delve deeper into the execution phase and explore the GTM strategies that outbound product marketers employ to win in the market. These strategies will provide practical guidance on effectively launching and promoting products to achieve market success.

Part 3
Outbound: Strategies for Product Adoption and Exponential Growth

This section shines a spotlight on the tactical side of product marketing, with a keen focus on execution and the pivotal role the key functions of outbound product marketing play in driving product adoption and accelerating growth. It encompasses the art of crafting compelling messaging and positioning that truly resonates with a target audience, as well as the strategic development of a robust GTM strategy. Additionally, it explores the implementation of a highly effective sales enablement program, all of which synergistically contribute to maximizing revenue and propelling overall growth.

This part has the following chapters:

- *Chapter 8, Competitive Positioning and Messaging for Growth*
- *Chapter 9, GTM Strategies for Exponential Growth*
- *Chapter 10, Enable Your Sales Team and Maximize Effectiveness*

Competitive Positioning and Messaging for Growth 8

Positioning is like finding the perfect spot for your product in the market. It effectively addresses the question of why customers should choose us at this moment and it's the crucial first step before diving into messaging. It involves deeply understanding your product, its features, its unique value, what sets it apart from competitors, where it fits in the market landscape, and why your product will succeed in this market. This forms the foundation of your positioning, which is typically an internal document used to align your team and create effective messaging. Messaging, on the other hand, is how you bring your positioning to life and communicate it to the market and different customer personas. It's the story you tell consistently across all your communication channels, whether it's presentations, product demos, or any other form of interaction. Your messaging is what shapes the perception of your product in the minds of your target audience.

Crafting a strategic and focused positioning and messaging strategy is like unleashing a powerful force that propels your launch toward success. It becomes even more crucial when you're faced with the challenge of navigating preconceived notions and biases surrounding similar product categories. To truly stand out in the market, you need a deep understanding of how your product will differentiate itself from the competition.

Taking the time and effort to meticulously shape your messaging and positioning is the key to effectively conveying the unique value proposition of your product. It's about showcasing the specific benefits and advantages that make your offering shine amidst the sea of competitors and adjacent products. By crafting compelling messaging, you can captivate your audience, address their pain points, and highlight the distinctive features that set your product apart.

In this chapter, we will embark on a comprehensive exploration of positioning and messaging, delving into their intricate nuances and crucial components. Throughout this exploration, we aim to provide comprehensive answers to key questions such as the following:

- How do you craft competitive positioning?
- Does narrative design replace positioning?
- How do you build effective messaging?

Driving growth with positioning

Positioning is the art of establishing your product as a frontrunner in delivering something that matters greatly to a specific group of customers. In the words of April Dunford, a renowned expert in the field, *"Positioning defines how your product is a leader at delivering something that a well-defined set of customers cares a lot about."*

Positioning refers to the process of defining and establishing a distinct place for a product or service in the market. It involves identifying and highlighting the unique attributes, features, and benefits of the product that differentiate it from competitors and resonate with the target audience. The goal of positioning is to create a perception in the minds of consumers about the value and relevance of the product. It helps establish a competitive advantage by clearly articulating how the product meets the specific needs and desires of customers better than alternative offerings.

Positioning influences various aspects of marketing, including messaging, branding, pricing, and distribution. It guides the development of marketing materials, such as advertisements, website content, and sales collateral, to ensure consistent and compelling communication of the product's unique selling points. Effective product positioning aligns customer needs with the product's value proposition, creating a strong and persuasive message that resonates with the target audience.

Stripe serves as an exemplary case of a company that has expertly implemented a strong positioning strategy. Positioned as a leading global payments processing platform, Stripe provides businesses with a seamless and highly secure solution to accept online payments and efficiently manage transactions. The key to their positioning lies in their commitment to simplifying the complexities of online payments. Stripe places great emphasis on their developer-friendly APIs and intuitive tools, enabling businesses to effortlessly integrate payment processing functionality into their websites and applications. Through their strategic positioning, Stripe establishes itself as a trusted partner, empowering businesses to optimize their online payment workflows and provide customers with a frictionless checkout experience.

Reliability and security are key elements of Stripe's positioning strategy. They showcase their robust infrastructure, advanced fraud detection systems, and adherence to industry standards, providing reassurance to businesses and customers alike regarding the safeguarding of payment data. Stripe also establishes its position as a global solution, facilitating payment acceptance from customers worldwide in diverse currencies. They highlight their broad range of payment methods and expertise in handling complex payment scenarios, including recurring subscriptions and marketplace transactions.

By aligning its positioning as a user-friendly, secure, and globally accessible payments platform, Stripe has successfully attracted a wide customer base, spanning start-ups, small businesses, and enterprise-level organizations. Their positioning as a trusted and innovative payment solution has solidified their standing as a prominent industry player within the online payments landscape.

The Stripe example illustrates the pivotal role of positioning as the fundamental pillar in the equation of your business growth. Recognizing that your product doesn't exist in isolation, but rather within a competitive marketplace, it becomes essential to navigate this crowded landscape. By strategically positioning your product, you can carve out a space in the minds of your customers, securing a distinct and advantageous position that sets you apart from rivals while aligning with customer expectations. Embracing this position allows you to establish a robust foundation for growth, significantly enhancing your chances of success.

Now, let us delve into a comprehensive exploration of the essential components that constitute effective positioning.

What are the key components of positioning?

Crafting an effective positioning strategy requires a meticulous process that entails thorough market research to gain insights into customer preferences, industry trends, and the competitive landscape. Armed with this valuable information, companies can then construct a compelling positioning statement or message that effectively communicates the product's unique value proposition, target market, and distinctive advantages.

Drawing from April's insightful analysis, positioning involves combining essential components to create a strong impact. To develop a robust positioning strategy, we can break it down into its elements, address each one carefully, and then assemble them into a coherent positioning statement. This approach ensures that each component is thoroughly examined and optimized to achieve the desired positioning outcome.

Deconstructing positioning into its parts is manageable because there is a consensus on the key elements that form the foundation of a positioning statement. These components are like the missing pieces in the puzzle of positioning. According to April Dunford, they include the following:

- **Competitive Alternatives:** This component involves understanding the landscape of competitors and alternative solutions available to customers. It requires analyzing the strengths and weaknesses of competitors and identifying the unique value proposition that sets your product apart.

- **Differentiated "Features" or "Capabilities":** Here, the focus is on highlighting the unique features or capabilities of your product/service. It's essential to identify the key attributes that differentiate you from competitors and resonate with the needs and preferences of your target customers.

- **Value for Customers:** This component centers around understanding and articulating the value and benefits your product's unique features/capabilities provide to customers. You have to clearly communicate how your product/service addresses their pain points, fulfills their needs, and delivers tangible value that surpasses other alternatives.

- **Target Audience:** Defining and segmenting your target customer base is crucial for effective positioning. By identifying customer groups who care about the value that your product provides and understanding their demographics, behaviors, and preferences, you can tailor your positioning and messaging to resonate with their unique needs and motivations.

- **Market Category:** Establishing the appropriate market category for your product/service is vital for positioning it effectively. This involves defining the context in which your product or service operates and differentiating it from other categories. It helps customers understand where your product/service fits and why it is the best choice for their specific requirements.

April emphasizes that the preceding components are interconnected and reliant on each other. The value proposition presented to customers is closely linked to the distinct features offered by the product or service. These features gain importance and set the offering apart when compared to other alternatives in the market. Identifying the ideal target customers entails comprehending their keen interest in the unique value being provided. Lastly, selecting the appropriate market category establishes the context in which the product's exceptional value becomes evident to the target customers.

Considering the interplay between these components, it raises the question: Where should we commence? According to April, the flow should follow the sequence shown in the following figure:

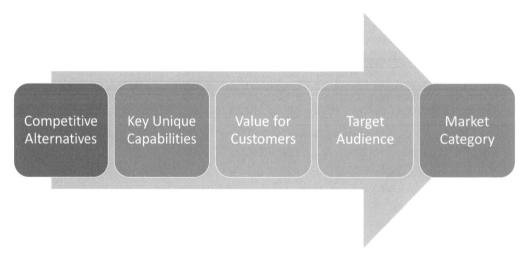

Figure 8.1 – Key components of positioning according to April Dunford

According to April's analysis, a highly effective method to initiate the positioning process is by conducting a thorough analysis of competitive alternatives. This entails gaining profound insights into the actions customers would take in the absence of your solution. Equipped with this invaluable knowledge, the subsequent step involves pinpointing the distinctive attributes and features that set your offering apart from these alternatives. Once these unique differentiators are identified, the focus then shifts toward evaluating their significance for customers. This entails determining the specific advantages and value that these capabilities provide to buyers. By truly grasping the distinctive value proposition you bring to the table, a comprehensive understanding of the impact and relevance of your solution within the market is achieved.

Moving forward, the attention turns to customer segmentation. While there may be a range of customers who appreciate your value, it is essential to identify those who prioritize and deeply care about it. This involves examining the characteristics and attributes of customers who exhibit a strong affinity with your differentiated value. Through this process, you can define your best-fit customers, enabling targeted marketing and messaging efforts to effectively reach and engage with them.

Lastly, you need to turn your attention to the critical aspect of the market category. The objective is to position your solution within a distinct market context where the value you offer becomes immediately apparent to your target customers. This involves precisely defining the market you aim to conquer and strategically establishing the positioning required to flourish within it. By carefully selecting the appropriate market category, you guarantee that your unique value proposition harmonizes effortlessly with the expectations and requirements of your intended audience.

By adhering to this systematic and sequential approach, beginning with competitive alternatives and advancing through differentiated features, customer value, customer segmentation, and market category, you have the ability to construct a comprehensive positioning strategy that deeply resonates with your customers and fuels substantial growth.

When it comes to positioning, it is crucial not only to grasp the process but also to remain vigilant about avoiding common pitfalls that can undermine its effectiveness. Let us delve into two prominent pitfalls that April Dunford (and I concur with her viewpoint) strongly advocates for avoiding at any expense:

- **Avoiding a broad definition of competitive alternatives**: One common error is defining competitive alternatives too broadly. Rather than considering every potential competitor, it is vital to focus on understanding the actions customers would take if your offering were absent. Sometimes, customers may stick to their existing problem-solving methods or opt for no action at all. Positioning yourself against the status quo becomes paramount in motivating customers to take decisive steps. It is advisable to avoid including "phantom competitors," referring to companies that could theoretically compete with you but are not encountered in real deals. By directing your attention toward competitors that customers genuinely consider, you can reinforce your positioning and avoid diluting your message by positioning against unlikely competitors.

- **Avoiding assumptions about the necessity of creating a new market category**: When selecting a market category, there are two options to consider: positioning your product within an existing category or aiming to establish a new category in customers' minds, positioning your product as the leading solution within that category. Opting for an existing category allows you to leverage customers' existing knowledge and understanding of the market. By associating your product with a familiar category and highlighting its unique attributes, you can effectively differentiate it from other solutions and cater to specific buyer needs within that specific niche. On the other hand, creating a new market category involves introducing a fresh perspective to customers. This approach requires significant effort to educate customers and establish the significance and relevance of the new category. While it might be assumed that creating a new category leads to market dominance, historical evidence suggests that companies pioneering new categories often face challenges in the long run. Competitors who enter the market after the category has already been established can often gain a competitive advantage.

By carefully evaluating the options and considering the potential outcomes, you can make an informed decision about whether to position your product within an existing category or venture into the endeavor of establishing a new market category.

Having gained a comprehensive understanding of positioning, it is now time to delve deeply into one of its pivotal components, which also holds significance in messaging: the value proposition.

Value proposition and competitive positioning

A value proposition is the core statement that captures the essence of the value your product/ service provides to your customers. It outlines the unique benefits, solutions, or outcomes that customers can expect from a particular product or service. The value proposition addresses the specific pain points or needs of customers and explains how your product/service is specifically designed to address those challenges and deliver value in a way that sets it apart from competitors.

In today's fast-paced and fiercely competitive business world, the importance of value propositions has become more pronounced than ever before. With intense competition, evolving customer expectations, dynamic market forces, information overload, well-informed decision-making, and a customer-centric approach, it is crucial for businesses to effectively communicate the unique value they offer. A compelling value proposition serves as a key differentiator, capturing the attention of customers and establishing trust by addressing their needs and highlighting the benefits and solutions provided.

The value proposition plays a crucial role in driving business growth by effectively conveying the unique value and benefits that a particular product or service offers to customers. It goes beyond the surface-level features and specifications and focuses on demonstrating how the offerings can positively impact customers' lives or address their specific pain points. By highlighting the advantages and benefits of the product, the value proposition makes it easier for customers to recognize the value they would gain by choosing your solution. Furthermore, a well-crafted value proposition serves as a persuasive tool that convinces customers that your product is the best option to meet their needs or solve their problems. It differentiates your product from competitors by clearly communicating the distinct benefits and advantages it brings, ultimately encouraging customers to choose your product over others.

How to create a strong value proposition

A strong value proposition plays a crucial role in your company's growth as it effectively communicates the value and benefits of your products or services to your target customers. By clearly articulating the unique value your offering provides, you enable customers to understand why they should choose your product over alternatives. When crafting your value proposition, there are key components that you might need to consider to make it effective and compelling:

- **Target audience:** Identify the specific target audience for your product/service
- **Customer needs:** What specific needs or problems does your product address for the target audience if they choose to adopt it?
- **Benefits/solutions:** How does your product address and fulfill the needs of the target audience?
- **Differentiation:** What sets your product apart from competitors in the market?

Once you have thoroughly addressed the questions mentioned earlier, you are well prepared to craft your compelling value proposition. In my experience, an effective framework for developing value propositions includes the following:

Our [unique product/service] *that helps* [target audience] *who want to* [specific goal or desire] *by* [key benefits or solutions], *unlike* [competitors], *we* [unique differentiator].

This framework ensures that our value proposition is precisely aligned with the needs and aspirations of your target audience. It effectively communicates the value they can expect and prominently highlights what sets you apart from the competition. To illustrate, let's delve into an example:

"Our cloud-based project management software is designed for tech companies that need streamlined collaboration and project tracking. With our platform, teams can easily manage tasks, timelines, and resources, ensuring efficient project execution and improved productivity. Unlike other project management tools, our solution offers seamless integrations with popular development tools and provides advanced analytics for data-driven decision-making."

In this particular case, the framework takes the following shape:

Our [cloud-based platform] *helps* [tech companies] *who want to* [optimize project management processes] *by* [providing easy management of timelines, tasks, and resources], *unlike* [other project management tools], *our* [solution offers seamless integrations with popular development tools and provides advanced analytics, enabling data-driven decision-making].

Once we have thoroughly examined the value proposition framework, it's time to explore the essential elements involved to be able to develop a value proposition. The development of a compelling value proposition involves five key components that require careful consideration and analysis. To begin, it is crucial to identify and thoroughly analyze your target audience. This entails gaining a deep understanding of their demographics, behaviors, pain points, and the ways in which your product can address their problems or enhance their lives. Additionally, it is important to comprehend their roles in the buying process and what motivates them. This comprehensive understanding will enable you to create an ideal buyer persona.

The next step involves delving into market understanding. This entails identifying new trends and, more importantly, conducting a thorough analysis of your competitors' activities. By understanding their value propositions, analyzing their product features and functionality, and examining user reviews, you can gain valuable insights. This analysis will help you identify gaps in the market and differentiate your product/service.

After completing the initial steps, it becomes crucial to identify and articulate the unique value proposition of your product. Clearly conveying how your product directly addresses the specific pain points and challenges of your target audience is essential. To enhance credibility, it is important to provide verifiable evidence and measurable results. For instance, showcasing how your product helped customers to reduce time spent by X hours each month or increase their revenues by X% establishes its effectiveness in resolving pain points. By incorporating this compelling information into your sales and marketing materials, you can effectively highlight the concrete benefits your product offers.

After establishing your value proposition, it is important to test it to ensure its effectiveness. This testing phase allows you to gather feedback and make iterative improvements if necessary. It provides an opportunity to refine and enhance your value proposition based on real-world responses and insights. The following figure provides a concise and comprehensive overview of the essential components necessary for creating a compelling value proposition:

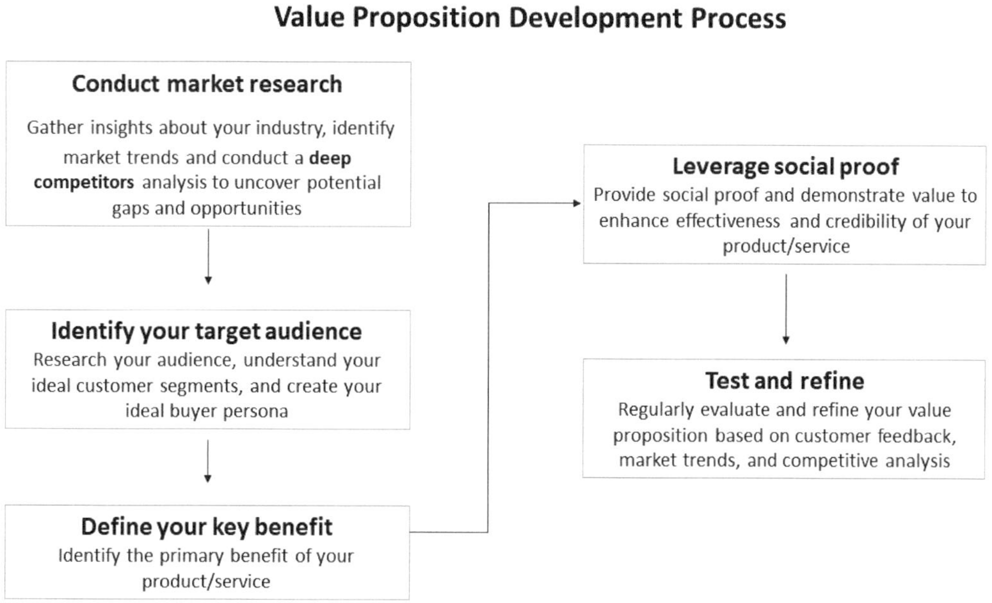

Value Proposition Development Process

Conduct market research

Gather insights about your industry, identify market trends and conduct a **deep competitors** analysis to uncover potential gaps and opportunities

Identify your target audience
Research your audience, understand your ideal customer segments, and create your ideal buyer persona

Define your key benefit
Identify the primary benefit of your product/service

Leverage social proof
Provide social proof and demonstrate value to enhance effectiveness and credibility of your product/service

Test and refine
Regularly evaluate and refine your value proposition based on customer feedback, market trends, and competitive analysis

Figure 8.2 – Value proposition development process

The value proposition plays a vital role in the competitive positioning of a product. It helps define the unique value and benefits that distinguish your products from competitors' products. By clearly articulating the value proposition, you can effectively position your product in the market and highlight its competitive advantages.

Competitive positioning is a strategic process wherein a company establishes a distinctive stance for its products or services, setting them apart from competitors in the market. The aim is to create a unique position or angle that makes the offering more appealing to customers. This positioning can be achieved through various means, including pricing strategies, product features, exceptional customer service, or a combination of these elements.

In a competitive market, every company needs to position its products effectively to stand out and succeed. Understanding and leveraging competitive positioning is crucial for companies to differentiate their products, attract customers, and outperform competitors. By assessing the competitive landscape and identifying unique selling points, companies can refine their overall positioning and make strategic decisions to gain a competitive edge.

Competitive positioning can be considered as a more specific and detailed version of overall positioning. While overall positioning establishes a product's/service's position in the market as a whole, competitive positioning specifically focuses on how the product or service compares to specific competitors. It hones in on the competitive landscape and provides a clearer understanding of the product's unique position in relation to a particular competitor or a defined set of competitors.

One notable example of bold and tasteful competitive positioning in the market is the rivalry between Apple and PC, exemplified by Apple's "Get a Mac" campaign. This campaign serves as a classic illustration of effective positioning without resorting to overt negativity. The "Get a Mac" campaign cleverly showcased the perceived benefits of using a Mac over a PC, emphasizing simplicity, reliability, and creative capabilities.

In these iconic advertisements, Apple employed actors to personify the Mac and PC, presenting their target customer (the Mac) as young and laid-back, and portraying the PC as representing an older, outdated, and less intelligent persona. This creative approach allowed Apple to differentiate itself from the competition by emphasizing its products' key differentiators. The dialogue between the Mac and PC characters became an engaging narrative that illustrated Apple's advantages in a charming and relatable way.

For instance, in one ad, the PC character sneezes, prompting the Mac character to ask if he's okay. The PC replies, "No, I've got that virus that's going around." This light-hearted interaction subtly points out that PCs were more susceptible to viruses compared to Macs. By employing humor and clever scenarios, Apple effectively communicated a key differentiator without directly attacking PC users or resorting to negative messaging.

The "Get a Mac" campaign remains a remarkable example of competitive positioning done right. It showcased Apple's ability to highlight the strengths of its products while maintaining a respectful tone toward competitors. By focusing on the advantages of its offerings rather than disparaging the competition, Apple successfully differentiated itself in the market, solidifying its brand identity as a modern, user-friendly, and reliable technology company.

Competitive positioning and value proposition are closely related and interdependent concepts that play a crucial role in shaping a product's market positioning strategy. While they are distinct, they work together to communicate the unique value a product provides to its target customers. Competitive positioning involves defining how you want your product to be perceived in relation to competitors and the unique space it aims to carve out. In essence, competitive positioning is about the desired market position and differentiation from competitors, while the value proposition focuses on the specific benefits and value that the product delivers to customers. Competitive positioning defines the context and perception, while the value proposition communicates the specific problem-solving capabilities and value that set the product apart. Together, competitive positioning and value proposition work hand in hand to create compelling messaging that resonates with the target audience.

Airbnb serves as a prime example of a company that effectively aligned its value proposition with its competitive positioning by positioning itself as a distinctive option in contrast to traditional hotels. Within the travel industry, Airbnb disrupted the conventional hospitality model by offering a personalized and unique accommodation experience for travelers. By diverging from the traditional hotel approach, Airbnb set itself apart by providing a platform for individuals to rent out their homes, apartments, or distinct properties to travelers. This strategic positioning allowed Airbnb to present a value proposition that catered to travelers seeking a more personalized and authentic journey. Through connecting these travelers with local hosts, Airbnb emphasized the opportunity to gain insider insights and recommendations, granting them an immersive experience unlike that of standardized hotel rooms.

This alignment between Airbnb's value proposition and its competitive positioning allowed it to gain a competitive edge in the market. It successfully attracted a customer base looking for alternatives to traditional hotels and tapped into the growing demand for more personalized and authentic travel experiences. Through its customer-centric approach and disruptive business model, Airbnb challenged the dominance of traditional hotels and became a leading player in the accommodation industry, redefining how people think about travel accommodation.

Before we delve into the messaging session, it is essential to explore the concept of narrative design and its relationship with positioning. Let us take a moment to explore the essence of narrative design and its connection to positioning, paving the way for a deeper understanding of their combined impact.

Strategic narrative, narrative design, and positioning

In recent times, narrative design has garnered significant attention as an influential subject, prompting discussions among prominent companies such as HubSpot about its potential to supplant positioning. This presents a remarkable opportunity to delve into the essence of narrative design and discern its distinctive nature compared to positioning. A strategic narrative serves as a guiding force, molding and directing the activities of a business while encapsulating its fundamental values, purpose, and vision. It furnishes a cohesive framework that underpins decision-making and facilitates effective communication. Conversely, narrative design represents the methodology employed to artfully craft and convey this narrative. By leveraging storytelling techniques, messaging strategies, and visual elements, narrative design creates a compelling and captivating narrative that deeply resonates with the intended audience. Its primary focus lies in constructing a new paradigm or category within a crowded market, harnessing the transformative power of storytelling. While narrative design and positioning both play integral roles in marketing and communication, they diverge in their approach, purpose, and impact.

Positioning chiefly concerns itself with communicating value and differentiation within established markets, whereas narrative design transcends those boundaries by fostering immersive storytelling experiences that not only cultivate new markets but also instigate organic demand. HubSpot stands as an exceptional exemplar of effective narrative design within notable companies. They have skillfully crafted a compelling narrative around the concept of inbound marketing. With a focus on attracting and engaging potential customers through valuable content, personalized experiences, and the cultivation of long-term relationships, HubSpot positions itself as a thought leader in the industry. Their narrative design serves as a guiding force, directing businesses toward a more impactful and customer-centric marketing approach. By championing the principles of inbound marketing, HubSpot has successfully established itself as a trusted authority, empowering businesses to achieve greater effectiveness and success in their marketing endeavors.

Let's delve deeper into the comparison between narrative design and product positioning:

- **Communication Approach:** Product positioning focuses on clearly communicating the value and benefits of a product or brand to the target audience. It provides context and structure to help buyers understand the solution quickly and make informed decisions. The emphasis is on delivering a concise and compelling message that resonates with the customers' needs and positions the product favorably in the market. On the other hand, narrative design takes a different approach. It goes beyond communicating product features and benefits by creating a whole new universe or storytelling experience in the audience's mind. It aims to immerse the audience in a narrative that engages emotions, captures their attention, and fosters a connection with the brand or product on a deeper level.

- **Market Strategy:** In the realm of marketing, product positioning plays a crucial role in well-established markets where competition is prevalent. Its primary objective is to distinguish a product from its competitors by highlighting its unique value proposition. By effectively communicating a clear and compelling advantage, the aim is to capture market share and entice customers away from other alternatives. In contrast, narrative design offers a different approach that can be leveraged to create or redefine a new market category. This involves the construction of a captivating and distinct narrative or universe that sets the company apart as a trailblazer or sole participant in that particular space. Through the art of storytelling, narrative design generates interest, intrigue, and curiosity among the audience, thereby establishing a market for a product or service that may not have existed before.

- **Sales Impact:** Product positioning plays a crucial role in supporting sales efforts. Clearly communicating the value and benefits of a product enables sales teams to effectively articulate the offering's advantages to potential customers. Product positioning ensures that salespeople have a solid foundation to engage with prospects, address their needs, and ultimately close deals. On the other hand, narrative design can build new markets in such a way that the product or service becomes self-explanatory. The narrative itself generates interest and creates a desire for the offering, potentially eliminating the need for extensive sales efforts. When the narrative design successfully captivates the audience and establishes a compelling story, it can generate organic demand and attract customers without the need for traditional sales tactics.

Product positioning and narrative design can work together synergistically. While narrative design focuses on creating a compelling overarching story for our companies and categories, product positioning is tailored to specific launches and individual products. The ideal approach is to design a narrative that remains consistent over time, providing a cohesive and enduring brand story. Each product launch can then be positioned within the larger narrative framework, bringing it to life and highlighting its unique features and benefits. By aligning positioning with the broader narrative, we ensure consistency and strengthen the overall brand identity.

Indeed, as product marketers, our role primarily revolves around developing compelling positioning, launching products, and contributing to the design of the overall narrative. However, it is crucial to acknowledge that the responsibility for crafting the narrative design lies with the CMO and CEO. These key individuals serve as the chief architects of the narrative design, as they possess the strategic vision and holistic understanding of the company's objectives and brand story. They play a pivotal role in shaping the narrative design, ensuring that it aligns with the company's values, resonates with the target audience, and guides the organization's activities. While, as product marketers, we can contribute to the narrative design process by providing valuable insights and inputs, the ultimate responsibility for creating and driving the narrative design rests with the marketing leader and CEO.

Effective product messaging for growth

Effective messaging serves as the vital conduit for communicating your value proposition to customers, demonstrating how your product surpasses alternative offerings. It plays a pivotal role in establishing the context around your product and guiding your organization's competitive positioning, paving the way for success. The true significance of messaging lies in its ability to captivate your target audience's attention and persuade them to choose your product over competing options. Messaging plays a strategic role in conveying the value, benefits, and unique selling points of your product or service to your intended audience. It involves carefully crafting language, tone, and content that effectively communicates your product's value proposition and distinguishes it from competitors in the market. The ultimate aim of product messaging is to captivate and persuade your target customers by compellingly communicating the advantages and benefits of your product. It is essential to tailor your messaging to resonate with the specific needs, desires, and pain points of your target audience, ensuring a strong connection and engagement. An effective product messaging strategy extends beyond concise value proposition communication. It aims to establish an emotional connection with the audience, address their concerns, and highlight the distinctive qualities that differentiate your product. Through impactful messaging, you not only capture potential buyers' attention, generate awareness, and ignite their interest but also influence their decision-making process, guiding them to choose and purchase your product. Ultimately, successful product messaging results in a clear and concise articulation of your value proposition while forging a deep emotional connection with your audience. By addressing their specific needs and showcasing the unique qualities of your product, you can effectively differentiate yourself from competitors and resonate with your customers, fostering growth and achieving success.

Messaging serves as a vital cornerstone in the role of product marketers (PMMs), forming the foundation of our core responsibilities. However, crafting compelling and consistent messaging is a challenging task. As PMMs, our primary objective is to develop messaging that deeply resonates with our target audience while effectively conveying the value proposition of our product. This requires us to ensure that our messaging seamlessly aligns with the needs and preferences of our intended audience. To accomplish this, we must shift our perspective and gain a comprehensive understanding of how our product or service can be presented in a way that captivates the attention and piques the interest of our target audience.

In our role as orchestrators, we bear the responsibility of harmonizing messaging efforts across the organization. This entails collaborating with various teams and individuals to ensure that our messaging remains consistent and aligned throughout all channels and touchpoints. From C-level communications to the content displayed on our website and other external or internal collaterals, our goal is to weave together a cohesive narrative that accurately represents our brand and resonates with our target audience. By orchestrating these efforts, we create a powerful and unified message that reinforces our brand identity and builds strong connections with our customers.

Our success lies in fostering collaboration and synergy among teams. We strive to craft messaging that not only grabs attention but also sparks genuine interest in our product or service. This requires an in-depth understanding of our audience's pain points, aspirations, and motivations. By speaking their language and providing compelling solutions, we can address their needs effectively. Through our strategic orchestration, we ensure that every facet of our messaging ecosystem works in harmony, amplifying the impact and reach of our message, and ultimately driving the success of our marketing efforts.

The key elements of effective messaging

Leveraging my expertise in the field of messaging, I have identified four pivotal attributes that act as catalysts in driving the effectiveness of messaging. To ensure messaging resonates with the intended audience and yields optimal results, it should embody the following characteristics:

- **Relevance**: Effective messaging is crafted to align with the specific needs, interests, and challenges of the target audience. It takes into account their pain points and clearly articulates how the product or service can address those pain points, offering a solution that resonates with their unique requirements. By demonstrating relevance, messaging captures the attention of the audience and establishes a strong connection. For example, *"Get there. Your day belongs to you."* – Uber's message highlights the relevance of the ride-sharing service in providing convenient transportation options, while also conveying authenticity by acknowledging the importance of personal time.

- **Credibility**: Messaging that is backed by tangible evidence, such as testimonials, case studies, or data, enhances its credibility. Providing concrete proof of the product's effectiveness, reliability, and positive impact bolsters the audience's confidence in the offering. Credible messaging strengthens trust, mitigates skepticism, and reinforces the belief that the product can deliver on its promises. For example, *"Music for everyone."* –

Spotify's message reflects its authenticity in making music accessible to a wide range of listeners, demonstrating its credibility as a leading music streaming platform.

- **Consistency**: Consistent messaging is vital for reinforcing and establishing a cohesive image across various channels and touchpoints. By consistently conveying core messages and the product's/service's value proposition, messaging creates a unified and recognizable presence. This consistency helps customers develop a clear understanding of what the product/service stands for, fostering a sense of familiarity and trust. For example, *"See what's next."* – Netflix's message signifies its commitment to delivering innovative and engaging content, showcasing its consistency in providing a platform for discovering new and exciting entertainment.

- **Authenticity**: This plays a pivotal role in crafting effective messaging. The human-centered approach remains paramount, avoiding an overuse of technical jargon or passing fads. Striking a delicate equilibrium between simplicity and clarity is crucial, enabling the messaging to resonate across diverse individuals. By upholding an authentic tone, the messaging establishes a genuine bond with the audience, fostering trust and relatability that result in heightened engagement. For example, *"Where work happens."* – Slack's concise message conveys its authenticity by positioning the platform as the central hub for collaboration and productivity in the workplace.

Having grasped the key elements of effective messaging, let's now delve into the strategies to truly nail your messaging.

Crafting compelling messaging

Crafting compelling messaging requires a methodical and strategic approach to ensure that it resonates with the intended audience and effectively conveys the value of the product. This process entails a series of interconnected steps that work together to shape the messaging strategy and ensure its success. Crafting your messaging can be done in a few steps:

1. Conducting market research
2. Understanding your target audience
3. Developing your value proposition
4. Crafting key messages
5. Channeling adaptation
6. Testing and refining
7. Rolling out, measuring, and optimizing

Now, let's dive into each of the essential steps of the messaging process to gain a more comprehensive understanding.

Conducting market research and competitive analysis

To ensure a strong foundation for your messaging strategy, it is crucial to conduct comprehensive market research and competitive analysis. This involves delving into market trends, evaluating your competitors' positioning strategies, and identifying gaps and opportunities in the market. Thorough market research plays a crucial role in enabling you to attain a profound understanding of your target audience, including their needs, preferences, and pain points. By conducting comprehensive research, you can uncover valuable insights into emerging trends, market demands, and customer behavior, thus empowering you to align your messaging effectively with the evolving market landscape.

Simultaneously, performing a comprehensive competitive analysis offers valuable insights into how your competitors position their products and communicate their messages. By thoroughly evaluating their strengths, weaknesses, and unique value propositions, you can identify strategic opportunities to differentiate your product and stand out in the market. This analysis allows you to pinpoint gaps and unmet needs that your product can effectively address. By leveraging these insights, you can strategically craft messaging that emphasizes your product's distinct advantages and positions it as the ideal solution for your target audience. Through clear and compelling communication, you can highlight the unique selling points that set your product apart from the competition, demonstrating credibility and relevance to your customers.

Through the integration of market research and competitive analysis, you acquire a thorough grasp of market dynamics, the competitive landscape, and customer preferences.

Understanding your target audience

To craft impactful messaging that truly resonates with your intended audience, it is crucial to possess a deep understanding of their needs and preferences, which can be achieved by creating detailed buyer personas. This involves gathering comprehensive insights about your target audience, such as their characteristics, motivations, pain points, and behavior patterns.

The process begins by conducting extensive market research to collect demographic data, such as age, gender, location, education, and profession. This foundational information provides a basic understanding of your target audience's key attributes. Furthermore, it is essential to explore psychographic details, including their interests, values, lifestyle choices, and purchasing behaviors. By delving into these aspects, you can gain valuable insights into their preferences, aspirations, and decision-making processes.

To effectively tailor your messaging and address the diverse needs of your target audience, it is essential to segment them based on relevant criteria such as behavior, needs, or preferences. This segmentation enables you to create distinct buyer personas that represent different customer segments. Each persona should encapsulate a specific set of characteristics, goals, challenges, and purchasing patterns. By developing multiple personas, you can customize your messaging to cater to the unique needs of each segment and effectively address their pain points.

To build accurate and detailed buyer personas, go beyond general demographics and delve into their motivations and pain points. Conduct interviews, surveys, and focus groups with existing customers, prospects, and internal teams such as sales to gather qualitative insights. Ask questions about their challenges, goals, priorities, and their perception of your product or service. This qualitative data provides rich information that helps you understand why they decided to use your product, how they're using it, and what problems your product is helping them solve. Furthermore, leverage quantitative data to support your understanding of your target audience. Analyze customer behavior data, website analytics, and customer feedback to uncover patterns, preferences, and purchase patterns. This quantitative data adds another layer of insights to refine your buyer personas and messaging strategy.

By thoroughly understanding your target audience and creating detailed buyer personas, you can develop messaging that speaks directly to their needs, desires, and pain points.

Defining your value proposition

It is essential to articulate the unique value and benefits your product provides. Clearly highlight the problems it solves, the outcomes it enables, and the advantages it offers over competitors. This forms the foundation of your messaging, allowing you to effectively communicate why customers should choose your product.

Crafting key messages

Once you have gathered all the essential information regarding your target audience, the subsequent imperative step is to embark on the process of crafting your messaging. This pivotal stage involves the meticulous creation of various components that serve as the building blocks for your messaging framework. Now, let us delve into a closer examination of those components outlined:

- Buyer personas: Dive deep into understanding your target buyers. Define their characteristics, preferences, pain points, motivations, and how they make purchasing decisions. By crafting detailed buyer personas, you can tailor your messaging to resonate with each specific audience segment, addressing their unique needs and aspirations.

- Unique value proposition (UVP): Your UVP lies at the core of your messaging. It encapsulates the distinct value and benefits your product or service offers to your target audience. Clearly articulate how your offering solves their problems, fulfills their needs, and delivers a unique advantage over competitors.

- Competitive positioning: Analyzing the competitive landscape is crucial to differentiate your product or service from competitors in your messaging. It allows you to identify your product capabilities and effectively highlight them. This strategic positioning helps you stand out and effectively showcase the specific advantages you offer to potential customers.

By emphasizing these differentiators, you can create messaging that effectively sets your product or service apart from competitors in the market.

- **Elevator pitch**: Developing an engaging elevator pitch is essential for effectively conveying your product's essence and making a memorable impact on your audience. It is crucial to ensure that your pitch is concise, conversational, engaging, compelling, and easily comprehensible.

- **Capabilities**: Incorporating these capabilities into your messaging framework enables you to communicate the benefits of your product or service while underscoring the value it delivers to your customers. It involves detailing how your solution empowers or facilitates your customers in accomplishing tasks they previously struggled with or could not accomplish as efficiently before your product or service became available.

- **Proof points**: These are the supporting evidence or data points that substantiate the claims and benefits mentioned in your messaging. Proof points add credibility and build trust with your audience. Identify relevant data, case studies, or customer testimonials that can reinforce the value and effectiveness of your offering.

- **Use cases**: Use cases play a crucial role in showcasing the practical applications of your offering and demonstrating its value in action. By highlighting specific scenarios where your product excels, you help your audience visualize how it can enhance their lives or businesses. It is important to carefully craft use cases that align with the pain points and aspirations of your target audience. This allows you to showcase the unique selling points and advantages of your solution in a compelling way.

By incorporating these key elements into your messaging framework, you can create a comprehensive and persuasive messaging strategy. This framework acts as a guide to ensure consistency, clarity, and impact in your communications. As you move forward in the messaging process, these components will help shape your messaging content and provide a solid foundation for compelling and effective communication.

Now, let's explore the framework outlined in the following table in more detail and illustrate it with an example of a company called "DataTech," which specializes in offering an AI-powered data analytics platform specifically designed for enterprise businesses:

Messaging Framework Template		
Primary Persona	Chief Data Officers (CDOs) and Data Analysts of enterprise businesses. Responsible for managing and analyzing large volumes of data	
Secondary Persona	Not relevant	
Core Message		
AI-powered data analytics platform that data analysts enthusiastically embrace, heavily rely on, and effortlessly integrate into their		
Elevator Pitch		
DataTech's AI-powered analytics platform helps you drive revenue, save time and resources, and enhance your operational efficiency		
Value Proposition		
DataTech is a cutting-edge, AI-powered platform: it seamlessly integrates with your existing systems. DataTech provides advanced		
Capability 1	Capability 2	Capability 3
Drive revenue	Save time and resources	Enhance your operational efficiency
Proof Points	Proof Points	Proof Points
Our customers experienced +20% increase in revenue within six months	80% of our customers reduced their data processing time by +50%	90% of our customers achieved cost savings of up to 30% and enhanced overall productivity
Use Case 1	Use Case 1	Use Case 1
Pricing optimization

Used machine learning algorithms to analyze pricing data, market trends and customer behavior to make informed pricing decisions | Achieve [desired outcome] leveraging the power of [product features associated with capability2] | Achieve [desired outcome] leveraging the power of [product features associated with capability3] |
| Use Case 2 | Use Case 2 | Use Case 2 |
| Full List of Features | Full List of Features | Full List of Features |
| Real-time analytics dashboards
Historical pricing analysis
Customer purchase pattern analysis | Which features are applicable to this capability? | Which features are applicable to this capability? |

Table 8.1 – Example of a messaging framework
(for textual detail please refer to the downloadable image package)

Please keep in mind that this internal messaging framework is still in its early stages of development, designed to guide the rest of the company. It's essential to emphasize that the next critical step is testing, which calls for the creation of multiple messaging variations. This approach enables experimentation and the gathering of valuable insights to determine what truly resonates with the audience.

Channeling adaptation

Before proceeding to the testing phase of your messaging, it is crucial to invest time in tailoring your messaging to suit the specific requirements of different communication channels. This includes adapting your messaging for social media platforms, websites, email campaigns, and sales materials. While maintaining consistency in your core messaging, it is essential to consider the unique characteristics and preferences of each channel to ensure maximum impact and engagement with your target audience. By customizing your messaging for various channels, you can effectively deliver your message in a way that resonates and connects with your audience across multiple touchpoints.

Testing and refining

At this stage, refining your messaging becomes a priority, and testing plays a crucial role in this process. Test your messaging with a select group of target customers or through A/B testing. Gather feedback, measure effectiveness, and refine your messaging based on the results. Testing can take various forms and may require a significant amount of time. To ensure an effective testing approach, it is recommended to create a comprehensive test plan that outlines the specific channels and messaging variations to be tested.

Being thoughtful about the channels you choose for testing is essential. Consider the channels that align best with your target audience and have the potential to yield valuable insights. Each channel may require a unique approach to messaging, taking into account its format, audience behavior, and engagement patterns. For instance, when testing messaging in email campaigns, consider the recipients' familiarity with your product and their position in the customer journey. For subscribers who are new to your product, focus on introducing your unique value proposition and building trust. For existing customers, tailor the messaging to highlight personalized offers, upselling opportunities, or exclusive benefits. On the other hand, when testing within the product itself, such as through in-app messaging or onboarding flows, the audience is already engaged and actively interacting with the product. In this case, it is important to tailor the messaging to be more specific and relevant to the features, benefits, or actions within the product. This helps to deepen the user's understanding and create a seamless experience. Additionally, it is important to carefully consider the type of messaging you test within each channel. This can involve experimenting with different value propositions, calls-to-action, tones of voice, or specific features and benefits. By diversifying the testing scenarios, you can gather a broader range of data and insights to inform your messaging refinement.

A well-structured and thoughtful testing plan allows you to measure the effectiveness of your messaging and identify which approaches resonate most strongly with your audience. This iterative testing process empowers you to make data-informed decisions and optimize your messaging strategy for maximum impact and engagement.

Rolling out, measuring, and optimizing

Let's further deconstruct this step into smaller components:

- **Rollout**: In the context of larger companies with multiple stakeholders, the rollout process becomes more complex and typically involves multiple phases. To effectively manage the rollout, I recommend adopting a two-fold approach: the internal rollout and the external rollout. These phases are crucial in ensuring that the messaging is thoroughly communicated and understood within the company before being presented to external audiences.

  - **Internal rollout**: Before releasing the messaging externally, it is crucial to ensure internal alignment throughout the organization. To achieve this, you can create a "hub/wiki" where you can use it as a repository for all materials related to the messaging rollout. This includes key insights and data derived from testing, documentation of the final messaging work, value propositions, elevator pitches, buyer personas, and more. By consolidating this information, you provide a comprehensive resource that enables consistency and clarity across teams. On the other hand, I recommend proactively organizing meetings with various teams and stakeholders, where you present the core messages and concepts, guiding them through the entire process. During these sessions, emphasize the key insights, learnings, methodologies, and results that shape your messaging strategy. This proactive approach ensures that teams and individuals are well-prepared for the messaging rollout, allowing them to provide valuable feedback and actively participate in the messaging process.

- **External rollout:** In the external rollout phase, collaboration with channel partners plays a critical role. Having involved them throughout the process increases the likelihood of their support and ownership. To ensure a successful external rollout, here are some steps to follow:

    - **Involve different channel owners:** Engaging channel partners and enlisting their assistance is essential. By including them in the messaging journey, you build stronger relationships and increase the likelihood of their active participation and support.

    - **Audit all marketing channels:** Assess the existing marketing channels to identify any areas that require updating or aligning with the new messaging. This may involve revising website content, refreshing outdated materials, or aligning messaging across various touchpoints.

    - **Prioritize changes over time:** Going forward, any new projects or initiatives should incorporate the new messaging from the outset. This ensures consistent and unified messaging across all customer-facing materials and interactions.

- **Measure and optimize:** The final step in the process involves measuring the impact of the messaging rollout and optimization. While it can be challenging to measure the direct impact of messaging alone, you can apply various strategies to assess its effectiveness:

    - **Campaign performance:** Analyze the performance of marketing campaigns and look at metrics such as engagement rates (CTR), open rates, and so on. In addition, analyze the **conversion rate (CVR)** at various stages of the sales funnel, the number of new customers acquired, the customer retention rate, and revenue growth. By comparing the performance of campaigns before and after the messaging rollout, you can evaluate its impact on campaign effectiveness.

    - **Sales confidence:** Conduct a survey among your sales team to gauge their confidence levels. Repeat this survey quarterly to track any improvements in sales confidence as an indicator of success.

    - **Customer feedback and satisfaction:** Gather feedback from customers through surveys, reviews, and testimonials.

○ **Analyst briefings and reviews:** Revisit the analysts who were involved in the early stages of the process, share the new messaging, and observe their reactions. Their response can serve as an additional measure of success, as it indicates the effectiveness of the messaging in addressing previously identified challenges.

Continuously monitor and analyze the performance of your messaging. Incorporate customer feedback, market trends, and insights to refine and optimize your messaging strategy over time.

Crafting consistent messaging can indeed be a challenging task, and effectively rolling out and managing messaging can add complexity to the process. To address this challenge, we will now explore the topic of messaging automation in the upcoming section. We will explore how messaging automation tools can be valuable assets in streamlining and optimizing your messaging processes, ultimately helping you achieve greater efficiency and effectiveness in your communication efforts.

Messaging automation

Whether you're a solo product marketer in a corporate setting or working in a start-up, the process of rolling out messaging and managing it effectively can be complex. Regardless of the size of the organization, the challenge remains the same: ensuring consistent messaging across teams, channels, and touchpoints. In this regard, messaging and AI content platforms and messaging automation technologies offer invaluable support. These platforms provide a centralized solution for storing, organizing, and managing messaging elements. They act as a hub where you can house persona-specific copy, and use case descriptions, pain points, benefits, and features in an organized and easily accessible manner. By eliminating duplicates and enforcing standardized messaging practices, these platforms help maintain consistency and alignment throughout the organization.

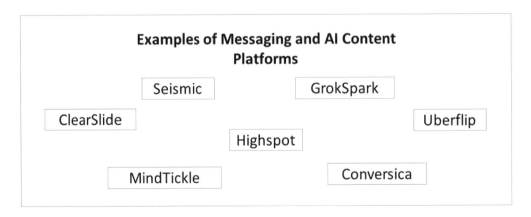

Figure 8.3 – Examples of messaging and AI content tools

Messaging and AI content platforms and messaging automation technologies can greatly assist product marketers in several ways:

- **Centralized messaging management**: They offer a centralized hub for product marketers to store and manage all messaging elements, ensuring easy access, updates, and consistency across marketing channels. This includes persona-specific copy, use case descriptions, pain points, benefits, and features.

- **Efficient messaging creation**: Messaging automation technologies on these platforms empower us as product marketers to efficiently generate customized messaging content. AI-powered content templates and automation tools streamline the process, enabling the quick creation of tailored messages for different personas, industries, or use cases.

- **Consistency and alignment**: Messaging and AI content platforms enforce consistency in messaging by eliminating duplicates and promoting standardized practices, allowing PMMs to align messaging across channels and teams. This builds a stronger brand identity and enhances overall brand strategy and positioning.

- **Collaboration and cross-team alignment**: These platforms foster collaboration between PMMs and teams such as sales, customer success, and marketing. By sharing messaging resources and templates, teams can align efforts and deliver a unified customer experience across the buyer's journey.

- **Dynamic updating and real-time access**: Messaging and AI content platforms provide real-time updating of messaging materials, ensuring immediate reflection of changes across all connected platforms and tools. This enables all teams to access the most up-to-date messaging content, minimizing the risk of using outdated or inconsistent messaging.

- **Streamlined product launches and updates**: PMMs can leverage these platforms to streamline the messaging process during product launches and updates.

- **Data-driven insights**: Messaging and AI content platforms often provide analytics and reporting capabilities. Product marketers can gain valuable insights into the performance of their messaging, such as which messages resonate most with target audiences or which pain points are most compelling. These insights can inform future messaging strategies and optimizations.

To summarize, effectively managing messaging across teams and channels can be challenging, regardless of organizational size. However, messaging and AI content platforms and automation technologies provide valuable assistance. These platforms centralize messaging elements, streamline creation processes, ensure consistency, and foster collaboration among teams and channels.

Summary

In this chapter, we have covered several essential topics that form the foundation of effective messaging and positioning strategies. We explored the art of crafting compelling positioning and messaging, ensuring that your solution stands out and resonates with your target audience. We also delved into the process of creating a strong value proposition, which involves identifying and articulating the unique benefits and advantages your product or service offers. Furthermore, we discussed the concept of narrative design, understanding how creating a captivating narrative can help forge deeper connections with customers. Additionally, we explored the strategy of creating a new category, which involves positioning your offering as a groundbreaking solution that fills a distinct gap in the market.

Armed with this knowledge, we are well-prepared to dive even deeper into the intricacies of building an effective go-to-market strategy in the upcoming chapter. That chapter will enable you to explore strategies and tactics to successfully introduce your product or service to the target market and promote it.

GTM Strategies for Exponential Growth   9

In today's rapidly evolving marketplace, businesses are constantly challenged to stand out and increase their market share. Crafting a comprehensive and well-executed **go-to-market** (**GTM**) strategy can be the key to achieving success. Such a strategy involves integrating various business functions and leveraging market and customer intelligence to effectively introduce products and establish a strong market presence.

A robust GTM strategy serves as the backbone of successful product launches, market penetration, and revitalizing existing products or driving sales growth. It begins by strategically identifying target audiences, understanding their needs, and crafting compelling messaging that resonates. This comprehensive strategy guides companies in developing well-rounded marketing plans, implementing effective distribution strategies, and formulating sales tactics to maximize their chances of capturing market share. At its core, a well-executed GTM strategy seamlessly integrates marketing, content creation, and customer intelligence to engage target customers and spark their interest. It encompasses vital aspects such as pricing, packaging, positioning, messaging, launch campaigns, enablement, and promotion. Moreover, a GTM strategy is not limited to new product introductions. It also plays a crucial role in revitalizing existing products and driving sales growth. Whether your company is venturing into uncharted markets, introducing a new product, or seeking to breathe new life into existing products, a thoughtfully constructed GTM strategy serves as a valuable compass, guiding them through the complexities of the market landscape.

To ensure success, continuous evaluation and refinement of the GTM strategy are essential. You should monitor **key performance indicators** (**KPIs**), analyze customer feedback, and adapt your approach to evolving market dynamics. This approach empowers your company to stay agile and responsive, enabling you to make informed decisions that not only maintain a strong market presence but also drive sustainable growth. This chapter aims to explore the pivotal components of a successful GTM plan, providing practical insights and strategies to help you as product marketers achieve your GTM objectives in today's competitive business environment. We will delve into the following key aspects:

- Exploring the key components of an effective GTM strategy
- Identifying ideal markets to ensure a product–market fit
- Laying out a distribution strategy
- Creating your own content strategy
- Measuring and optimizing your efforts

- Unveiling the blueprint for a successful product launch

Join me as we embark on a deeper exploration of these topics, uncovering the essential elements that comprise a robust GTM strategy. Together, we will gain valuable insights into the significance of this approach in driving business growth and expanding market reach.

Exploring the key components of an effective GTM strategy

Developing a well-executed GTM strategy is an imperative undertaking for businesses aiming to effectively deliver their product/service to their target audience. Whether introducing a new product or enhancing an existing one, a comprehensive GTM strategy serves as a roadmap that guides every step of the customer journey. With its holistic approach, a GTM strategy aims to address several pivotal questions pertaining to how you effectively reach your target audience and deliver your product or service. The following are crucial questions and what they encompass:

- **What**: What product or service are you offering to the market? What problem does your product solve? What is the job to be done?
- **Who**: Who is your target audience? Who are your top segments?
- **Why**: Why should customers choose your product or service over a competitor's? This entails understanding the value proposition and competitive advantages that differentiate your offering in the market.
- **Where**: Where will you sell and distribute your product or service? This involves identifying the initial touchpoints or entryways to the acquisition funnel, as well as the channels that are effective in reaching and engaging your target audience.
- **How**: How will you price your product or service?

Let's take a deeper look into the key components that form the foundation of an effective GTM strategy, highlighting their significance and providing insights into how they contribute to overall success:

- **Defining target markets**: Defining target markets is a pivotal step in crafting a highly effective GTM strategy. The primary objective is to identify specific markets or segments that warrant focused attention and the allocation of resources. This necessitates a comprehensive understanding of market intricacies, including size, growth potential, and competitive dynamics. Market definition requires meticulous research and analysis, gathering extensive data on customer demographics, preferences, and behaviors. A thorough examination of industry trends and competitor landscapes is crucial. By scrutinizing these factors, we identify promising segments that align with our product or service offerings. Assessing growth potential, market size, and barriers to entry informs our market penetration strategy. By carefully considering these factors, we can identify the most promising and appealing market segments to target. This involves understanding the specific tasks or "jobs to be done" by customers and effectively articulating how the product solves their problems. Additionally, acknowledging the unique challenges of different markets and seeking insights from in-market experts enhances our GTM strategy's effectiveness.

- **Target audience:** Creating a successful GTM strategy relies on thoroughly understanding your target audience or buyers (the individuals or groups that will benefit most from your product or service), which emphasizes the need to cater to their specific requirements. By identifying your target audience, you can discern their defining characteristics, encompassing demographics, psychographics, and role considerations. Exploring their challenges and pain points will provide insights that guide your messaging and positioning, helping you effectively communicate how your offering brings value to them by directly addressing their pain points. Identifying the channels and platforms where your audience discovers and interacts with products in your industry is crucial, as it ensures that your presence aligns with their preferences. Leveraging customer feedback and insights helps to gain a deeper understanding of your target audience, enabling you to fine-tune your GTM strategy accordingly. Here's why targeting your audience is essential in a GTM strategy:

  - **Effective messaging:** Understanding your audience enables you to craft messages that directly address their needs and differentiate your product from competitors. By applying the appropriate messaging based on the target audience and funnel stage, you can capture their attention and drive engagement.

  - **Marketing channels:** Customer insights enable you to identify the most effective channels to reach and engage your target audience. This allows you to allocate your marketing resources wisely and focus on platforms where your audience is most likely to be present and receptive.

  - **Buyer journey:** Defining your target audience helps you map out the buyer journey and identify touchpoints for effective engagement. By creating tailored marketing materials and resources, you can guide them through the purchasing process, building trust and facilitating conversion.

    Acquiring a profound comprehension of your target audience necessitates extensive research into their demographics, preferences, behaviors, and requirements. By utilizing this knowledge, you can customize your marketing approach, product positioning, and messaging to resonate effectively and engage with your target audience. This empowers you to craft compelling value propositions that emphasize the distinct benefits of your product or service, choose the most suitable communication channels, and establish yourself as a unique solution in the market.

- **Positioning and messaging:** Developing a strong GTM strategy relies heavily on a well-defined value proposition and messaging. These foundational elements are essential for effectively communicating the value proposition of your product or service to the target audience.

Start by creating a comprehensive positioning document that encompasses key aspects such as personas, the problem being addressed, solution definition, competitive landscape, positioning statement, and relevant use cases. This document sets the stage for developing messaging that resonates with your audience and clearly articulates the benefits and solutions your offering provides. Once the positioning is established, craft messaging that is tailored to your target audience's needs, preferences, and pain points. Emphasize the unique value proposition and differentiators that set your product apart from competitors. Utilize persuasive language, storytelling techniques, and emotional appeals to connect with customers on a deeper level and highlight the outcomes they can expect.

Consistency is crucial across all marketing channels and touchpoints. Whether it's advertising, website content, social media, or sales presentations, ensure that your messaging remains cohesive and aligned with the established positioning. This creates a unified brand experience and reinforces your value proposition in the minds of your customers.

- **Pricing**: Price plays a pivotal role in the success of a GTM strategy, as it directly influences how a product or service is perceived in terms of value and profitability. When determining the pricing strategy, several factors must be carefully considered to strike a balance between generating revenue and maintaining competitiveness in the market.

First and foremost, gaining a profound understanding of your target customers and their purchasing preferences is essential. This involves researching their preferred methods of buying and assessing whether providing upfront pricing information enhances their buying process. A thorough customer research helps you acquire in-depth knowledge of your target audience's preferences and buying behaviors, enabling you to make well-informed decisions regarding pricing transparency. Another crucial aspect of pricing strategy is understanding the production costs associated with your product or service. This entails evaluating factors such as raw materials, manufacturing, labor, and overhead expenses. When you assess these costs, you can establish a baseline for setting the price that ensures profitability. Perceived value also plays a significant role in pricing. It is essential to assess how your target customers perceive the value of your product or service and the benefits it offers. Aligning the price with the perceived value helps you enhance customer satisfaction and increase their willingness to pay. Conducting a competitive pricing analysis is crucial in determining the optimal price point. This involves evaluating the prices of similar products or services offered by competitors in the market. This way you can ensure that your pricing remains competitive and compelling to customers. Understanding the target customers' willingness to pay is another vital aspect of pricing strategy. This requires market research and customer insights to gauge the price sensitivity and affordability of your target audience. In some cases, businesses may adopt a pricing structure that caters to different customer groups or segments. This can involve tiered pricing, where different levels of features or services are offered at varying price points. This is a great way to maximize revenue potential and meet the diverse needs of your customers.

It is important to regularly review and adjust pricing strategies based on market conditions, customer feedback, and your business goals. Pricing decisions should also consider long-term profitability and sustainability, ensuring that your pricing strategy remains effective and aligned with your overall GTM strategy.

- **Distribution strategy:** Crafting an effective GTM strategy requires careful consideration of the distribution model, which determines the optimal approach to deliver the product or service to customers. By selecting the right distribution channels, businesses can enhance accessibility, manage costs, and cater to customer preferences. Here's what you need to know about the distribution model in your GTM strategy:

  - **Identify the right distribution channels:** Choose the channels through which your offering will be distributed, such as direct sales, online marketplaces, retail stores, or partnerships. Consider a combination of channels for broader reach. To determine the optimal distribution model, assess the various options available, including direct sales, retail partnerships, e-commerce platforms, and distribution networks. Each channel has its own advantages and considerations depending on factors such as the nature of your product, the target market, and your business objectives. Direct sales provide control over the customer experience and enable direct engagement, while retail partnerships leverage existing customer reach and infrastructure. E-commerce platforms offer global reach and convenient purchasing, requiring investment in online platforms and logistics. Distribution networks tap into existing networks for broader geographic coverage.

  - **Understand customer buying behavior:** Gain insights into your customers' purchasing habits and preferences. Determine where they typically learn about products in your category and identify the most effective channels at each stage of their buying journey. In addition, consider your product accessibility, cost implications, and desired level of customer experience control when choosing the distribution model.

  - **Align distribution with product type:** Tailor your distribution model based on the type of product you are launching. Understand your product's unique attributes and the problem it solves to align your distribution strategy accordingly.

  - **Collaborate with cross-functional teams:** Engage with cross-functional teams, such as sales, marketing, and product teams, to develop a successful distribution model. Leverage their insights and align with them for the best approach to distribution.

  - **Evaluate and adjust:** Continuously evaluate and adjust your distribution strategy based on performance metrics and market dynamics to ensure its effectiveness.

    Selecting appropriate channels and considering factors such as accessibility, cost, and customer preferences helps your company ensure efficient delivery and customer satisfaction, ultimately driving the success of its offerings.

- **Content strategy:** This encompasses a range of activities designed to generate interest and convince the target audience to make a purchase. In essence, it serves as the primary touchpoint that initiates the acquisition funnel. The plan starts with lead generation, where strategies such as content marketing, **search engine optimization** (SEO), social media, and partnerships are utilized to attract potential customers. Once leads are generated, the focus shifts to lead nurturing, involving personalized communication and targeted marketing efforts to build relationships and guide leads through the sales funnel. The plan also outlines customer acquisition tactics, such as sales presentations, demos, trials, and incentives, aimed at converting leads into paying customers. To foster loyalty and retain existing customers, customer retention strategies are implemented, including ongoing communication, customer support, and loyalty programs. The plan further identifies the specific marketing channels and tactics to be used, allocates resources, and establishes KPIs to measure success. By developing a well-defined sales and marketing plan, businesses can align their efforts, optimize resources, and achieve their GTM objectives with precision and effectiveness.

Crafting an effective GTM strategy is the cornerstone of successfully launching and promoting a product or service. It requires a comprehensive plan that aligns all the essential elements needed to target markets, engage customers, and drive revenue growth. By addressing key components such as market definition, target audience understanding, product messaging and positioning, pricing strategy, distribution and channel strategy, and a well-defined sales and marketing plan, you can create a GTM strategy that stands out with authenticity, clarity, structure, and excellence.

To begin, market definition involves identifying specific markets or segments based on size, growth potential, and competition, while understanding customers enables you to create tailored strategies that consider demographics, preferences, behaviors, and needs. The development of precise product messaging and positioning resonates with the target audience, emphasizing unique value propositions and differentiators. A pricing strategy incorporates factors such as production costs, perceived value, competition, and customer willingness to pay to ensure competitiveness and profitability. Distribution and channel strategies determine efficient delivery methods that consider accessibility, cost, and preferences. Finally, a sales and marketing plan outlines specific activities for lead generation, lead nurturing, customer acquisition, and customer retention to promote and sell the product or service effectively. By integrating these elements seamlessly, product marketers can create an effective GTM strategy that drives success in the market, captivates customers, and fuels revenue growth.

In the forthcoming sections of this chapter, our focus will be on identifying target markets, developing a distribution strategy, and crafting an effective content strategy. As we have already covered positioning and messaging, segmentation and personas, and market research in previous chapters, we will now move on to edifying the ideal markets to target.

Identifying your ideal market

To develop an effective GTM strategy, it is crucial to have a deep understanding of the market environment in which your product or service will be introduced. Before delving into the details of GTM planning, comprehensive research and analysis are of utmost importance. To accomplish this, it's crucial to fully immerse yourself in the intricacies of the market. This entails gaining a comprehensive understanding of its dynamics and delving into the pain points that potential customers are experiencing. Additionally, evaluating the existing solutions currently accessible in the market becomes imperative to determine what options are already in place.

By examining the competitive landscape, you can gain valuable insights into the market gaps and opportunities that your offering can fill. Understanding how your product or service differentiates itself from similar offerings is crucial for effective positioning. It allows you to showcase its unique value proposition, emphasizing the distinctive features and benefits that set it apart. Clearly communicate these differentiators to capture the attention of potential customers and establish a strong market position.

In addition to differentiation, a comprehensive understanding of the market's intricacies is vital. This involves assessing its size, growth potential, and competitive dynamics. Gather insights into these factors so you can identify potential areas for growth and tailor your GTM strategy accordingly. Understanding the market's size helps you gauge the overall opportunity and potential customer reach. Evaluating its growth potential allows you to determine whether the market is expanding or saturated, influencing your market penetration strategy. Analyzing competitive dynamics provides valuable information about the existing players, their market share, and the competitive landscape you'll navigate. Let's explore the essential strategies and steps to confirm that you have chosen the correct market for your product or service.

Determining whether you're in the right market

Making sure your product or service fits the right market requires carefully studying different factors and providing strong evidence that shows it meets the needs and preferences of your intended customers. You can enhance your confidence in the market's viability and make well-informed decisions to drive your GTM strategy by taking the following steps:

1. **Market Research:** Thorough market research is crucial to fully understand the trends, and dynamics of your target market. Identifying key players and potential customers is essential for making informed decisions. Valuable insights about the market's growth potential and consumer behavior can be gathered by utilizing market reports, industry publications, and online resources.

    Before proceeding, let's pause and focus on an essential stage: evaluating the market's potential and calculating its size. By thoroughly examining these factors, we can gain valuable insights to validate whether the market is the right fit for your product or service. Among the key metrics to evaluate the market potential of your product are the **total** addressable market (TAM), serviceable addressable market (SAM), and share of market (SOM). These are key metrics that help you assess market potential, segment your target audience effectively, and determine your market share aspirations. The TAM represents the total demand for a particular product or service. It quantifies the maximum potential revenue opportunity if you were to capture 100% of the market share. Understanding the TAM provides valuable insights into the overall market size and growth potential, allowing you to evaluate the market's attractiveness and set realistic goals. The SAM is a subset of the TAM that represents the portion of the market you can effectively target and serve with your product or service. It considers factors such as geographical limitations, customer preferences, and resource constraints. Evaluating the SAM helps you identify the specific segments and customer profiles that align with your value proposition and allows you to focus your efforts on the most promising market opportunities. The SOM represents the percentage of the SAM that you aim to capture within a specific timeframe. It reflects your market share aspirations and growth targets. By defining the SOM, you establish a benchmark against which you can measure your progress and determine the effectiveness of your GTM strategy.

In the process of calculating your TAM, the first crucial step is to collect pertinent data regarding the potential number of customers and the average revenue each customer generates within your target market. This data can be generated from various resources, such as market research reports, industry associations, government statistics, and internal database records. Let's take an example of a company that offers CRM software specifically designed for small- and medium-sized businesses (SMBs) to calculate the TAM, SAM, and SOM:

I. To calculate the TAM, we need to estimate the potential number of customers and the average revenue per customer in the target market:

    i. **Estimating potential customers:** Let's assume that the target market for the CRM software is SMBs in the United States. Based on data from government statistics and reputable market research reports, the estimated number of SMBs in the United States is approximately 30 million.

    ii. **Estimating average revenue per customer:** The average revenue generated per customer can differ based on various elements, including pricing models, offered features, and market positioning. Let's assume that the average annual revenue per customer for the CRM software is $5,000.

    Now, let's calculate the TAM:

    TAM = estimated number of potential customers × average revenue per customer

    TAM = 30 million customers × $5,000 revenue

    TAM = $150 billion

Therefore, the TAM for the CRM software targeting SMBs in the United States is $150 billion.

II. Regarding SAM, it represents the portion of the TAM that a company can realistically target based on its resources, capabilities, and GTM strategy. Let's assume that the company has the capacity to reach and serve 10% of the SMB market in the United States effectively.

SAM = TAM × serviceable market percentage

SAM = $150 billion × 10%

SAM = $15 billion

Therefore, the SAM for the CRM software targeting SMBs in the US is $15 billion.

III. The SOM is the portion of the SAM that a company can realistically capture within a specific timeframe. Suppose the company's objective is to secure 20% of the SAM during its initial three years of operation.

SOM = SAM × serviceable market percentage

SOM = $15 billion × 20%

SOM = $3 billion

Therefore, the SOM for the CRM software targeting SMBs in the US is $3 billion. To illustrate this better, see the following diagram:

Market Size - Example

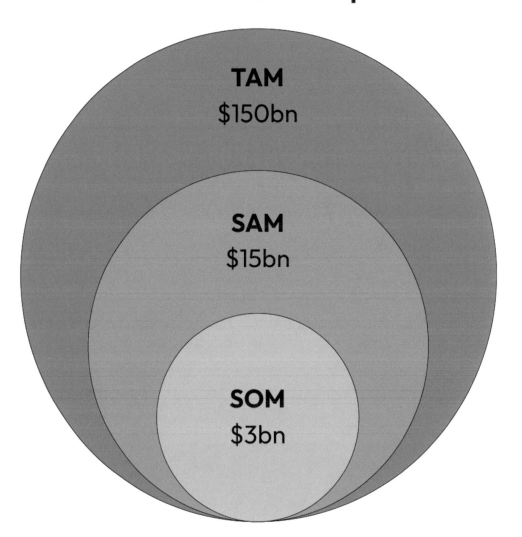

Figure 9.1 – An example of market size with a breakdown of TAM, SAM, and SOM

Now, let's proceed with the rest of the steps to assess the viability of the market and make well-informed decisions:

2. **Customer interviews**: Conduct one-on-one interviews to better understand your target audience's pain points and preferences. Utilize open-ended questions to uncover their

challenges, what they value most in a product or service, and their satisfaction with existing market solutions.

3. **Prototype testing:** Start by developing a prototype or **minimum viable product (MVP)** and conduct testing with your target customers. Seek feedback on its functionality, usability, and value proposition. Utilize this feedback to iteratively refine your product, aligning it more effectively with the market's needs and requirements.

4. **Competitive analysis:** Assess your competitors' offerings and their positioning in the market. Understand their strengths, weaknesses, and unique selling propositions. Identify gaps or opportunities where your product can provide additional value or differentiate itself from the competition.

5. **Beta testing:** To validate your product in a real-world context, consider launching pilot programs or conducting beta testing. Offer a selected subset of your target market the chance to try your product or service. Collect valuable feedback on their experience, identify areas for improvement, and gauge their levels of satisfaction and engagement

6. **Market validation metrics:** Define key metrics that indicate market validation, such as customer acquisition rate, conversion rate, customer satisfaction scores, or repeat purchase behavior. Monitor these metrics over time and compare them with your targets or industry benchmarks to assess your progress and the level of market acceptance.

7. **Industry expert consultation:** Seek guidance from industry experts, advisors, or consultants who have experience and knowledge in your target market. They can provide valuable insights, validate your approach, and offer suggestions based on their expertise.

8. **Partnerships and alliances:** Explore potential partnerships or alliances with complementary businesses in your market. Collaborating with established players or leveraging their distribution channels can provide further validation and increase your market reach.

Keep in mind that market validation is a continuous process, necessitating constant monitoring, adaptation, and iteration driven by customer feedback and market trends.

Market validation helps you assess whether a product has achieved or is progressing toward product–market fit. Product–market fit represents the alignment between a product or service and its specific target market, indicating that it effectively meets the needs of customers in that market. Through various activities, such as market research, gathering customer feedback, and competitive analysis, market validation enables you to validate the alignment between your product and the market's demands, ensuring it adequately addresses customer needs.

Let's thoroughly explore all aspects related to achieving product–market fit.

Product–market fit

Checking product–market fit is an important step in the GTM process. It should be done before you start filling out your GTM plan. Product–market fit serves as the fundamental basis for developing an effective GTM strategy. It involves thoroughly understanding the target market's needs, preferences, and pain points and ensuring that the product aligns with and addresses those demands. When a product achieves product–market fit, it signifies that there is a strong demand and acceptance for the product within the market.

Once product–market fit is established, the GTM strategy can leverage this understanding to effectively position and promote the product. The GTM strategy takes into account the insights gained during the product–market fit assessment and market validation, such as customer feedback, market research, and competitive analysis. These insights inform key decisions and actions related to marketing, sales, distribution, pricing, and customer support.

The GTM strategy harnesses the understanding of product–market fit to align messaging, positioning, and targeting with the unique needs and preferences of customers. This approach ensures that the most relevant message is effectively delivered through appropriate channels, making the product stand out and draw the attention of potential customers. By leveraging insights from product–market fit, the strategy drives customer acquisition and revenue generation by identifying promising customer segments and implementing tailored approaches to convert them into loyal paying customers. The GTM strategy showcases the product's distinct value proposition and addresses specific customer pain points, compelling them to embrace and adopt the product wholeheartedly. Furthermore, the strategy takes into account the competitive landscape and ever-changing market dynamics intending to position the product as the preferred solution for the target customers.

Product–market fit lays the vital groundwork for the GTM strategy, ensuring that the product perfectly aligns with the demands of the market. This process is ongoing and adaptive, continuously refined based on valuable customer feedback and market trends

What is product–market fit?

Product–market fit refers to the state where a product answers the needs and demands of a specific target market. It is the alignment between a product's value proposition, features, and user experience with the requirements, preferences, and pain points of the target audience. When a product achieves product–market fit, it indicates that there is a strong match between what the market wants and what the product offers.

Product–market fit is crucial because it signifies that a product has found a viable market and has gained significant traction with its target customers. It means that the product is delivering value and addressing a real problem or need in the market. Achieving product–market fit is often considered a major milestone for start-ups and new businesses, as it lays the foundation for sustainable growth, customer acquisition, and market success.

Signs of product–market fit can include positive customer feedback, high user engagement, a growing customer base, low churn rates, and increasing market demand. It indicates that customers are not only using the product but also deriving value from it, leading to satisfaction and loyalty. They may even become advocates or promoters of the product. However, it's important to note that product–market fit is not a one-time achievement. Market dynamics change and continuous efforts are required to maintain and adapt the product to meet evolving customer needs and preferences. Regular monitoring of key metrics, customer feedback, and market trends is essential to ensure that the product remains in sync with the market and sustains its fit over time. Here are several key aspects of product–market fit that contribute to its success:

- **Desirability and feasibility**: Product–market fit entails discovering a product or service that satisfies the specific needs and desires of a target market while ensuring its feasibility and viability for delivery to that market.

- **Target audience**: Product–market fit involves identifying and narrowing down the target audience that the product aims to serve. It focuses on providing a must-have solution to the collective problem experienced by that specific group of customers.

- **Gauging demand and satisfaction**: Product–market fit is about understanding the level of interest and demand for the product within the target market. It explores how the product satisfies the appetite and fills the gap in the market.

- **Organic growth and willingness to pay**: Product–market fit is characterized by organic growth, where satisfied customers become advocates and spread the word about the product. It also considers whether customers are willing to pay for the product, indicating its value and perceived benefit.

- **Consistent messaging**: Achieving product–market fit involves ensuring that everyone involved in the product's development and marketing consistently communicates the same message.

Quibi, a now-famous example of a startup that faced failure due to a lack of product–market fit, was a short-form mobile video streaming platform launched in 2020. With a vision to deliver high-quality content tailored for mobile viewing, Quibi aimed to capture the attention of viewers on the go. However, despite significant investment and the involvement of notable industry figures, Quibi struggled to resonate with its target audience and failed to achieve the desired level of success. The misalignment between Quibi's solution and consumer preferences, particularly in terms of content format and pricing, ultimately led to its downfall. Despite significant investment and the involvement of high-profile industry figures, Quibi faced numerous challenges. One of the main reasons for its failure was the misalignment between its solution and consumer preferences. Quibi positioned itself as a premium streaming service targeting millennials and Generation Z, with content produced by well-known celebrities and filmmakers.

However, Quibi's belief that there was a significant demand for short-form, premium content on mobile devices was incorrect. The platform struggled to attract and retain subscribers, as potential customers were already subscribed to free or lower-cost streaming alternatives and preferred longer-form content available on platforms such as YouTube and Netflix. Quibi's inability to resonate with its target audience and provide compelling value ultimately led to its end. The lack of product–market fit was evident through the low viewership numbers and negative reviews. Quibi shut down just months after its launch.

The case of Quibi offers valuable lessons, emphasizing the criticality of comprehending market demand and customer preferences before introducing a product. The inability to achieve product–market fit can substantially hinder a startup's chances of success in the highly competitive tech industry.

What are the benefits of product–market fit?

Achieving product–market fit holds immense strategic value, as it encompasses the crucial intersection between a business, its products, and its customers. Mastering this concept not only enhances the understanding of customer needs and how to fulfill them, but it also drives bottom-line growth. The benefits of nailing product–market fit are manifold. First, it translates into increased sales, as a well-aligned product meets the demands of an eager market, resulting in revenue growth. Second, it helps control customer churn by providing a product that customers appreciate and desire, leading to a decrease in attrition rates. Additionally, positive customer feedback becomes prevalent as customers begin to rave about the product and share their favorable experiences, which amplifies the power of word-of-mouth marketing. This organic form of promotion by satisfied customers contributes to visibility and growth. The satisfaction of having customers act as advocates for your product is unparalleled. Furthermore, product–market fit establishes a competitive advantage by setting your offering apart from competitors and positioning your product as a leader in the market. The understanding of customer needs and the ability to meet them effectively allows for focused and efficient resource allocation, streamlining product development, marketing strategies, and sales efforts. Finally, achieving product–market fit in one segment opens doors for expansion into new markets or customer segments, leveraging the gained insights and knowledge to replicate success. In summary, product–market fit is a strategic milestone that drives sales, customer retention, positive word-of-mouth marketing, competitive advantage, focus, efficiency, and growth opportunities, all contributing to long-term business success and profitability.

How to measure product–market fit?

Product–market fit refers to the alignment between a product and its target market. It indicates the degree to which a product satisfies the needs, preferences, and demands of the market it is intended for. Measuring and validating product–market fit involves a combination of methods and metrics to assess the alignment between your product or service and the target market. Monitoring and analyzing the four key metrics—activation, engagement, retention, and loyalty—can provide valuable insights into product–market fit. Here's how these metrics relate to assessing product-market fit:

- **Activation**: If the activation metric is positive and improving over time, it suggests that new users are successfully transitioning into active users of your product. It indicates that your value proposition and initial user experience resonate with customers, motivating them to start using your product. High activation rates imply that your product addresses a real need or pain point in the market and effectively communicates its value to users.

- **Engagement**: A positive and increasing engagement metric signifies that active users find value in your product and are actively using its features. It demonstrates that your product is delivering on its promises and meeting the expectations of users. High engagement levels indicate that your product is sticky and provides an enjoyable, useful, or efficient experience that keeps users coming back for more.

- **Retention**: If the retention metric is positive and improving, it suggests that users are finding enough value and reasons to continue using your product over time. It shows that your product is able to retain its user base and prevent churn. Strong retention rates indicate that your product satisfies ongoing needs, provides continuous value, or builds habits among users. This is a key aspect of achieving long-term success and sustainable growth.

- **Loyalty**: A positive loyalty metric implies that users are not only satisfied with your product but also willing to become advocates and recommend it to others. It indicates a high level of customer satisfaction and loyalty. Users who are loyal to your product can contribute to organic growth by spreading positive word-of-mouth marketing and attracting new customers. Loyalty reflects the strong connection between your product and its target market.

While no single approach fits all situations, several common methods are used to assess product–market fit. One method is conducting customer surveys to gather feedback on satisfaction levels, the value proposition of your product, and the likelihood of customer recommendations. A high **net promoter score** (**NPS**) or positive customer satisfaction ratings can indicate a strong product–market fit. Usage and engagement metrics provide valuable insights into user behavior. Analyzing active users, retention rates, time spent on your product, and frequency of use can reveal the extent to which your offering meets customer needs. Customer interviews and feedback are valuable for understanding customers' pain points and needs and how effective your product is at addressing them. Positive feedback and testimonials from customers can signify a good product–market fit. Market share and growth are important indicators of product–market fit. Monitoring your market share and growth rate compared to competitors can help determine if your product is meeting customer demands and outperforming alternatives. Referrals and word-of-mouth marketing are indicative of customer satisfaction and fit. Assessing the number of referrals and recommendations from existing customers demonstrates how well your product satisfies customer needs and generates positive market buzz.

By consistently monitoring these metrics and observing positive trends over time, you can gain confidence that your product is achieving product–market fit. However, if any of these metrics consistently show low or declining performance, it indicates areas of improvement. It may suggest that your product is not fully meeting the needs of the market or that there are aspects of the user experience that require refinement. In such cases, reassessing your value proposition, product strategy, or user feedback can help you iterate and enhance your product to better align with the market. Now, let's move on to the next component of an effective GTM strategy: distribution.

Laying out distribution strategy

As mentioned earlier, a key component of a well-crafted and effective GTM strategy is the development of a distribution strategy, which involves making informed decisions about the best means of delivering the product to customers. This entails considering various channel options, such as direct sales, resellers, or distributors, to ensure efficient access to the intended market.

To identify the most effective distribution models for a target market, it is crucial to gain a deep understanding of the target market's demographics, preferences, and buying habits. By analyzing customer data, including purchase patterns, preferences, and satisfaction levels with existing distribution channels, valuable insights can be obtained. This analysis helps to identify any gaps or areas for improvement, enabling informed decisions when selecting distribution models. Additionally, actively seeking customer feedback plays a vital role in understanding their preferences and experiences with different distribution methods.

In order to develop a robust distribution strategy, conducting thorough market research is essential. This research allows you to uncover commonly used distribution channels within your industry or market segment. Furthermore, analyzing competitors within the same market to evaluate their distribution strategies is vital.

When assessing distribution channels to effectively reach and serve your target market, it is recommended to consider market accessibility factors such as geographical coverage, logistics, and cost-effectiveness. To evaluate the effectiveness of different distribution channels, it is beneficial to implement a pilot or test phase, if possible. This allows you to gather valuable insights into their performance. Moreover, exploring the potential for integrating multiple distribution channels can create a seamless and convenient experience for customers, thereby enhancing satisfaction and overall performance.

Continuous monitoring and evaluation of the chosen channels play a crucial role. KPIs such as sales volume, customer satisfaction, and market reach serve as great indicators of each channel's success. Based on the KPIs, you can make necessary adjustments and optimize your distribution strategy accordingly. Regularly assessing and adapting your approach will ensure your distribution channels remain effective and aligned with your business objectives. Let's take a look at some of the most common distribution methods/channels.

Exploring common distribution methods

Effective distribution is crucial for successfully delivering products or services to customers. There are several distribution methods to choose from, each serving as a channel through which your offerings reach the market. The most common distribution models include direct sales, indirect sales through resellers or distributors, marketplaces, and partners/resellers. Here's a breakdown of these distribution models:

1. **Direct sales:** This refers to selling a product or service directly to customers without involving intermediaries. It involves the company pushing its products through advertising and promotional activities or by waiting for potential customers to actively search for the products. This can be done through various channels, such as a company's own website (such as Netflix), physical stores (such as Apple), or direct sales teams (such as Google AdWords). These direct sales teams may engage in two different sales approaches: inside sales and field sales.

     I. **Inside sales:** These sales activities are conducted remotely. It typically involves sales representatives reaching out to customers via phone calls, emails, or online meetings. Inside sales teams focus on prospecting, qualifying leads, and closing sales remotely without the need for in-person visits.

     II. **Field sales:** Sales representatives meet customers face-to-face, either by traveling to customer locations or attending trade shows or events. Field sales teams often build relationships with customers, provide product demonstrations, and negotiate sales terms directly.

     Both inside sales and field sales are effective methods for engaging customers directly and closing sales. The choice between these approaches depends on factors such as the nature of the product or service, the target market, and the company's resources and objectives.

2. **Indirect sales:** These sales involve diverse strategies that expand a product's reach beyond direct interactions. These methods leverage partnerships, online platforms, licensing, franchising, and reseller networks to effectively tap into broader markets and distribution channels.

     I. **Strategic partnerships:** Collaborating with strategic partners who have an established customer base can help expand the product's reach. This can involve joint marketing efforts or bundling the product with complementary offerings.

     II. **E-commerce platforms:** Selling products through popular online platforms or marketplaces such as Amazon, eBay, or Shopify can be an effective distribution method, particularly for reaching a wide customer base.

     III. **Licensing or franchising:** Licensing the product to other companies or allowing them to operate under a franchise model can help expand its reach into different markets or geographies.

     IV. **Resellers:** This distribution method involves partnering with third-party resellers who sell the product on behalf of the company. Resellers can include retailers, wholesalers, or **value-added resellers (VARs)**.

These are just a few examples of common distribution methods, and the selection of the most appropriate methods depends on several factors. The nature of the product, the characteristics of the target market, industry dynamics, and business goals all play a role in determining the most suitable channels for distribution. Careful evaluation of each option is essential to ensure that the chosen methods align with the overall GTM strategy and effectively meet the needs of the target audience.

B2B versus B2C distribution strategies

Crafting a winning distribution strategy hinges on the mastery of customization to align the approach with the unique characteristics of the target market and product. Remarkably, distribution strategies diverge considerably when comparing **business-to-business (B2B)** and **business-to-consumer (B2C)** target markets. These distinct business landscapes demand tailored approaches to seamlessly connect with and captivate their respective audiences. Now, let's delve deeper into the distribution strategies for each market segment.

B2B distribution strategy

B2B distribution strategies place great importance on direct contact with customers, employing various channels and interactions. Sales representatives are central to this process, possessing extensive product knowledge and expertise. They engage in one-on-one interactions, delivering detailed product demonstrations that allow customers to experience the software first-hand and gain a comprehensive understanding of its capabilities.

The personalized customer service extends throughout the entire buying process. Sales reps actively listen to customer inquiries, address concerns, and provide guidance to facilitate informed decision-making. By offering tailored advice and solutions, they ensure that the product meets the specific needs and requirements of each customer.

Consultations play a vital role in B2B distribution strategies as well. Sales reps engage in meaningful discussions with customers, asking relevant questions to comprehensively understand their pain points and challenges. This deep understanding enables them to propose customized solutions that precisely align with the customer's unique requirements.

Negotiations and contract discussions are integral components of B2B transactions. Sales reps act as knowledgeable guides, closely collaborating with customers to navigate pricing discussions, contract terms, and service-level agreements. This direct contact fosters real-time feedback, streamlining negotiations and ensuring mutually beneficial agreements are reached.

Post-sale, B2B distribution strategies prioritize ongoing support and relationship-building. Sales reps maintain regular contact with customers, providing assistance with product onboarding, addressing any technical issues, and offering post-sale support. Some B2B companies, such as big enterprises, even assign dedicated account managers to their customers, ensuring personalized attention and tailored solutions as their needs evolve over time.

To further enhance customer understanding and optimize product utilization, B2B distribution strategies may include training and educational resources. Sales reps may organize training sessions, workshops, or webinars to educate customers on the software's features, functionalities, and best practices. These initiatives empower customers, enabling them to fully leverage the product's capabilities and derive maximum value from their investment.

A relevant example of a company implementing a multi-channel distribution strategy in the B2B market is Microsoft. Microsoft, a well-known technology company, offers a diverse range of software, hardware, and cloud-based solutions tailored for businesses.

To effectively distribute their products and services, Microsoft employs various channels. First, they utilize a direct sales force to engage with enterprise customers, gaining insights into their specific requirements and providing customized solutions. In addition to direct sales, Microsoft partners with resellers and system integrators. These intermediaries possess expertise in Microsoft's solutions, offering support and implementation services while promoting and selling Microsoft products to customers.

To expand its presence further, Microsoft leverages digital marketing channels, industry events, and collaborations with other technology providers. These efforts enable Microsoft to extend its reach, establish credibility, and position themselves as a trusted partner within the market.

Implementing a multi-channel distribution strategy enables Microsoft to successfully reach a wide customer base, provide tailored solutions, and solidify its position in the market.

As a product marketing manager in a B2B company, you focus heavily on equipping the sales team with the necessary tools and resources. This includes developing sales collateral, product documentation, case studies, and presentations that enable sales representatives to effectively convey the value of the software to potential customers. Ensuring a smooth customer onboarding process and ongoing support is also important. As the product marketing manager, you play a role in guiding new customers through implementation and providing support resources to maintain customer satisfaction.

Maximizing product utilization requires proper training and education. As a product marketing manager, you have to facilitate training sessions, webinars, or workshops to educate customers, sales representatives, and other stakeholders on product features, benefits, and best practices.

B2C distribution strategy

B2C distribution strategies are centered around creating a seamless customer experience and ensuring the accessibility of products or services for consumers. B2C companies employ various methods tailored to the preferences and needs of their target audience.

Partnering with marketplaces and aggregators, such as Amazon, eBay, and Alibaba, is a common approach. These platforms offer a vast consumer base and established infrastructure for order fulfillment and customer support. Listing products on these platforms allows B2C companies to leverage their extensive reach, increasing visibility and potential sales.

Collaborating with resellers and retailers is another effective method in B2C distribution strategies. By forming partnerships with established retail networks, B2C companies can tap into the reseller's customer base and benefit from their expertise in specific markets or regions. This expands product availability and offers convenience for consumers who prefer purchasing through physical stores or specific online platforms.

Building a strong community is a crucial aspect of B2C distribution strategies. This is achieved through fostering engagement on social media platforms, online forums, user groups, or dedicated online communities. Comprehensive customer support and resources are essential in B2C distribution strategies. B2C companies offer multiple customer service channels, such as phone, email, and live chat, to promptly address inquiries and resolve issues. They also provide valuable resources such as tutorials, FAQs, user manuals, and troubleshooting guides to assist customers in effectively using their products and overcoming common challenges.

Leveraging third-party software is another tactic employed by B2C companies to enhance product offerings and provide additional value to customers. For example, a camera manufacturer might partner with a reputable photo editing software provider to bundle their product with high-quality editing software, creating a more comprehensive and appealing solution for customers.

Digital marketing is an essential component of B2C distribution strategies. Companies allocate resources to various online marketing techniques, such as online advertisements, SEO for their websites, leveraging social media platforms for brand promotion, and partnering with influencers to endorse their products. These strategies are implemented with the goal of achieving several key objectives, including creating brand awareness, directing traffic to online channels, generating consumer interest, and ultimately boosting conversion rates and sales.

Apple is a prime example of a highly successful B2C company with a distinctive distribution strategy. Apple has revolutionized the consumer electronics industry with its innovative products, such as the iPhone, iPad, and Mac computers. Apple uses a multi-channel distribution strategy to reach its customers. They sell products through their online store and physical retail stores, such as Apple stores. Additionally, they have partnerships with carriers, which play a significant role in distributing their products, particularly iPhones, through carrier stores and contracts. Their e-commerce platform provides customers with a seamless online shopping experience, featuring detailed product information, easy ordering, and secure payment options. Apple's physical retail stores located worldwide offer a unique and immersive environment where customers can explore and interact with the latest Apple devices and receive personalized assistance from knowledgeable staff. By integrating their online and offline channels, Apple ensures a consistent brand experience for customers across various touchpoints. Additionally, Apple's distribution strategy emphasizes strong logistics and supply chain management to maintain efficient inventory levels and meet customer demands.

As a product marketing manager in a B2C company, your role is essential in creating a seamless customer experience and ensuring the accessibility of products or services. You collaborate with various stakeholders to implement effective methods tailored to the target audience's preferences and needs. This includes partnering with marketplaces and aggregators to leverage their reach, collaborating with resellers and retailers to tap into their customer base and expertise, and building a strong community through social media and online engagement. Additionally, you prioritize comprehensive customer support, providing multiple channels and valuable resources to assist customers. You also explore partnerships with third-party software providers to enhance product offerings and employ digital marketing strategies to generate brand awareness, drive traffic, and increase consumer interest for higher conversion rates and sales.

Summing it up

To summarize, the distribution strategy for a B2B target market differs from that of a B2C target market in several ways. B2B distribution involves more direct contact with customers, such as sales reps, product demos, and one-on-one interactions, as B2B buyers have specific requirements and need in-depth information. B2C distribution, on the other hand, relies more on online reviews and digital marketing, as B2C buyers have less contact with the seller. B2B strategies focus on building relationships, offering personalized solutions, and educating customers about complex products, while B2C strategies prioritize convenience, quick transactions, and reaching a larger consumer audience through mass marketing and e-commerce platforms. These B2C approaches aim to create a seamless and accessible customer experience, maximize product visibility, generate brand loyalty, and ultimately drive consumer interest and sales. Selective channel partnerships are common in B2B, while B2C emphasizes creating a strong online presence and leveraging multiple online marketplaces.

Overall, the distribution strategies are customized to address the specific characteristics and requirements of each target market. Now, brace yourself for a thrilling transition as we shift gears and venture into the upcoming session—a deep dive into the art of crafting an impactful content strategy.

Creating your content strategy

Crafting a successful GTM content strategy requires careful consideration of several key elements. To begin, a deep understanding of your target audience is crucial. This involves conducting comprehensive market research to gather insights into their demographics, psychographics, pain points, and preferences. When you understand your audience's needs, motivations, and the jobs to be done, you can create content that resonates with them effectively.

Moreover, it is crucial to have a well-defined value proposition and messaging framework. This framework plays a vital role in shaping the perception of your product or service within the market and differentiating it from competitors. It serves as a cohesive basis for all your content initiatives, guaranteeing that your messaging resonates with your intended audience and effectively conveys the distinct value of what you offer.

Compelling content development is another critical aspect of a successful GTM content strategy. This entails creating high-quality, relevant, and engaging content that educates, informs, and entertains your audience. Whether it's through blog posts, articles, videos, infographics, case studies, or other formats, your content should provide value and address your audience's pain points.

Equally important is effective content distribution. This involves selecting the most appropriate channels and platforms to reach your target audience. Your website, social media platforms, email marketing, industry publications, partnerships, and other avenues can all play a role in distributing your content. A well-planned distribution strategy ensures that your content reaches the right people at the right time, maximizing its visibility and impact.

Content development

Crafting compelling content for your GTM strategy requires careful consideration of the following elements:

1. **Deep audience understanding:** Conduct thorough research and analysis to gain a profound understanding of your target audience. Identify their pain points, challenges, and aspirations to create content that resonates with their specific needs.

2. **Tailored messaging and value proposition:** Clearly articulate the unique value and benefits of your product or service. Tailor your messaging to different stakeholder groups, highlighting how your solution addresses their specific problems and delivers value.

3. **Alignment with GTM goals:** Ensure that your content development aligns with the overarching goals and objectives of your GTM strategy. Your content should support the GTM campaign approach and effectively communicate the value proposition of your offering.

4. **Integration of social proof and beta results:** Incorporate social proof, testimonials, and results from beta testing into your content. Highlight positive feedback and successful outcomes to build credibility and trust with your target audience.

5. **Continuous evaluation and adaptation:** Regularly assess the effectiveness of your GTM content strategy and make necessary adjustments. Stay agile and responsive to changing market dynamics and customer feedback. Continuously refine and optimize your content to ensure it remains relevant and impactful.

Steps to Impactful Content Creation

Figure 9.2 - Steps to impactful content creation

To sum it up, craft impactful GTM content by deeply understanding your audience, aligning messaging with value, and integrating social proof. Continuously adapt and evaluate to ensure alignment with your GTM goals and the audience's needs.

Types of content

Effectively utilizing a variety of collateral materials can yield substantial results. These resources serve as tangible evidence and validation of the value proposition your product brings to potential customers. They play a crucial role in fostering trust, establishing credibility, and influencing purchasing decisions. Here are some impactful types of collaterals worth considering:

- **Social proof:** Utilize social proof to enhance your credibility and showcase the positive impact of your product. Incorporate case studies, customer success stories, awards and recognitions, and endorsements from industry influencers or partnerships logos to highlight customer testimonials and endorsements. These valuable resources can be featured on your website, incorporated into your social media posts, and integrated into your marketing materials, providing real-world examples that further demonstrate the value of your product.

- **Video testimonials:** Video testimonials offer a dynamic way to capture customer feedback. Whether through product demonstrations, customer interviews, event highlight reels, tutorials and how-to videos, video case studies, or webinar recordings, hearing customers share their experiences and success stories adds authenticity and builds trust with prospects.

- **Use case content:** Develop content specific to different use cases, such as blog posts, YouTube videos, case study whitepapers, step-by-step guides, industry-specific webinars, success stories, interactive tools, and calculators or infographics. These resources provide practical examples of how your product solves specific problems and addresses customers' needs.

- **Thought leadership content:** Create thought leadership content that establishes your expertise and educates customers about industry trends, challenges, and the solutions your product offers. This can include whitepapers, eBooks, webinars, or podcast episodes.

- **Leave-behinds:** Provide comprehensive leave-behind materials for both buyers and users. These resources can include product guides, user manuals, cheat sheets, and FAQs, enabling customers to better understand and make the most of your product.

Utilizing these different types of collaterals enables you to capture customer feedback effectively, showcase social proof, highlight use cases, establish thought leadership, and provide valuable resources to enhance your customer experience.

Content distribution

The effectiveness of a GTM strategy heavily relies on a well-crafted content distribution and channel strategy that enables reaching and engaging the intended audience, thereby maximizing the impact of product marketing endeavors. By purposefully selecting suitable channels and optimizing content distribution, it becomes possible to adeptly convey your message, cultivate awareness, and stimulate customer engagement.

A Sneak Peek to Launch Checklist - Content

Foundations	Responsible Department	Accountable	Approver	Priority	Due Date	Status
Content Marketing						
Press Release						
Reports						
Whitepaper						
Solutions Page						
Blog content						
Customer Marketing						
Monthly Newsletter						
Customer Email						
Video & Podcasts						
"How to" Product Video						
Launch Video						
Podcast						

Figure 9.3 – A sneak peek to launch checklist: content

> **NOTE**
>
> The preceding table does not encompass all content types within each category. As mentioned, this is a sneak peek, and the complete list is available at https://sites.google.com/view/theproductmarketingcode/.

When developing a content distribution and channel strategy, several factors should be taken into consideration to ensure its effectiveness. Here are key elements to consider:

- **Target audience:** To maximize your impact, it is essential to possess a profound understanding of your target audience, including their content consumption habits and preferred channels. Armed with this invaluable knowledge, you can strategically select the most appropriate channels to engage and effectively reach your specific audience.

- **Channel selection:** Choose the channels that align with your target audience's preferences and behaviors. Consider a mix of online and offline channels, such as social media platforms, industry-specific websites, email marketing, paid advertising, events, print media, and more. Select the channels that offer the best reach and engagement opportunities.

- **Content relevance:** Tailor your content to the specific channels you choose. Adapt your content format, tone, and messaging to resonate with the audience of each channel. For example, create visually appealing content for social media, in-depth articles for industry publications, and interactive videos for your website or YouTube channel.

- **Timing and frequency:** Determine the optimal timing and frequency for distributing your content. Consider factors such as peak usage times for different channels, industry trends, and the preferences of your target audience.

- **Measurement and analysis:** Implement tracking and analytics to measure the performance of your content distribution efforts. Monitor key metrics such as reach, engagement, conversions, and audience feedback. Use the insights gained to refine your distribution strategy, optimize channel selection, and improve content relevance for better results.

- **Integration with GTM strategy:** Ensure that your content distribution strategy aligns with your overall GTM strategy. Coordinate your content distribution efforts with other marketing initiatives, sales activities, and customer touchpoints to create a cohesive and integrated approach.

- **Iteration and optimization:** Through iteration and optimization, it is crucial to consistently assess and enhance your content distribution approach by analyzing performance metrics and incorporating market feedback. Remain receptive to experimenting with fresh channels, formats, and strategies in order to determine the most effective methods for engaging your specific target audience.

Key Elements to Ensure Content Distribution Effectiveness

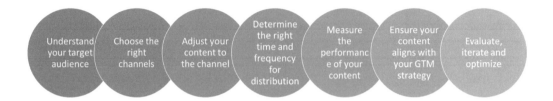

Figure 9.4 - Content distribution effectiveness

Developing a well-structured distribution strategy is vital to ensure the successful reach and impact of your content across various stages of the buying funnel or customer journey. Firstly, it is essential to carefully choose the appropriate channels. Analyze the platforms and channels where your target audience actively participates and engages. This may encompass social media platforms, industry-specific websites, email marketing, paid advertising, influencer partnerships, and other relevant avenues. By selecting channels that align with your audience's preferences, you enhance the visibility and consumption of your content among the intended individuals.

In addition to selecting the right channels, it's important to distribute your content at the right time and stage of the buying funnel. Each stage of the buyer's journey, from awareness to loyalty and advocacy, requires different types of content and messaging. For example, during the awareness stage, you might focus on creating content that introduces your brand and highlights the value you offer. In the consideration stage, you can provide in-depth information and comparison resources to help potential customers evaluate their options. As customers move through the decision stage and make a purchase, you can provide support materials and onboarding resources. Furthermore, during the loyalty and advocacy stages, you can nurture customer relationships through valuable content that encourages repeat purchases and referrals.

Content by Buying Journey Stage

Awareness	Interest	Consideration	Purchase	Advocacy
• Social media content	• Webinars	• Product comparisons	• FAQs	• Personalized emails
• Digital advertising	• Video content	• Guides/whitepapers	• Product pages	• Customer newsletters
• Print media	• Infographics	• Demo videos	• Customer reviews	• Exclusive content
• TV advertising	• Case studies	• Testimonials	• Pricing and packaging	• Social media engagement
• Paid content	• e-books	• Case studies	• Comparison charts	• Customer surveys
• Tradeshows	• Whitepapers	• Free trials Customer reviews		
• Podcasts	• Social media content			
• Industry reports				
• Research papers				

Figure 9.5 – Content by buying journey stage
(for textual detail please refer to the downloadable image package)

By aligning your content distribution with the various stages of the buying funnel, you ensure that your content is relevant, timely, and engaging for your audience. This not only maximizes the visibility of your content but also increases its impact. It helps guide potential customers through their decision-making process, educates them about your product or service, and encourages them to take the desired actions.

Let's now proceed to the next phase of the GTM strategy, which involves measuring its effectiveness and optimizing its performance.

Measuring and optimizing your efforts

When it comes to ensuring a successful GTM strategy, measuring and optimizing your efforts is crucial. This allows you to effectively track the performance of your tactics, identify areas for improvement, and make data-driven decisions to drive better results. Here are some key steps to consider when measuring and optimizing your GTM strategy:

1. **Define key metrics**: A crucial first step involves identifying relevant KPIs aligned with your specific goals and objectives. These metrics may encompass **conversion rate** (**CVR**), **customer acquisition cost** (**CAC**), and **lifetime value** (**CLTV**). Regularly monitoring and analyzing these KPIs allows for a comprehensive evaluation of your GTM strategy's effectiveness and enables data-driven decision-making.

2. **Implement analytics tools:** Utilize analytics tools such as Google Analytics, Mixpanel, and HubSpot to gather relevant data on user behavior, website traffic, and conversion rates. These tools provide valuable insights into how customers interact with your GTM efforts and help you identify specific areas for improvement.

3. **Track campaign performance:** Evaluating the success of your marketing endeavors requires vigilant monitoring of campaign performance. Consistently analyzing metrics such as **click-through rate (CTR)**, CVR, and **return on investment (ROI)** yields valuable insights.

4. **Analyze customer feedback:** Collect feedback from customers through surveys, interviews, or user testing. This qualitative data provides valuable insights into customer preferences, pain points, and opportunities for improvement. Incorporating this feedback into your GTM strategy allows you to refine your messaging and targeting for better results.

5. **Continuously iterate:** Remember that GTM is an iterative process. Regularly review your metrics, identify areas for improvement, and make data-driven adjustments to your GTM tactics. Embrace a mindset of continuous improvement and optimization based on the insights and feedback you gather.

Key Steps to Measure and Optimize Your GTM Strategy

Figure 9.6 - Steps to measure and optimize GTM strategy

To ensure an accurate measurement of GTM activities' success, it is vital to establish clear and measurable objectives. By setting specific deliverables, you can effectively track progress and evaluate the effectiveness of your GTM strategy. For instance, if the goal is to enhance user adoption, a specific objective could be to achieve a 30% increase in new customers within a four-week timeframe. This objective provides a tangible and measurable target to assess the success of your GTM efforts and make data-driven adjustments accordingly.

In addition, it's important to remember that measuring and optimizing your GTM strategy is an ongoing and iterative process. By maintaining agility and responsiveness to user feedback and performance data, you can continuously refine your strategy and achieve improved outcomes. Embracing a proactive and adaptive approach allows you to make data-driven adjustments, stay ahead of market trends, and drive better results over time.

A well-executed GTM strategy is essential to ensure a successful product launch. It enables the delivery of the right message to the appropriate audience through effective channels at the optimal timing. By defining target markets, understanding the audience, and tailoring messaging and positioning, the GTM strategy maximizes the chances of capturing customer interest and engagement during the launch phase. In the upcoming section, we will explore a comprehensive framework that sets the stage for a successful product launch.

Unveiling the blueprint for a successful product launch

Product launch and GTM both play vital roles in the success of introducing a new product or service. While a product launch focuses on the actual process of bringing a new offering to the market, a GTM strategy encompasses the comprehensive plan that guides how a company will effectively reach and deliver value to its target customers. Creating a successful product launch requires careful consideration of various elements. Let's take a look into the key components of a product launch:

1. Aligning the launch process
    I.   Clear launch goals (and accountability)
    II. Launch timeline
    III. Launch tier
    IV. Roles and responsibilities (DACI model)
    V.   Success measurement and tracking

2. Developing a solid GTM strategy
    I.   Market and competitive intelligence
    II. Ideal customer profile and target personas
    III. Product messaging and differentiation (and message testing)
    IV. Product/feature
    V.   Pricing and packaging
    VI. Content plan
    VII. Distribution plan

3. Collaborating on an effective execution plan
    I.   Product readiness
    II. Sales and customer success teams' enablement
    III. Partner enablement
    IV. Analyst briefings

By including these fundamental elements in your launch plan, you can establish a robust framework for a successful product launch. A well-developed launch plan brings immense clarity to the diverse range of stakeholders involved, fostering effective communication, seamless coordination, and collaboration throughout the launch process. In this section, our primary focus will be on the various aspects of aligning the launch process, as this is the ideal opportunity to delve into this topic. While we have either covered or will touch upon the remaining elements in previous or upcoming chapters, it is essential to dedicate our attention to ensuring alignment with the launch process, as it's a crucial component of a successful product launch. Let's now delve into the significance and intricacies of achieving stakeholder alignment in the context of a successful launch.

Aligning with the launch process

When it comes to launching a new product or feature, a well-structured and coordinated approach is key to achieving success. Aligning on the launch process and establishing clear goals are essential to keeping everyone on the same page and ensuring accountability. A comprehensive launch timeline helps you organize activities and set realistic deadlines. Assigning roles and responsibilities using the DACI model ensures that every team member knows their tasks and can contribute effectively. Lastly, measuring and tracking success allows you to evaluate the impact of your launch and make data-driven decisions. In this section, we will delve into each of these components, exploring how they contribute to a smooth and impactful product launch.

Stakeholder alignment

Effective stakeholder alignment is a crucial element in driving the success of a GTM strategy. It involves bringing together relevant stakeholders from various departments, such as product marketing, product management, sales, and customer success, to collaborate toward a common goal and foster synergy.

The process of stakeholder alignment initiates with the establishment of a clear and shared understanding of the goals and objectives of the GTM strategy. This encompasses defining the target audience, pinpointing the specific product or service being introduced, and determining the desired business outcomes. By ensuring that all stakeholders possess a comprehensive grasp of these goals, they can better comprehend how their unique roles and responsibilities contribute to the overall success of the strategy.

Once the roles and responsibilities within the organization have been clearly defined, the significance of effective communication cannot be overstated. It is crucial to provide your stakeholders with precise guidelines and expectations, ensuring that they have a comprehensive understanding of their specific tasks and obligations. Clear communication plays a pivotal role in aligning stakeholders and fostering collaboration. It is equally important to provide each team with the necessary resources and support to accomplish their tasks effectively and execute their responsibilities with confidence.

In addition to role clarity, a well-defined timeline is crucial for executing the strategy effectively. The timeline serves as a roadmap that outlines key milestones and deadlines, providing a clear structure for all teams involved. By establishing a timeline, everyone is aware of the sequence of activities and the expected timing for each step. Assigning owners to different tactics and utilizing a centralized document with a structure such as **Responsible, Accountable, Consulted, Informed (RACI)** further enhances role clarity and accountability within the GTM strategy. The RACI framework helps identify who is responsible for executing specific tasks (the "Responsible" role), who ultimately takes ownership and is accountable for the success of those tasks (the "Accountable" role), who should be consulted for input and expertise (the "Consulted" role), and who should be kept informed about progress and outcomes (the "Informed" role). Utilizing the RACI framework enables teams to align their efforts and responsibilities, ensuring effective coordination and collaboration. It helps avoid confusion, the duplication of efforts, and communication gaps. Each team member understands their role and contribution to the overall strategy, fostering a sense of ownership and accountability. *Figure 9.7* presents an exemplary table that incorporates stakeholder accountability according to the RACI model:

Stakeholders by Department	Responsible	Accountable	Consulted	Informed
Product Marketing	PMM ▾	Simona ▾		
Product	PM ▾	Antonella ▾		
Marketing	Marketing Manager ▾			
Sales	Sales Executive ▾			
Customer Success	Customer Manager ▾			
Sales Enablement [in case relevant]	Sales Enablement Manager			

Figure 9.7 – Stakeholders accountability (RACI model)

To maintain stakeholder alignment, it is essential to establish regular check-ins that cater to cross-functional collaboration and individual one-on-one meetings. These check-ins should consider different time zones, especially in global companies, to ensure inclusive participation. Also, maintaining ongoing communication channels, such as Slack, is vital to facilitating seamless information-sharing among stakeholders.

Regular check-ins and ongoing communication play a significant role in keeping stakeholders informed and accountable. These interactions create valuable opportunities for stakeholders to come together, discuss progress, and address any challenges or concerns that may arise during the strategy's implementation. Through collaborative discussions, stakeholders can openly exchange ideas and insights, ensuring that everyone is aligned and working toward a common goal.

It is crucial to keep your stakeholders well-informed about any changes or updates to the strategy. Timely and transparent communication enables stakeholders to actively contribute their input and suggestions for improvement at the right time. Keeping everyone informed and engaged fosters a sense of ownership and commitment to the strategy's success.

Effective GTM planning involves the participation of stakeholders not only within the organization but also from external sources. The engagement and collaboration of both internal and external stakeholders are fundamental to the success of a comprehensive GTM strategy. These stakeholders, who are customers, industry influencers, sales teams, and executives, among others, actively contribute to shaping the strategy and play vital roles in its effective implementation.

Effective collaboration with external stakeholders is crucial, as they bring valuable insights, market influence, and expertise. Customers, industry analysts, and channel partners are among the key external stakeholders who contribute to the GTM plan. Understanding their needs, preferences, and market dynamics is essential to aligning the strategy with the target audience and maximizing its impact. Leveraging the expertise of industry analysts and partnering with channel partners can significantly enhance the success of the GTM plan, as their insights, market knowledge, and established connections can open doors to new opportunities and expand market reach.

Internally, stakeholders such as the sales team, marketing team, product managers, executives, and customer support are instrumental in executing and supporting the GTM plan. Collaborating closely with these internal stakeholders is crucial to leveraging their collective expertise and resources. By working together, we ensure the seamless implementation of the plan, aligning product features, messaging, and marketing strategies with customer needs and organizational objectives.

Furthermore, measuring the success of the GTM strategy is an integral component of stakeholder alignment. This process entails tracking and analyzing KPIs, such as customer satisfaction, sales performance, and product usage. By monitoring metrics, stakeholders gain valuable insights into the strategy's effectiveness and can identify areas that require improvement or adjustment. The data obtained from these measurements serves as a foundation for making informed, data-driven decisions to refine the strategy and maximize its impact. In the final section of this chapter, we will dive into a comprehensive and in-depth discussion on this specific aspect.

Let's now delve into the remarkable GTM strategy implemented by Spotify for the launch of their video ads. This endeavor serves as a prime example of the profound impact achieved through stakeholders' alignment, collaboration, and adept handling of challenges. The launch of Spotify video ads was built upon a multidisciplinary approach that seamlessly intertwined various stakeholders, orchestrating a harmonious symphony of expertise and insights.

At the helm of this endeavor was a visionary product team, leading the charge by spearheading the conceptualization process. Drawing from a deep well of comprehensive user research, they diligently sought to understand the preferences and aspirations of their target audience. Simultaneously, meticulous attention was paid to the technical logistics, as the team precisely engineered the optimal format for video ads. The aim was to curate a rewarding user experience that not only captured attention but also incentivized viewers to engage fully with the content.

Strategic considerations formed the bedrock of this GTM strategy, effectively navigating the ever-evolving dynamics of the market landscape. With a keen eye on the surging popularity of mobile video and the fragmented nature of the TV ad market, Spotify deftly adapted to the swiftly evolving industry. The team's astute decision-making ensured the success of the strategy, aligning it with the demands and preferences of the target audience.

As the GTM strategy unfolded, meticulous modules and intensive training programs were deployed to empower the sales team with the necessary skills and knowledge. This step proved to be pivotal in effectively presenting and selling video ads, considering the novelty of the advertising format. The team expertly balanced trade-offs, striking the delicate equilibrium between ad consumption and the amount of ad-free listening time users could enjoy. Such decisions were guided by rigorous user research and insightful inventory analysis, enabling informed choices that resonated with both audience preferences and business imperatives.

Throughout the entire process, the collaboration between internal and external stakeholders played an instrumental role. Within the organization, internal peers worked synergistically, overcoming challenges and ensuring the flawless execution of the strategy. External stakeholders, including industry partners and customers, made invaluable contributions by providing insights and feedback that critically shaped the launch. The collaborative approach among stakeholders ultimately amplified the effectiveness and resonance of Spotify's video ads in the market.

By examining this compelling example, we gain valuable insights into the significance of strategic stakeholder engagement, cohesive internal teamwork, and the artful navigation of technical and market complexities in crafting and executing a triumphant GTM strategy.

Launch goals

When strategizing the goals for product launches, it is essential to take into account both short-term and long-term objectives. By doing so, we can effectively evaluate the success and impact of the product in the market.

In the short term, our primary goals revolve around acquisition, engagement, and awareness. Our aim is to attract a specific number of new users or generate a certain level of buzz on social media within the weeks following the launch. These objectives allow us to gauge the resonance of our product with the intended target audience and provide us with valuable early feedback for potential improvements. By focusing on acquisition, we strive to increase the number of individuals who are aware of our product and actively consider using it. Engagement is another key metric that helps us understand how well users interact with our product and its features, as it indicates the level of interest and satisfaction experienced by users during their initial experience.

Conversely, our long-term objectives revolve around establishing a foundation for continuous product usage and widespread adoption. While acquiring new users remains important, our ultimate focus lies in nurturing enduring relationships and fostering a sense of loyalty and commitment among users. To achieve this, we set goals that revolve around user retention and activation rates, which allows us to measure the proportion of users who sustain their engagement with the product over an extended period or exhibit behaviors that indicate a deeper level of involvement. Consistently monitoring these metrics helps us gain valuable insights into the product's ability to deliver ongoing value and meet the evolving needs of our users, enabling us to make necessary refinements and enhancements to further drive sustained usage and satisfaction.

Furthermore, we emphasize measuring user engagement frequency as a long-term goal. This entails tracking the regularity and depth of interactions users have with the product. By encouraging users to engage with the product on a consistent basis, we enhance their overall experience, reinforce the value proposition, and increase the likelihood of sustained usage. This can be measured through various indicators such as daily or monthly active usage, time spent on the product, feature usage, or user-generated content.

Considering both short-term and long-term goals for product launches enables us to holistically assess the performance of our product. The short-term objectives provide immediate feedback, allowing us to make timely improvements and iterate on the product. Simultaneously, the long-term goals guide us toward fostering lasting user relationships, driving adoption, and ensuring the sustained success of the product in the market.

Launch tier

The utilization of launch tiering is a valuable technique for classifying product launches based on their strategic importance and the allocation of resources dedicated to them. By implementing a well-defined tiering system within your PMM organization, you can gain numerous advantages, such as improved efficiency, clear expectations, and effective communication. Employing a tiering system provides a structured framework for evaluating and prioritizing launches, allowing you to allocate resources efficiently in line with expected outcomes. This approach ensures that your efforts are concentrated on initiatives that offer the highest potential for success, optimizing resource utilization and maximizing returns.

There are two compelling reasons to embrace launch tiering:

- First and foremost, it is imperative to align resources and investments with the projected outcomes of each launch. By implementing a tiered approach, your company can appropriately allocate resources, optimizing its efforts and maximizing returns. This enables the efficient utilization of resources, ensuring that focus is directed toward initiatives that hold the greatest potential for success.

- It is important to note that not every feature or product enhancement requires a separate announcement. Grouping related features together can result in a more powerful and compelling narrative. This approach enables you to present a coherent story that deeply connects with customers. It also highlights the significance of strategic customer activation, ensuring that each communication holds value and enhances their overall experience.

Indeed, the implementation of a tiering system can differ from company to company. It is crucial to tailor the tiering approach according to the unique requirements and goals of the organization. A widely utilized and successful method for classifying launches based on their impact on the business and market is the three-tiered approach. When evaluating the market impact, it is crucial to consider how the launch changes the company's position within the market. This assessment includes factors such as whether the launch introduces a unique offering that competitors do not have or offers its products in a similar manner. It also involves considering whether the launch aligns with major industry trends that analysts and buyers are currently focused on and discussing. Considering both the business and market impact enables your company to better understand the significance of each launch and determine the appropriate level of resources and support required. This approach allows you to prioritize launches, allocate resources effectively, and ensure your company capitalizes on opportunities to differentiate itself in the market.

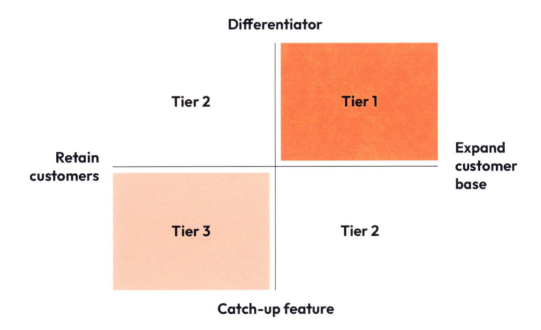

Figure 9.8 – Launch tier by business goals

Launches that have the most significant business and market impact are designated as *Tier 1*. These include new products, new product plans, or key features that bring substantial benefits to customers and establish a competitive edge. They represent strategically important offerings, which the company aims to generate buzz and discussion around both internally and externally. These launches often involve major platform news or game-changing developments. In some cases, a bundle of lower-tier announcements may be included. For *Tier 1* launches, consider incorporating impactful elements such as client events, customized video content, or press coverage.

Tier 2 launches embody initiatives that hold a moderate level of business and market impact. These launches often revolve around the introduction of new features or enhancements to existing ones. While they may not bring about the same transformative effects as *Tier 1* launches, they nonetheless provide value and contribute to the overall product offering. Notably, they possess the potential to resonate with a significant number of customers. When orchestrating *Tier 2* launches, it is advisable to include a diverse array of content elements to effectively engage the target audience. This can entail crafting compelling blog posts, developing captivating web pages, producing relevant sales collateral, ensuring extensive social media coverage, and offering campaign and creative support.

Tier 3 launches encompass updates or enhancements with the lowest level of business and market impact. These launches typically focus on minor improvements that fill specific gaps or enhance the user experience without significantly altering users' workflows. They are often related to product upgrades or changes that primarily affect a small subset of customers. Typically, *Tier 3* launches are included within quarterly launch programs or release notes, depending on their impact and scope. Content elements for *Tier 3* launches are more streamlined in comparison. A blog post announcement can be used to inform the audience about the updates, while an internal heads-up in the sales bulletin ensures internal stakeholders are aware of the changes.

Launch metrics/measurement

Establishing metrics and KPIs is of utmost importance prior to a product launch. Typically included in the marketing brief or GTM plan, these metrics should align with the launch goals. Collaborating with cross-functional teams, such as product and marketing analytics teams, is crucial to developing a measurement plan or dashboard for tracking progress against these goals. Monitoring progress at different stages, such as immediately after the launch, a few days post-launch, and one or two weeks post-launch, can yield valuable insights and allow for necessary adjustments to marketing strategies. This approach enables the ability to accelerate or decelerate adoption based on observed results. While the specific metrics will vary depending on the product and business, there are a few standard metrics to consider, which we will look at next.

Awareness and early adoption

This refers to the process of customers embracing and using a new product or feature. It is important to measure the rate of adoption to assess the success and impact of the product launch. Here are some key metrics and indicators that can be used to measure product adoption:

- **Number of active users**: This metric focuses on quantifying the number of users who have actively engaged with the product within a defined timeframe. It serves as a fundamental indicator of product adoption and usage.

- **User engagement**: User engagement metrics evaluate the extent of user interaction and involvement with the product. These metrics encompass factors such as the frequency of product usage, duration of time spent using the product, or specific actions taken by users within the product.

- **Product usage**: These metrics provide detailed insights into how customers are utilizing the product. This can include specific actions performed within the product, feature usage rates, or the depth and breadth of product usage. For example, tracking the number of transactions completed, the amount of content created, or the features accessed can give a clearer picture of how customers are adopting and using the product.

Other relevant metrics for measuring product adoption may include customer onboarding success rate, conversion rates from trial to paid users, or customer satisfaction scores related to the product. These metrics provide valuable information on how effectively customers are integrating the product into their workflows or deriving value from its use.

Channel performance

Channel performance evaluation involves assessing the effectiveness of different marketing channels in terms of how well they deliver your message and drive customer engagement. While open rates and CTRs are important metrics for measuring channel performance, there are additional metrics that provide valuable insights. Consider the following metrics:

- **Conversion rate**: The conversion rate is a metric that calculates the percentage of users or visitors who successfully complete a desired action, such as making a purchase or filling out a form. It serves as a valuable tool for evaluating the efficacy of different marketing channels in driving conversions and can identify areas that require enhancement.

- **Cost per conversion**: Cost per conversion calculates the average cost incurred for each conversion generated through a specific marketing channel. By comparing the cost per conversion across different channels, you can identify the most cost-effective channels and allocate your budget accordingly.

- **Return on ad spend (ROAS)**: ROAS quantifies the revenue generated per dollar spent on advertising. It serves as a valuable metric for assessing the efficiency and profitability of your advertising campaigns across various channels. A higher ROAS indicates a more successful campaign in terms of revenue generation.

- **Customer Engagement:** Customer engagement metrics, such as time spent on the site, page views, or average session duration, provide insights into how users interact with your website or other digital channels. These metrics help assess the engagement level and the effectiveness of your marketing efforts in capturing and retaining user attention.

- **Social Media Metrics:** If you are utilizing social media channels as part of your GTM strategy, metrics such as follower growth, engagement rate, likes, comments, and shares can provide insights into the reach and impact of your social media campaigns. These metrics help evaluate the effectiveness of your social media presence and engagement with your target audience.

- **Cost per thousand impressions (CPM):** CPM measures the cost of reaching one thousand users or impressions through a specific advertising channel or campaign. It helps assess the cost efficiency and reach of your advertising efforts, especially in display or programmatic advertising campaigns.

By considering these additional metrics, you can gain a more comprehensive understanding of how each marketing channel performs and make informed decisions to optimize your channel mix and improve overall marketing effectiveness.

A Sneak Peek to Metrics by Channels and Launch Tier

			Week 1			Week 2			Week 3		
Tier	Activity	Metric	Target	Performance	Δ	Targets	Performance	Δ	Targets	Performance	Δ
1	PR	#Press mentions									
1	Early access	#Exclusive previews									
1, 2	Email Marketing	Email open rate									
1, 2	Email Marketing	Email click through rate (CTR)									
1, 2	Email Marketing	Email conversion rate									

Figure 9.9 – A sneak peek of a metrics checklist by channel and launch tier

Regularly monitoring and analyzing these metrics will help you identify strengths and areas for improvement, enabling you to refine your GTM strategy and achieve better results.

Product retention

This refers to the ability of a product to retain customers over time. It is a critical metric that measures customer loyalty, satisfaction, and ongoing engagement with the product. Tracking customer churn rates, which represent the percentage of customers who stop using or cancel their subscription to the product, is one way to assess product retention. A high churn rate may indicate issues with product quality, user experience, or customer support, while a low churn rate suggests that customers are satisfied and continue to find value in the product.

Apart from monitoring churn rates, it is essential to gauge customer satisfaction and loyalty as key indicators of product retention. This evaluation can be conducted through methods such as distributing surveys, soliciting customer feedback, or utilizing NPS assessments. By gathering insights into customer satisfaction levels and understanding how likely they are to recommend the product to others, you can acquire valuable information about the product's ability to retain customers and gauge its overall effectiveness.

Monitoring product retention metrics allows you to identify areas of improvement and take necessary actions to enhance the overall customer experience. By addressing pain points, improving product features, or enhancing customer support, you can increase customer satisfaction and reduce churn rates, leading to improved product retention.

Regularly analyzing these metrics and data provides valuable insights into the success of your product launch and its long-term impact on customer retention. It helps you make data-driven decisions to optimize your marketing strategies, refine your GTM approach, and drive better results. By focusing on product retention, you can build a loyal customer base, drive customer advocacy, and achieve sustainable business growth. Here are a few additional metrics related to product retention and revenue:

- **Customer lifetime value (CLTV)**: CLTV represents the predicted net profit generated from a customer over their entire relationship with your business. It helps measure the long-term value of a customer and assess their profitability. By calculating CLTV, you can identify high-value customers and make informed decisions on customer acquisition and retention strategies.

- **Annual recurring revenue (ARR)**: ARR is the predictable annual revenue generated from subscription-based products or services. It provides a snapshot of the annual revenue stream and helps measure the growth and stability of the recurring revenue model. ARR is particularly useful for businesses with subscription-based pricing models.

- **Average revenue per user (ARPU)**: ARPU is a metric that calculates the average amount of revenue generated by each active user of your app within a specific time period.

- **Churn rate**: Churn rate measures the percentage of customers or subscribers who discontinue their relationship with your product over a given period. It directly impacts product retention and revenue. Monitoring the churn rate helps identify the reasons why customers are leaving and allows you to take proactive measures to reduce churn and retain customers.

- **Expansion Revenue**: Expansion revenue refers to the additional revenue generated from existing customers through upselling, cross-selling, or expanding their usage of your product. It measures the ability to increase revenue from your customer base without acquiring new customers. Tracking expansion revenue provides insights into the effectiveness of your customer growth and expansion strategies.

- **Renewal rate**: This measures the proportion of customers or subscriptions that opt to continue their contract or subscription at the end of its term. It is a valuable metric for assessing customer loyalty and satisfaction. A high renewal rate indicates a solid product–market fit and effective customer retention, suggesting that customers are satisfied with the offering and choose to stay.

These metrics provide insights into product retention and revenue generation. By monitoring and analyzing these metrics, you can identify areas for improvement, optimize your customer retention strategies, and drive sustainable revenue growth. It's important to choose the metrics that align with your business model, pricing structure, and customer lifecycle to gain a comprehensive understanding of your product's performance and financial health.

Since we're addressing the product launch, let's discuss some best practices for a global product launch.

A global product launch

When developing a global product distribution strategy, several crucial aspects must be considered. One of the key factors is the early identification of priority markets. Thoroughly assessing which markets offer the most potential for substantial growth and demand enables the customization of a targeted GTM plan. This involves tailoring specific strategies for each priority market while also providing baseline efforts, such as product localization and basic marketing assets, for other markets. Defining the countries within each priority group and outlining precise GTM activities for each one is essential for a successful execution. Investing larger media budgets in priority markets allows for the launch of focused local campaigns that effectively engage potential customers and create brand awareness. Due to their higher growth prospects and strategic significance to the overall plan, priority markets warrant a more intensive approach. Conversely, markets outside the priority group can be approached with a more measured and controlled strategy. While still pursuing basic marketing efforts and product localization, these markets do not require the same level of extensive resources as allocated to priority markets. This balanced approach allows for efficient resource allocation and strategic expansion into diverse markets.

Considering the timing of your product launch is a critical aspect of a global distribution strategy. While the allure of a simultaneous launch across all geographies may be tempting, it's essential to weigh internal limitations and resource availability. Launching in numerous markets simultaneously can strain internal teams, potentially leading to suboptimal execution and a lower overall launch quality. Instead, focusing on a more selective approach by initially targeting fewer markets allows your teams to dedicate more attention and effort to each launch, resulting in a higher level of precision and effectiveness. Conducting a thorough evaluation of available resources, including manpower, budget, and logistical support, is crucial to determining the number of markets you can realistically target in one go without compromising on quality. This assessment helps strike a balance between ambitious expansion and ensuring that each launch receives the attention it deserves. Staggered launches offer additional benefits. Adopting a phased approach allows you to gather valuable insights and learnings from the initial launches, which can then inform and improve subsequent ones. This iterative process facilitates adjustments and refinements based on real-world market feedback, thereby increasing the chances of success in subsequent markets.

Product localization plays a crucial role in the success of international product launches. While professional translations are an important initial step, relying solely on them may not suffice. If translations are not carefully adapted, they may come across as unnatural or overly complex for the local audience, potentially leading to misunderstandings and reduced customer engagement. To ensure that your product effectively resonates with the target audience in each market, thorough testing and validation of translations within the product's **user interface (UI)** and marketing assets are essential. This process goes beyond linguistic accuracy and involves understanding local cultural nuances and preferences. Conducting local testing enables you to gather valuable feedback directly from the target audience. By doing this, you can ensure that your product's messaging and user experience align with customer expectations and preferences. In situations where dedicated local product marketing support is not readily available due to resource constraints or other factors, a practical approach is to leverage the language skills of employees from other functions within your company.

To ensure marketing assets' local relevance during international product launches, it is beneficial to establish a scalable model for asset adaptation. While creating completely unique materials for each market may not be feasible due to resource constraints, prioritizing certain assets for customization and adding a local touch can significantly enhance their effectiveness. Identifying key marketing assets that play a crucial role in conveying your product's value proposition or resonating with the target audience allows you to focus on customizing these assets for each market. This includes core messaging, visuals, and calls to action that directly influence customers' decision-making processes. For priority markets with significant growth potential or strategic importance, it becomes essential to invest in creating genuinely local materials that cater to the audience's preferences, culture, and language. On the other hand, markets with fewer pronounced differences or lower priority may only require basic localization efforts, such as adjusting language, currency, and contact information to align with local norms without a complete overhaul of marketing materials. A scalable asset adaptation model strikes a balance between customization and efficiency, optimizing resource utilization. By strategically investing in adapting key assets for priority markets while maintaining basic localization for others, you can efficiently reach a broader audience without compromising the impact of your marketing efforts. This approach allows for effective engagement with diverse markets and increases the chances of a successful international product launch.

Unpaid channels play a crucial role in a comprehensive GTM strategy, especially when dealing with limited marketing budgets for international launches. Leveraging owned channels becomes imperative to maximizing the effective use of available resources. By adopting creative and resourceful approaches, additional avenues for reaching the target audience can be explored, reducing reliance on expensive paid campaigns. One effective approach is to explore cross-selling opportunities with existing products. This involves promoting the new product to the customer base of already-established products. By strategically aligning the new offering with complementary products, awareness and interest in the target market can be generated.

Leveraging the existing trust and loyalty of the customer base increases the likelihood of successful adoption of the new product. In-product messages are another valuable tool for promoting adoption. By incorporating targeted messages within the product itself, you can effectively reach your existing user base without incurring additional marketing costs. These messages can educate users about the new product's features, benefits, and any special offers, encouraging them to explore and adopt the new offering. Integrating these unpaid channels into your GTM strategy enables you to effectively reach and engage with your target audience while optimizing resource allocation.

By incorporating these key factors into your global product distribution strategy and tailoring it to each market's unique requirements, you can significantly increase your chances of success in diverse regions. This comprehensive approach allows for the optimization of resources, ensures your product's relevance to local audiences, and maximizes the effectiveness of your launch efforts.

Summary

In this chapter, we have thoroughly explored the essential components of an effective GTM strategy. Three key topics took center stage, offering fresh insights not previously covered in this book: content strategy, distribution strategy, and the crucial process of identifying the right target markets.

Moreover, we dedicated considerable attention to a critical aspect of any successful product launch—the alignment process. By meticulously addressing various aspects, such as setting goals, defining launch tiers, establishing timelines, assigning roles and responsibilities, and outlining key success metrics, we aimed to equip you with the knowledge needed to orchestrate a seamless and impactful product launch.

Before concluding this strategic chapter, it is worth noting that our next focus will be on another key area that is particularly relevant to B2B product marketers—sales enablement. In the upcoming chapter, we will delve into the strategies and practices to enable sales teams to drive success in the market.

Stay tuned for more insightful content as we continue our journey to uncover the core principles and tactics that underpin effective GTM strategies.

Enable Your Sales Team and Maximize Effectiveness 10

In the ever-evolving and highly competitive marketplace of today, sales enablement has emerged as a strategic imperative to empower sales teams and foster business growth. With customers being more informed than ever and their preferences continuously changing, sales enablement becomes instrumental in equipping salespeople for success. By providing comprehensive support, tailored training, and essential resources, sales enablement ensures that sales teams can navigate the dynamic landscape, effectively convey the value of their company's solutions, and secure successful deals.

At its core, sales enablement recognizes the vital role that sales professionals play as the driving force behind revenue generation and the achievement of the organization's sales objectives. It encompasses a range of carefully designed initiatives that support sales teams throughout the entire sales process, starting with comprehensive training and coaching programs. These programs equip salespeople with the latest sales techniques, product knowledge, and negotiation skills, enabling them to navigate complex sales scenarios with confidence.

Additionally, sales enablement ensures that sales representatives have access to relevant and compelling sales content. This includes well-crafted sales collateral such as impactful sales presentations, informative product brochures, persuasive case studies, and compelling customer testimonials. Armed with these resources, salespeople can effectively communicate the unique value proposition of the company's offerings, address customer pain points, and differentiate themselves from competitors.

Incorporating sales technologies and tools is another crucial aspect of sales enablement. Implementation of **customer relationship management (CRM)** systems, sales automation software, and analytics tools streamline sales processes, enhance efficient customer management, and provide valuable insights for data-driven decision-making.

In conclusion, through ongoing training, the provision of relevant content, and the effective utilization of sales technologies, organizations empower their salespeople to engage effectively with prospects, communicate value convincingly, and successfully close deals.

In this chapter, we will explore the pivotal role of a product marketer in enabling sales teams, covering topics such as the following:

- Building an effective sales enablement program
- Creating impactful sales enablement collateral
- Measuring the success of sales enablement initiatives

Building an effective sales enablement program

In today's dynamic market context, buyers are more informed and demand explicit demonstrations of value. To meet these evolving expectations and drive business success, sales enablement is essential for equipping sales teams with the right information, tools, and practices.

Sales enablement plays a crucial role in ensuring that sales teams promptly access relevant information for each buyer at the opportune moment. It effectively addresses challenges such as competitive pressures, time to deal, and enhancing customer experience and retention. The impact of sales enablement on a company's growth can be substantial, leading to various positive outcomes.

By implementing effective sales enablement practices, your company can experience faster ramp-up and increased productivity, resulting in confident and high-performing sales teams. Moreover, it empowers sellers to target the right buyer with the appropriate conversation at the correct time, leading to expedited sales cycles and improved conversion rates through the buying funnel. This, in turn, helps achieve sales quotas and fosters deeper customer relationships. Additionally, sales enablement equips sellers with the skills and resources to effectively communicate the value of products, resulting in higher deal sizes, expansion within existing accounts, and improved customer retention. Lastly, it enables sellers to compete successfully against the competition, driving up win rates and increasing market share.

Sales enablement is equally vital for product marketers, empowering the sales team to excel in effectively presenting the product and its capabilities. When providing the necessary information, content, resources, and tools, sales enablement ensures accurate and impactful product selling, avoiding both overselling and underselling.

Furthermore, sales enablement enhances the prospect and customer experience by equipping sales teams with up-to-date knowledge of buyer behavior and best practices. This enables them to effectively address customer needs throughout the buying journey, reducing friction and ensuring consistency in approach and messaging.

Ultimately, sales enablement contributes to a positive customer experience and builds trust in your company. Learning from successful sales reps and implementing effective strategies while eliminating ineffective ones ensures alignment with key stakeholders, leading to increased deal closures and revenue generation.

In some companies where there is no dedicated sales enablement team, product marketing may take on the responsibility of sales enablement. The primary goal is to ensure that the sales team has the right information and tools at their disposal to meet buyer expectations and drive business success.

Crafting a comprehensive sales enablement program involves integrating essential components into your strategy to empower your sales teams for success:

- **Sales enablement strategy:** Crafting a successful sales enablement strategy is essential for aligning all initiatives with the overarching business goals and sales objectives. This includes defining target markets, identifying buyer personas, establishing efficient sales processes, and implementing KPIs to assess the effectiveness and impact of the program.

- **Sales enablement collateral:** In the dynamic world of sales, having the right collateral is essential. This encompasses a diverse range of content and assets, from captivating sales presentations that showcase your products' or services' unique value to insightful case studies and informative whitepapers that instill confidence in potential clients. Additionally, providing training videos, playbooks, and battle cards equips your sales force with indispensable guidance to tackle everyday sales challenges.

- **Sales enablement tools and technology:** Embracing cutting-edge sales enablement tools is a game-changer for your sales professionals. These technology platforms and software solutions streamline sales processes, optimize customer interactions, and provide crucial insights to enhance sales performance. With a finger on the pulse of the latest tools and technologies, your sales team gains a competitive edge, making meaningful connections with clients and propelling your business forward.

- **Sales enablement onboarding, learning, and development:** Providing new sales representatives with comprehensive training and onboarding to ensure they have the necessary knowledge and skills to succeed in their roles. Moreover, it promotes a culture of continuous learning and development within the sales team, offering ongoing training sessions, workshops, and opportunities for skill enhancement.

- **Cross-functional collaboration:** Collaboration between sales, marketing, product, and customer success teams is essential for a holistic sales enablement approach. Ensure that your program encourages and facilitates cross-functional communication.

- **Sales enablement for customer success:** Extending sales enablement efforts to support customer success teams, ensuring they have the necessary resources to enhance customer retention and drive upsell and cross-sell opportunities.

- **Metrics and analytics:** Tracking and analyzing KPIs such as revenue generated, sales cycle length, and customer satisfaction are essential aspects of sales enablement. By evaluating these metrics, you can assess the effectiveness of their sales enablement program and identify areas for improvement. In addition, you can make data-driven decisions together with sales leaders to enhance overall sales performance and measure your program's ROI.

Crafting an effective sales enablement program requires tailoring it to suit your organization's distinct needs, considering factors such as industry, target market, and sales team requirements. Ensuring alignment with company objectives is crucial, and clear goals and objectives must be defined to drive the program's integration with the overall sales strategy. These defined goals empower sales teams, providing direction and focus to maximize productivity.

A successful sales enablement program should equip sales teams with the necessary resources, training, and support they need to excel in their roles. By establishing the program as a trusted and valuable resource, it becomes a central pillar of the sales organization.

Compelling and engaging content is essential for an effective sales enablement program. It should enable sales teams to effectively communicate the value proposition of the company's offerings, addressing customer pain points and driving lead generation, conversions, and customer retention.

Efficient sales processes play a pivotal role in any sales enablement strategy. A well-defined sales engagement process, with clear stages from prospecting to closure, ensures consistency and effective navigation through the customer journey. Understanding the customer journey, marketing funnel, and sales process is vital, and data from sources such as company intranets and department-level goals can help achieve this.

With valuable insights at hand, the focus shifts to developing sales enablement processes that drive efficiency and productivity. Analyzing both lost and won deals reveals patterns associated with successes and failures. Equipping sales representatives with uniform and compelling messaging to communicate the product's value to different buyers is crucial.

As the sales team grows, implementing a robust system to monitor progress and ensure the repeatability of the sales process becomes increasingly important. Data-driven activities such as tracking customer data within a CRM, conducting sales forecasting, and monitoring performance metrics facilitate this process.

Evaluating the efficacy of the sales enablement program is essential to understand its impact on sales performance and achievements. Monitoring KPIs such as product adoption, ROI, and sales cycle provides valuable insights. Regular feedback from the sales team and customers helps shape the program and adapt it to changing market dynamics. Leveraging sales enablement tools and technology enhances efficiency and impact, enabling better tracking of KPIs and measurable outcomes.

Crafting a personalized sales enablement program that aligns with the specific needs of the sales and customer success teams becomes achievable, when you carefully consider all the aspects previously mentioned. Let's now take a closer look at one of the critical pillars of a sales enablement program: sales collateral.

Building your sales collateral hub

Sales enablement content plays a crucial role in equipping sales teams with the resources and information they need to succeed. It encompasses three key categories: internal content, external content, and training materials.

Internal content provides exclusive guidance for sales reps, empowering them with the knowledge and tools to navigate the sales process effectively. This includes resources such as battlecards, product information sheets, and sales scripts. Such materials enable sales professionals to confidently articulate the value of products or services within the organization.

External content serves the specific purpose of engaging and influencing prospects and customers. It encompasses various resources, including pitch decks and product demos, which empower sales representatives to showcase the distinctive benefits and solutions offered by the company. Through these materials, sales reps effectively capture the interest and trust of potential buyers.

Apart from internal and external content, training materials play a vital role in fostering continuous development. Onboarding materials, training modules, and learning resources such as sales training, demo scripts, and video demos are designed to equip sales representatives with the necessary skills, knowledge, and industry insights to excel in their roles.

Sales enablement content encompasses a diverse array of valuable resources, including competitive battlecards, sales scripts, case studies, pitch decks, and product demos. These components empower sales professionals to skillfully communicate the value of products or services throughout the sales cycle. Moreover, sales enablement collateral plays a pivotal role in seamlessly guiding potential buyers through the buyer journey. Aligning your sales collateral with each stage is crucial to effectively engage prospects and facilitate their progression toward making a well-informed purchase decision.

Before we delve into sales enablement collateral, it's important to note that as a product marketer, while sales enablement is a crucial aspect of your role, creating content is typically not directly within your responsibility. In larger organizations, this task is usually owned by the content marketing team. However, even though content creation may not be your role, having a comprehensive understanding of the available content is essential. It enables you to identify additional resources your sales team might need to effectively engage potential customers at each stage of the buying funnel.

Now, let's dive deeper into the specific sales collateral needed at each stage of the buying journey.

Adjusting your sales collateral for every stage of the buying journey

As potential customers progress through the stages of awareness, consideration, and decision-making, their preferences and requirements undergo dynamic changes. Staying ahead in this competitive landscape and effectively influencing potential buyers' decisions demands a tailored approach to your sales collateral strategy. Customizing your sales collateral for every stage of the buying journey is imperative. This includes crafting compelling content to grab attention during the initial awareness phase and presenting persuasive evidence and testimonials during the decision-making stage. By optimizing your sales collateral and aligning it with the specific needs of prospects at each stage, your sales and customer success teams will be empowered to drive engagement and cultivate enduring customer relationships.

Let's take a deeper look into the internal sales collateral for each stage. Some of the external sales collateral will be shared here as well, and the rest of the sales collateral can be found on the book's website: https://sites.google.com/view/theproductmarketingcode.

Awareness and interest stage

During the awareness stage of the sales process, equipping sales teams with the right resources becomes paramount in effectively engaging potential customers and sparking initial interest. At this crucial stage, the primary goal is to capture a prospect's attention and demonstrate a profound understanding of the challenges they are facing. For this stage of the sales process, the primary objective is to encourage potential buyers to reach out and express their desire to learn more about your company and the solutions you offer for their specific problems.

During this stage of the funnel, sales enablement practices focus on providing content that sparks curiosity and captures the interest of potential buyers. The content should effectively showcase the value and benefits of your products or services, compelling prospects to take the next step and initiate contact with your sales team. At this stage, it is crucial to equip your sales reps with comprehensive information about the buyer personas. This empowers them to gain a deeper understanding of the diverse profiles of potential customers. With this valuable knowledge, sales reps can effectively identify the right individuals to contact, customize their approach, and establish personalized connections with prospects. The goal is to be efficient and minimize time spent in this stage, swiftly moving potential buyers toward meetings and progressing them along the sales pipeline. As a sales enablement professional, supporting your sales reps in this endeavor is paramount. By providing the necessary insights and resources, you can facilitate their ability to engage with prospects more effectively and accelerate the overall sales process. Let's take a look at the internal assets used at this stage of the funnel.

Sales scripts

Sales scripts play a crucial role in equipping your sales team with a well-prepared set of talking points and guidelines to navigate even the trickiest scenarios. These carefully crafted scripts are designed to provide structure and direction for your sales representatives during their interactions with prospects. The primary purpose of sales scripts is to help your reps confidently initiate conversations and identify whether the prospect meets the buying criteria for your product or service. In addition to initiating conversations and qualifying leads, sales scripts also empower your team to handle objections that may arise during the conversation.

Sales Scripts - Examples

Intro

Sales Rep: Hello, [**Prospect's Name**]. This is [**Your Name**] from [**Your Company**]. How are you today?

Prospect: I'm doing well, thank you. How about you?

Sales Rep: I'm great, thank you for asking. The reason for my call today is that I noticed [mention a specific trigger or reason for reaching out, such as a recent interaction with the prospect's company or an industry event]. I wanted to take a moment to introduce myself and see if I could learn more about your current needs and challenges.

Building Relationship with the Prospect

Sales Rep: Before we dive into business, I'd love to learn a bit more about you and your role at [Prospect's Company]. Can you tell me a little about your background and your responsibilities?

Prospect: Of course. I am [Prospect's Position] at [Prospect's Company]. I've been working here for [number of years], and my role involves [briefly describe their main responsibilities].

Sales Rep: That's impressive. It sounds like you have a wealth of experience in your field. I'd love to hear more about your experiences and challenges in your role. Is there anything specific that has been keeping you busy lately?

Prospect: Yes, we've been focusing on [mention recent initiatives or projects]. It's been both exciting and challenging.

Sales Rep: I can imagine. Taking on new initiatives can be quite demanding, but it's also an opportunity for growth and progress. If you don't mind sharing, what are some of the key objectives you are hoping to achieve through these initiatives?

Figure 10.1 – Sales script examples

Email templates

Efficient communication is the backbone of successful sales interactions, especially when reaching out to prospects through email. To empower sales representatives in this endeavor, email templates serve as indispensable tools. These templates offer a structured and consistent approach, enabling sales professionals to save precious time while ensuring that key messages are conveyed accurately.

In the fast-paced world of prospecting, where inboxes are flooded with emails, grabbing attention is a top priority. Crafting concise and focused messages becomes crucial in capturing the prospect's interest and keeping them engaged throughout the conversation.

Initial Outreach Email

Subject Line: Introduction and Opportunity for Collaboration

Hi [**Prospect's Name**],

I hope this email finds you well. My name is [**Your Name**], and I'm a Sales Representative at [**Your Company**]. I came across [**Prospect's Company**] and was impressed by your recent achievements in [**mention a relevant industry or project**].

At [**Your Company**], we specialize in [**briefly describe your product or service and its unique value proposition**]. Our solutions have helped companies like [**mention successful clients or case studies**] achieve significant results, such as [**mention specific outcomes or improvements**].

I believe there may be potential synergies between [**Your Company**] and [**Prospect's Company**], and I'd love to explore the possibility of collaboration. If you're open to a brief call to discuss how our offerings align with your goals, please let me know a date and time that suits you best, and I'll gladly arrange it.

Thank you for considering this opportunity. I'm looking forward to learning more about your organization and exploring how we can work together for mutual success.

Best regards,
[**Your Name**]
[**Your Job Title**]
[**Your Company**]
[**Your Contact Information**]

Figure 10.2 – Email templates

Consideration stage

In the consideration stage, potential customers have progressed beyond the initial awareness of a product or service and are actively evaluating their options to find the best fit for their needs. During this phase, they are seeking information to make a well-informed decision, narrowing down their list of potential solutions. Despite gathering relevant details about various offerings, they still require guidance from a sales representative to fully understand how the product or service can address their specific pain points and requirements. At this stage, the sales representative takes on a more consultative and advisory role. They engage in in-depth conversations with prospects to identify their unique needs and challenges. Moreover, during the consideration stage, there is an additional step involving the qualification of prospects to ensure they align with the customer criteria and genuinely express interest in the solution. This strategic approach allows sales efforts to be concentrated on prospects with a higher potential to convert into customers. Furthermore, during this phase, sales representatives often conduct initial product demonstrations to showcase the features and benefits of the offering. These demonstrations play a crucial role in helping prospects visualize how the product can solve their challenges and provide tangible benefits.

Battlecards

Battlecards are a vital resource, providing essential information and guidance to sales representatives about competing companies and their products or services. These succinct and targeted documents play a crucial role in helping sales teams comprehend the strengths, weaknesses, key messages, and strategies of specific competitors in the market. The central purpose of battlecards is to provide sales representatives with the knowledge and tools necessary to effectively navigate competitive situations.

Overview
Arch Cloud Solutions - Enterprise edition is a robust cloud computing platform designed to meet the complex needs of large-scale enterprises. It offers scalable infrastructure, advanced security features, and seamless integration with existing systems, enabling businesses to achieve optimal performance and efficiency in their digital transformation journey.

Customer pain points
- Security and compliance
- Integration challenges
- Scalability and flexibility
- Downtime and high availability
- Performance and latency
- Cost management

Key differentiators
- More robust and secure infrastructure compared to competitors, ensuring data protection and compliance
- The platform's seamless hybrid cloud integration sets it apart from other cloud providers, making it ideal for enterprises with complex IT environments
- Advanced data analytics capabilities enable enterprises to make data-driven decisions more effectively compared to other cloud offerings

Key features
- Scalability: Easily scale computing resources up or down to match varying workloads and business demands
- Security and compliance: Industry-leading security protocols and compliance measures to safeguard sensitive data
- Hybrid cloud integration: Seamlessly integrates with on-premises infrastructure for a hybrid cloud approach
- Performance optimization: Accelerates application performance
- Disaster recovery: Comprehensive disaster recovery options to minimize downtime and data loss
- Data analytics: Built-in analytics tools to gain valuable insights from large datasets in real time
- Enterprise support: 24/7 dedicated support and a dedicated account manager for prompt issue resolution

Why we win
- Better performance and reliability
- Scalability and flexibility
- Competitive pricing
- Ease of implementation and integration
- Security and compliance

Pricing
- Customized pricing based on enterprise needs
- No setup fees
- Monthly plans with many tiers - Basic, Advanced, and Enterprise
- Flexible contract length options - 1-year, 2-year, and 3-year
- Discounts available for long-term contracts, up to 20% off
- Includes 24/7 dedicated enterprise support.

Handling objections

Objection #1: *"Your pricing seems higher than competitors"*
Answer: While our pricing may appear higher initially, it's essential to consider the value you'll receive with our cloud solutions. Our platform offers industry-leading security, seamless hybrid cloud integration, and dedicated enterprise support.

Objection #2: *"How can I be certain that my data will remain secure on your platform?"*
Answer: Data security is our top priority. Our solution is equipped with the latest security protocols and undergoes regular audits to maintain compliance with industry standards. Our multi-layered security approach includes encryption, access controls, and real-time monitoring to safeguard your sensitive data.

Q&A

Q1: What your cloud solution stand out from other cloud providers?
A: Our cloud solution offers several unique advantages. Its seamless hybrid cloud integration, robust security measures, and advanced data analytics capabilities set it apart.

Q2: Our current IT infrastructure is complex. Can your solution handle the integration smoothly?
A: Absolutely! We specialize in handling complex IT environments. Our solution offers seamless integration with your existing on-premises systems, preserving your current IT investments while leveraging the benefits of the cloud.

Figure 10.3 – Example of a battlecard

Typically, battlecards include the following key components:

- **Competitor overview**: A summary of the competitor's business, industry position, target market, and customer base

- **Product comparison**: A comparison of the competitor's offerings with your own, highlighting key differences and advantages

- **Key messaging**: Core messages to communicate to potential customers about why your product is superior

- **Differentiators**: Unique selling points that distinguish your product from the competitor's

- **Objection handling**: Guidance on addressing common objections raised by prospects in relation to the competitor

- **Sales strategy**: Recommended tactics and strategies for winning deals against this specific competitor

- **Customer stories**: Examples of successful sales pitches or customer experiences where your product outperformed the competitor's

Through the use of battlecards, sales reps gain valuable insights into how to adeptly position products or services against competitors, articulate unique value propositions, address objections, and ultimately, achieve successful deals.

Pitch presentations

Pitch presentations serve as a strategic way to present your product or service to potential customers and create a lasting impression. Andy Raskin's framework (https://medium.com/the-mission/the-greatest-sales-deck-ive-ever-seen-4f4ef3391ba0) for an outstanding sales narrative comprises five essential elements:

1. **Show the shift**: Begin by illustrating the transformative impact your solution can create in the world of your target audience, making it urgent and compelling for them to take action. Emphasize how adopting your solution can address a critical pain point or capitalize on a significant opportunity that they cannot afford to overlook.

2. **Positive future impact**: Paint a vivid picture of the positive future that awaits the potential customer once they adopt your solution. Highlight the benefits and advantages they can expect to experience, both in terms of tangible outcomes and intangible benefits. Conversely, convey the potential negative consequences of not taking action or staying with the status quo.

3. **Teaser vision**: Offer a teaser vision of how your product or service will specifically help the potential customer achieve their goals. Present a compelling scenario of how their challenges will be overcome and their desired results will be positively realized with your solution. This teaser vision should resonate deeply with the customer's aspirations and needs.

4. **Introduce features and capabilities:** Articulate the key features and capabilities of your product or service that will empower the potential customer to overcome obstacles and attain their desired outcomes. Demonstrate how these features directly address their pain points and fulfill their unique requirements.

5. **Share evidence and case study:** Provide real-world evidence, such as a case study or customer success story, to back up your claims and build trust with the potential customer. Show how your product has delivered results for others in similar situations and highlight the measurable benefits achieved. This evidence helps validate the effectiveness and credibility of your solution.

This framework helps you effectively communicate the value of your product or service, instill a sense of urgency, and build trust, ultimately increasing the likelihood of converting potential customers into satisfied clients.

Product sheets

A product info sheet, also referred to as a datasheet or product data sheet, serves as a concise and well-organized document offering comprehensive details about a product or service. It acts as a reference point for sales teams, providing in-depth information about the product's features, specifications, benefits, and intended usage.

Product Info Sheet: CybShield

Product overview

CybShield is an advanced cybersecurity solution tailored for B2B enterprises seeking robust protection against evolving digital threats. With cutting-edge features and proactive defense mechanisms, CybShield ensures the utmost security for sensitive data and critical business operations.

Key features

- Threat Detection: AI-powered real-time monitoring identifies and neutralizes cyber threats before they breach your network
- Advanced Firewall Protection: A multi-layered firewall system to safeguard against unauthorized access and data breaches
- Endpoint Security: Comprehensive protection for all endpoints, including laptops, desktops, mobile devices, and servers
- Security Analytics: Detailed analytics and reporting to track security incidents, investigate vulnerabilities, and enhance overall security posture
- Data Encryption: Military-grade encryption protocols to protect sensitive information during transmission and storage

Technical Specifications
- Supported Platforms: Windows, macOS, Linux.
- Integration: Seamlessly integrates with existing security infrastructures and SIEM platforms.
- Compliance: Compliant with industry standards, including GDPR, HIPAA, and ISO 27001.

Benefits

- Protect valuable data and maintain customer trust
- Minimize downtime and ensure business continuity
- Achieve compliance with regulatory requirements
- 24/7 monitoring and support

Use Cases

- Enterprise Protection: Secure large-scale organizations against targeted attacks and data breaches.
- Remote Workforce Security: Extend protection to remote employees accessing sensitive data from diverse locations.
- Compliance Assurance: Ensure adherence to industry-specific data security regulations and maintain a strong security posture.

Figure 10.4 – Product info sheet

Having explored the comprehensive details of product info sheets, let's now transition our focus to product demo.

Product demo

A product demo is a presentation or showcase of a product's features and capabilities, typically conducted by sales representatives to potential customers or stakeholders. It serves as an opportunity to provide a hands-on experience with the product and demonstrate how it can address the specific needs and pain points of your target audience.

A product demo aims to create a compelling case for the product's adoption by showcasing its unique selling points and how it can solve the customer's problems effectively. It can take various forms, such as live demonstrations, interactive presentations, or guided walk-throughs. The format and content of the demo are tailored to suit your audience's preferences and level of technical understanding. This is why, during the demo, the presence of the right team members is vital. For complex products, have a solution architect or pre-sales engineer on hand to handle technical questions effectively.

A successful product demo captivates the audience, addresses their questions and concerns, and leaves them excited about the potential of the product. Be prepared to adapt if prospects ask questions or request specific demonstrations. Think modularly so you can adjust the demo seamlessly without losing your flow.

Case studies

A case study is a persuasive piece of content that acts as social proof for your product or service. It goes beyond just marketing claims and presents real-world evidence of how your offering has brought success to actual customers. By sharing the experiences and achievements of satisfied customers, a case study provides tangible proof of the value your product delivers.

With a meticulously crafted case study, you have the perfect opportunity to showcase the real impact of your product's key features in addressing the specific challenges and pain points your customers face. This powerful platform highlights the practical benefits and concrete outcomes that your product delivers, leaving no room for doubt about its value. As potential customers delve into the tangible evidence presented in the case study, they gain trust and confidence in your offering. Witnessing how your product has positively transformed the lives of others in similar situations, they become convinced that it is the ideal solution to meet their needs and overcome their challenges. The case study becomes a persuasive tool that resonates with potential buyers, guiding them toward making the right choice for their requirements.

The versatility of case studies is a significant advantage, as they can be effectively utilized at different stages of the sales funnel to influence prospects' decisions. In the consideration stage, potential customers are actively researching and evaluating various solutions. A carefully crafted case study can seize their attention and demonstrate how your product has successfully addressed challenges for others, making a compelling case for why it can do the same for them. In the purchase stage, when potential customers are evaluating their options and making a decision, a case study serves as a powerful tool to push them toward choosing your product. It provides the reassurance they need to proceed with confidence, knowing that your offering has been proven effective for others. Even after a purchase is made, a case study can continue to play a role in customer retention. By showcasing successful outcomes, it reinforces the customer's choice and fosters a sense of satisfaction and loyalty.

Here are the key steps to create a compelling case study:

1. **Define your main goal**: Define the purpose of the case study clearly. Identify the key aspects you wish to demonstrate, such as the product's efficacy, customer success stories, or problem-solving prowess, and pinpoint the specific outcomes you aim to emphasize.

2. **Decide the format of your case study**: Decide the format to effectively present your success story. The format can take different shapes:

    I. Written case study

    II. Video with the customer

    III. Review on a third-party website

    IV. Interview with customers over a podcast

     V. Customer presentations at events

3. **Identify the ideal candidate for your case study**: Select a customer who has achieved notable success using your product or service. Seek out customers who are eager to share their experiences and offer positive feedback.

4. **Prepare a list of questions to ask**: Create a list of well-thought-out questions to learn about your customer's unique story and gather essential insights for a powerful case study. The following are some examples of questions to get you started:

    I. Introduction and company overview:

       i. Can you please provide an overview of your company?

    II. Challenges and goals:

       i. Prior to utilizing our product, what difficulties or obstacles were you encountering?

       ii. What were your primary goals when you decided to seek a solution?

    III. Decision-making process:

       i. How did you discover our product, and what led you to choose us?

       ii. Were there any other potential solutions you considered before selecting ours?

    IV. Implementation and integration:

       i. How did the implementation of our product take place within your organization?

       ii. What were the key steps involved in integrating our solution into your existing workflow?

    V. Success and outcomes:

       i. What specific improvements have you experienced since using our product?

       ii. Can you share any measurable results or KPIs that have been positively impacted?

    VI. Unique selling points:

       i. In your opinion, what sets our product apart from others in the market?

       ii. How has our solution addressed your specific needs better than alternative solutions?

    VII. Recommendations:

       i. Would you recommend our solution to other businesses facing similar challenges? Why?

    VIII. Testimonial:

      i. Can you provide a brief statement summarizing your overall experience with our product?

5. **Craft a compelling story**: Organize the gathered information into a narrative format that flows logically and captures the reader's attention. Include an introduction, background, challenges faced, the solution provided, and the achieved results:

    I. **Highlight key metrics**: Incorporate quantifiable metrics and statistics to support the success of the case study. Use data to demonstrate the tangible impact of your product on the customer's business.

    II. **Incorporate quotes and testimonials**: Integrate authentic and direct quotes from the customer to enhance the case study's credibility. Let their own words serve as a testament to the value of your product.

    III. **Add visuals**: Include relevant visuals such as images, charts, graphs, and infographics to make the case study visually engaging and enhance the reader's understanding of the information.

    IV. **Review and approval**: Share the case study draft with the customer for their review and approval. Ensure that they are comfortable with the content and the way their success story is presented.

Let us now move on to the next stage of the buying journey.

Purchase stage

During the purchase stage, the customer has made their decision, and now it's time to finalize the details and uphold the commitments made during the sales process. This is a phase where you solidify your brand values and leave a lasting impression on your new client. Your sales representatives play a pivotal role in proposing the final solution, addressing any objections, and skillfully closing the deal through negotiation. During this stage, your reps should be well prepared to present the final proposal, which outlines the specific terms and conditions of the purchase. They need to ensure that the proposed solution aligns perfectly with the client's requirements and addresses their needs comprehensively.

As with any negotiation, there may be objections raised by the client. Your reps should be equipped to handle these objections with professionalism and tact. Active listening, understanding the client's concerns, and offering viable solutions are crucial in navigating through objections effectively. The negotiation phase is an opportunity to showcase your commitment to customer satisfaction and demonstrate the added value your product or service brings. Throughout this stage, it's essential to follow through on all promises made during the sales process. Deliver the product or service as per the agreed terms and ensure a seamless onboarding experience for the new client. Let's take a look at the most important assets at this stage next.

Dealing with objections

The objection addressing part of the sales process is a stage where sales representatives handle any concerns or doubts raised by potential customers. It involves actively listening to the customer's objections, empathizing with their perspective, and providing well-crafted responses to alleviate their concerns. The goal is to turn objections into opportunities by demonstrating the value and benefits of the product or service, ultimately moving the sales conversation forward.

To effectively handle objections, sales reps need to be well prepared and equipped with a deep understanding of the product or service they are selling. This knowledge allows them to address objections confidently and provide relevant information to support their responses. Here are some suggestions of how you can equip your sales representatives to handle objections:

- **Objection handling guide:** An indispensable resource that encompasses a wide range of common objections and presents suggested responses. This comprehensive guide includes various scenarios and outlines the appropriate strategies to effectively overcome each objection. This guide equips your sales team with the tools needed to navigate objections with confidence and finesse.

- **Objection handling script:** To address objections effectively, consider developing an objection handling script for your sales representatives. This scripted approach will provide your team with empathetic responses, supporting evidence, and persuasive arguments to skillfully counter objections.

Objection Handling

Prospect: Actually, I'm concerned about the cost. Your solution seems a bit pricey compared to some alternatives I've been considering.

Sales Rep: I appreciate your honesty, **[Prospect's Name]**. Cost is indeed an essential aspect when evaluating any solution, and I completely understand your concern. Allow me to provide some context on our pricing structure and the value our solution brings.

Prospect: Sure, go ahead.

Sales Rep: Our pricing is designed to reflect the extensive benefits and return on investment our solution offers. While it may appear higher initially, it's essential to consider the long-term impact and value it delivers. Clients who have implemented our solution have reported significant improvements in [mention specific metrics or outcomes achieved by your clients]. These tangible results translate into substantial savings and increased efficiency over time.

Prospect: I see. But I'm still not sure if it fits within our budget.

Sales Rep: I completely understand your need to adhere to your budget. To address this, I'd be more than happy to discuss flexible payment options, such as phased implementation or bundling features to meet your specific requirements. Additionally, we can explore any potential cost-saving opportunities without compromising the overall benefits our solution brings.

Figure 10.5 – Objection handling: scenarios for example

1. **FAQs:** Create a comprehensive list of commonly asked questions relevant to your product or service. Within this section, proactively address objections with clear and concise responses. These thoughtfully curated FAQs can be integrated into your sales collateral or

featured on your website, serving as a proactive tool to preemptively resolve common concerns and enhance customer satisfaction.

2. **Customer testimonials:** Gather testimonials from satisfied customers who have faced similar objections but ultimately chose your product or service. Use these testimonials as social proof to reassure potential buyers and build trust.

3. **Case studies:** Create case studies that showcase how your product or service helped other customers overcome challenges and achieve their goals. These real-life success stories can be compelling evidence to address objections.

4. **Comparison charts:** Develop comparison charts that highlight the strengths of your product compared to competitors. Use this content to showcase how your solution is better suited to address customer needs and concerns.

Finally, let's move to the last stage of the buying journey.

Advocacy/post-purchase stage

During the advocacy or post-purchase stage, the primary focus is on facilitating a seamless onboarding process and encouraging customer adoption of the product or service. The ultimate goal is to deliver value and benefits to customers promptly after their purchase. At this stage, you need to focus your collateral on the following:

- **Onboarding process:** Provide an onboarding guide and relevant support that different teams and customers can use to ensure they're using the product effectively and understand its features and functionalities.

- **Customer success enablement:** At this stage, it's important to collaborate with customer success and provide them with the collateral they might need to onboard customers, manage the relationship with them, and build VoC programs together with them.

- **Gathering feedback:** Collecting feedback from customers about their experience with the product helps identify areas for improvement and shows that the company values customer input.

- **Renewal readiness:** Creating positive experiences and building a strong relationship with the company all contribute to a higher chance of customer renewal.

Let's delve deeply into one of the key assets of this stage: handling pricing increases.

Pricing increases

During the advocacy stage, handling pricing increases is crucial as nurturing and retaining existing customers takes precedence. To ensure a positive approach, transparency, value communication, and personalized insights are essential. Transparently explain the reasons behind the adjustment, such as product improvements or market changes. Emphasize the value added to their business through enhancements and upgrades. Personalize the communication using customer-specific data to demonstrate the direct impact. Maintain a customer-centric focus, address concerns promptly, and reinforce dedication to their success. *Figure 10.6* is a great example of how Spotify handled the topic.

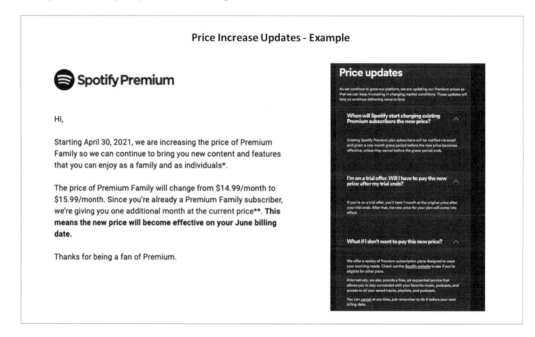

Figure 10.6 – Price increase updates example.
(For textual detail please refer to the downloadable image package)
source: www.businessinsider.com

Having covered the relevant sales assists at each stage of the buying journey, let's now shift our focus to discussing sales enablement tools.

Sales enablement tools

Recognizing the profound impact of sales enablement tools has evolved from a mere preference to a strategic necessity for businesses seeking to thrive in today's dynamic marketplace and achieve unparalleled sales excellence. These innovative solutions bestow sales teams with a wealth of invaluable resources, streamlined processes, and data-driven intelligence. By offering a robust repository containing marketing collateral, product information, and customer insights, sales enablement tools empower sales representatives to address customer inquiries with unwavering confidence, fortified by compelling evidence. Through dynamic automation features such as email templates and lead scoring algorithms, these tools streamline repetitive tasks, allowing sales teams to dedicate more time to nurturing meaningful relationships with prospective clients. By harnessing advanced data analytics, sales enablement tools provide actionable insights to optimize sales strategies, driving overall performance to new heights. Additionally, the capability to deliver personalized and tailored content empowers representatives to engage customers on a deeper level, fostering stronger relationships and fueling successful conversions. Let's delve into some key types of sales enablement tools that are reshaping the landscape of modern sales:

- **CRM systems:** CRM systems serve as a centralized database designed to efficiently manage customer and prospect information. Within these systems, a vast array of data is embraced, ranging from contact details and communication history to purchase records and other relevant information. For sales representatives, CRM systems offer invaluable tools for optimizing customer interactions. Every call, email, meeting, or touchpoint can be meticulously recorded and linked to specific customer profiles, ensuring a comprehensive view of engagement history. Beyond managing individual interactions, CRM systems also provide insights into the sales pipeline. Sales representatives can monitor the progress of deals and opportunities, thanks to built-in reminders and automation features that facilitate timely follow-ups. Notable examples of CRM solutions in the market include **HubSpot CRM, Salesforce,** and **Microsoft Dynamics 365.**

- **Sales content management platforms:** These platforms enable sales teams to efficiently manage and utilize their sales collateral, which encompasses a range of materials such as presentations, product information, case studies, and sales scripts. These platforms act as centralized repositories, ensuring content is stored and organized in a manner that allows easy access for sales representatives during the sales process. Key features such as tagging, categorization, version control, and robust search capabilities empower sales reps to quickly locate relevant content tailored to specific prospects. Additionally, the platforms offer valuable insights through analytics, enabling sales managers to track content effectiveness and make data-driven decisions. Integration with CRM systems and other sales tools further streamlines workflows, facilitating seamless access and content sharing. Prominent examples of such platforms include **Highspot, Seismic,** and **DocSend,** which are widely adopted by businesses to optimize sales content management and deliver more compelling messaging to prospects.

- **Sales automation software:** A category of tools that streamline repetitive sales tasks and workflows, such as email sequencing, follow-ups, and lead scoring. By using predefined rules and technology, these tools automate various sales-related activities, freeing up sales representatives' time to focus on high-value tasks that contribute to driving sales results. The software enables automated email scheduling, reminders for follow-ups, and lead prioritization based on scoring criteria. It also assists with task management, data entry, and record keeping, ensuring accurate and up-to-date CRM information. With real-time reporting and analytics, sales managers and reps can track progress and make data-driven decisions. Integration with CRM systems ensures a seamless flow of information, supporting personalized communication and enhancing overall sales efficiency, engagement, and effectiveness.

- **Sales intelligence tools:** These tools are specialized software solutions that empower sales representatives with personalized information on prospects and businesses matching their target profiles. These tools enable reps to search for organizations and individuals based on firmographics, demographics, and buying signals, creating detailed prospect profiles. With up-to-date contact information and lead scoring, sales reps can prioritize their efforts and engage with the right decision-makers. These tools also offer advanced search and segmentation, helping sales teams identify relevant prospects. Examples of such tools include **LinkedIn Sales Navigator, ZoomInfo,** and **DiscoverOrg** (now part of ZoomInfo).

- **Sales engagement platforms:** These tools facilitate seamless communication with prospects and customers across multiple channels, such as email, phone, and social media. These platforms offer features such as email tracking, scheduling, and templates to enhance engagement and responsiveness. Sales reps can reach out through their preferred channels, and email tracking provides valuable insights for follow-ups. Automated email sequencing ensures timely communication, while call management features streamline calling processes and gather call performance data. Social media integration allows reps to engage prospects on platforms such as LinkedIn, nurturing relationships. Sales cadences help create a systematic and strategic approach to sales outreach. Popular examples include **Outreach, SalesLoft,** and **Groove.** These platforms optimize sales communication, leading to improved customer relationships and higher conversion rates.

- **AI-powered sales assistants:** AI-powered chatbots and virtual assistants are innovative software solutions that utilize artificial intelligence and natural language processing capabilities to support sales representatives by offering real-time information, personalized recommendations, and automated responses to common queries. These virtual assistants and chatbots engage with prospects and customers, providing up-to-date information about products and services, personalized suggestions, and managing routine tasks without requiring human intervention. Moreover, these AI-powered sales assistants utilize language processing to understand and engage with customer inquiries in a way that closely resembles human communication. Some prominent examples of such tools are **Gong, Intercom,** and **Drift.** These platforms play a significant role in enhancing customer interactions, boosting lead conversion rates, and delivering a highly personalized and responsive sales experience.

Sales enablement tools are like trusty companions for sales teams, offering a helping hand with organizing content, automating tasks, and enabling smoother communication. With these tools by their side, sales reps can build strong connections with customers through personalized interactions.

Let's now focus on how to measure and assess the effectiveness of the sales enablement program. This step is crucial in understanding how well the program is working and what improvements can be made.

Sales enablement success indicators

Sales enablement metrics are measurable indicators used to assess the effectiveness of sales enablement initiatives and strategies within your organization. These metrics help measure the impact of sales enablement efforts on various aspects of the sales process and the performance of the sales team. Understanding and tracking these metrics provides valuable insights into areas for improvement and helps optimize sales enablement efforts to drive better outcomes. Here's a breakdown of what sales enablement metrics are, their significance, and what actions to take based on the measured metrics:

- **Average conversion rate:** The conversion rate is a metric used to gauge the percentage of leads or prospects that successfully convert into customers or closed deals within a specific time frame. It offers valuable insights into the efficiency and effectiveness of the sales process, providing a clear understanding of how well potential opportunities are converted into actual sales. This metric indicates the proportion of leads generated during a campaign that have been successfully converted into paying customers. It serves as a valuable tool for sales and marketing teams to assess the effectiveness of their lead generation and sales efforts and identify areas for improvement in the sales process. A higher average conversion rate signifies a more successful and efficient sales process.

  For example, let's assume a company generates 100 leads in a marketing campaign. The sales team actively engages with these leads, conducts sales calls, and follows up with each prospect. Out of the 100 leads, 20 of them become paying customers by making a purchase or closing a deal. To calculate the average conversion rate, divide the number of converted leads by the total number of leads and then multiply by 100 to express it as a percentage:

  *Average Conversion Rate = (Number of converted leads / Total number of leads) * 100*

  *Average Conversion Rate = (20 / 100) * 100 = 20%*

- **Average sales cycle length:** This measures the average amount of time it takes for a sales opportunity to progress through the entire sales process, starting from the initial contact with a prospect to the final closure of the deal. This crucial metric offers valuable insights into the efficiency of the sales process and how swiftly sales representatives can convert leads into closed deals. By analyzing this metric, teams can gain a better understanding of the typical time it takes to move a lead through the sales process and achieve deal closure. A shorter average sales cycle length indicates a more efficient sales process and faster deal closures, while also pinpointing areas where improvements can be made to accelerate the sales cycle. Let's illustrate this metric with an example.

  In a specific quarter, a company's sales team proactively engaged with prospects to successfully close the following deals, each having its respective sales cycle length:

  Deal 1: Sales cycle length – 30 days

  Deal 2: Sales cycle length – 45 days

Deal 3: Sales cycle length – 60 days

Deal 4: Sales cycle length – 50 days

Deal 5: Sales cycle length – 35 days

To determine the average sales cycle length, simply sum up the sales cycle lengths of all closed deals and then divide the total by the number of deals.

Average Sales Cycle Length = # of days to close all deals in a given period / # of total deals in a given period = (30 + 45 + 60 + 50 + 35) / 5 = 44 days

- **Win rate:** This measures the percentage of successfully won opportunities or deals out of the total number pursued by either a sales representative or the entire sales team. This critical metric offers valuable insights into the effectiveness of the sales team in converting potential opportunities into closed deals. By assessing how effectively the sales team achieved $X\%$ of the pursued opportunities, a higher win rate indicates a more successful sales team in meeting their sales objectives and closing deals. Sales leaders can leverage this metric to gain a comprehensive understanding of the team's performance, evaluate the efficacy of sales strategies and tactics, and identify areas for potential improvement in the sales process or the need for additional sales enablement support.

For example, a company's sales team pursues 50 opportunities or deals during a specific quarter. Out of these 50 opportunities, they successfully closed 20 deals. To calculate the win rate, divide the number of won deals by the total number of opportunities and then multiply by 100 to express it as a percentage:

*Win Rate = (# of won deals / Total # of opportunities) * 100 = (20 / 50) * 100 = 40%*

- **Win/loss rate:** This measures the ratio of won opportunities to lost opportunities for a sales representative or the entire sales team. It provides insights into the sales team's ability to win deals compared to the number of deals they have lost. This metric helps understand the balance between won and lost opportunities and provides insights into the team's overall effectiveness in closing deals. A win/loss rate greater than 1 indicates a positive performance, as the team is winning more deals than they are losing. Conversely, a win/loss rate below 1 suggests that the team is losing more deals than they are winning and may need to improve their sales strategies or sales enablement efforts.

For example, a company's sales team pursues 50 opportunities or deals during a specific quarter. Out of these 50 opportunities, they successfully closed 20 deals, but they also lost 30 deals. To calculate the win/loss rate, divide the number of won deals by the number of lost deals:

Win/Loss Rate = # of won deals / # of lost deals = 20 / 30 = 0.67

- **Customer lifetime value (CLTV):** This is a vital company metric that represents the total revenue anticipated from a single customer throughout their entire relationship with the company. Understanding CLTV is crucial for gauging the long-term value of customers and their impact on the company's profitability and growth. This metric enables companies to assess the value of acquiring and retaining customers effectively, aiding in resource allocation to maximize long-term revenue and profitability. A higher CLTV signifies the company's success in nurturing customer loyalty and extracting greater value from each customer, which is a strong indicator of a robust and sustainable business model.

For example, let's assume a company operates a subscription-based software service. The average customer stays with the company for 3 years and pays $500 per month for the service. To calculate the CLTV, multiply the average monthly revenue per customer by the average customer lifespan:

CLTV = Average monthly revenue per customer * Average customer lifespan = $500 * 36 months = $18,000

- **Churn rate**: This is a metric that calculates the percentage of customers or subscribers who terminate or cancel their business relationship with a company during a specific period. Commonly utilized in subscription-based businesses, **software-as-a-service (SaaS)** companies, and other industries with recurring revenue models, this metric offers valuable insights into customer attrition. A high churn rate indicates a faster rate of customer loss, potentially leading to a decline in recurring revenue and impacting the company's growth and profitability. Conversely, a low churn rate reflects satisfied and loyal customers, contributing to a stable and growing customer base. Regularly tracking the churn rate is imperative for identifying customer retention issues and implementing targeted strategies to reduce churn. These strategies may include enhancing customer service, refining product offerings, or conducting customer engagement campaigns to foster loyalty and retention.

For instance, consider a company running a subscription-based streaming service. At the start of the month, they had a total of 1,000 active subscribers. Over the course of that month, 50 subscribers decided to cancel their subscriptions. To calculate the churn rate, simply divide the number of canceled subscribers by the total number of active subscribers at the beginning of the month, and then multiply the result by 100 to express it as a percentage:

Churn Rate = (# of canceled subscribers / Total # of active subscribers) * 100 = (50 / 1000) * 100 = 5%

- **Customer retention rate**: This is a company KPI that measures the percentage of customers or subscribers retained by a company within a specific period. It serves as the inverse of the churn rate, providing valuable insights into the company's capability to maintain its existing customer base. A high customer retention rate indicates the company's success in fostering customer loyalty and satisfaction, contributing to a stable and growing customer base. This positive indicator showcases the company's ability to deliver value to its customers, build strong relationships, and offer exceptional customer service. Additionally, a high retention rate contributes to the increase in CLTV and overall revenue growth. Monitoring the customer retention rate is crucial for understanding customer churn dynamics and assessing the effectiveness of customer retention strategies and efforts.

Consider an example where a company runs a subscription-based e-commerce platform. At the start of the year, they had a total of 500 active customers. Over the course of the year, 450 customers either renewed their subscriptions or continued to make purchases. To calculate the customer retention rate, simply divide the number of retained customers by the total number of active customers at the beginning of the period, and then multiply the result by 100 to express it as a percentage:

*Customer Retention Rate = (# of retained customers / Total # of active customers) * 100 = (450 / 500) * 100 = 90%*

- **Time to first sale:** This measures the amount of time it takes for a sales representative to close their first deal from the time they start their job or when they become actively engaged in selling. It is the duration between a salesperson's onboarding or start date and the date of their first successful sale. This metric provides insights into how quickly a new sales representative can become productive and contribute to revenue generation for the company. A shorter "time to first sale" generally indicates that the onboarding process and sales enablement efforts are effective in preparing new hires for success.

For example, let's say your company hired a new sales representative, John, on January 1st. John went through the onboarding process, received product training, learned about the company's sales processes, and started engaging with potential customers.

After two weeks of training and preparation, John officially started actively selling on January 15th. Over the next few weeks, John reached out to prospects, conducted product demos, and negotiated with potential clients. On February 10th, John successfully closed his first deal and brought in revenue for the company. John's "time to first sale" would be calculated as follows:

Time to First Sale = February 10th–January 15th = 26 days

- **Time to meet quota:** This measures the time it takes for a sales representative to achieve their sales quota or target. It represents the duration between the start of a sales period (e.g., monthly, quarterly, or annually) and the date when the sales rep reaches their assigned quota. This metric provides insights into how quickly a sales representative can achieve their assigned sales target and contribute to the company's revenue goals. A shorter "time to meet quota" indicates strong sales performance and the ability to close deals efficiently.

For example, let's assume a company sets a quarterly sales quota for its sales team. The sales period for Q3 started on July 1st and ended on September 30th. John, one of the sales representatives, was assigned a quota of $100,000 for the quarter. Throughout the quarter, John actively engaged with prospects followed up on leads, and worked on closing deals. He faced some challenges in the early part of the quarter, but he persisted and managed to close multiple deals as the quarter progressed.

On September 20th, John successfully secured a significant deal that pushed his total sales for the quarter to $100,000. At this point, he has met his quota, and any additional sales will contribute to overachievement. In this example, John's "time to meet quota" would be calculated as follows:

Time to Meet Quota = September 20th–July 1st = 81 days

- **Number of closed deals**: This measures the total count of deals that a sales representative or the entire sales team successfully closed within a specific period. This metric provides a direct representation of the team's or individual's sales performance in terms of closing deals and generating revenue. This metric provides insights into the overall productivity and effectiveness of the sales team in converting leads into successful sales. A higher number of closed deals indicates better sales performance and revenue generation.

For example, let's assume a company has a sales team of five representatives. In the first quarter of the year (January 1st to March 31st), each sales representative actively engaged with prospects, conducted sales calls, and negotiated with potential clients. Here are the closed deals for each sales representative in the first quarter:

Sales rep 1: 15 closed deals

Sales rep 2: 12 closed deals

Sales rep 3: 18 closed deals

Sales rep 4: 14 closed deals

Sales rep 5: 16 closed deals

The total number of closed deals for the entire sales team in the first quarter would be as follows:

Total Closed Deals = Total count of deals = 15 + 12 + 18 + 14 + 16 = 75 closed deals

- **Average deal size**: This calculates the average value of closed deals for a specific period. It provides insights into the typical size or value of the sales transactions made by a sales representative or the entire sales team during that period. This metric provides insights into the typical value of deals closed by the team during that specific period. It helps sales leaders understand the revenue impact of individual sales transactions and aids in forecasting and setting sales targets. Let's illustrate this metric with an example.

Let's assume a company has a sales team that actively sells its products to various clients. In the first quarter of the year (January 1st to March 31st), the sales team closed the following deals:

Deal 1: $10,000

Deal 2: $15,000

Deal 3: $8,000

Deal 4: $12,000

Deal 5: $20,000

To calculate the average deal size, you add up the monetary values of all closed deals and divide by the total number of deals:

Average Deal Size = Total revenue in a specific period / # of closed deals in a specific period = ($10,000 + $15,000 + $8,000 + $12,000 + $20,000) / 5 = $13,000

- **Asset utilization:** This measures the usage and effectiveness of sales enablement assets and resources by sales representatives. It helps sales enablement teams and leaders understand how frequently and efficiently sales reps are using various content, tools, and resources provided to them to support their sales efforts. A high asset utilization rate suggests that sales reps are actively using the provided resources to support their sales activities, which can lead to more effective sales interactions and increased deal closures. On the other hand, a low asset utilization rate may indicate that sales reps are not fully leveraging the available sales enablement assets, which could lead to missed opportunities or inefficiencies in the sales process. Product marketers or sales enablement teams can use this metric to identify underutilized assets and work with sales reps to encourage better adoption and usage of the resources available to them.

  For example, a company provides its sales team with a variety of sales enablement assets, such as sales presentations, product brochures, case studies, and demo videos. The sales enablement team wants to track how often these assets are being used by the sales reps.

  To calculate asset utilization, the sales enablement team can use analytics from their sales enablement platform or content management system to monitor the number of times each asset is accessed or used by sales reps within a specific period, such as a month or a quarter.

  For example, in a given quarter, they see the following:

  Sales Presentation A was accessed 100 times

  Product Brochure B was accessed 50 times

  Case Study C was accessed 80 times

  Demo Video D was accessed 120 times

  The total number of asset accesses in the quarter is the sum of all asset accesses:

  Total Asset Accesses = 100 + 50 + 80 + 120 = 350

- **Time to onboard:** This metric quantifies the average length of time it takes for a new sales representative to become fully productive and self-sufficient in their role. This metric enables organizations to evaluate the effectiveness of their onboarding process and gauge how quickly new hires can begin contributing to the company's sales efforts. A shorter time to onboard indicates an efficient onboarding process, allowing new sales reps to achieve productivity and contribute to the company's revenue goals more rapidly. Conversely, a longer time to onboard may indicate the need for improvements in the onboarding program to expedite the readiness and success of new sales representatives. To optimize the time to onboard, companies should prioritize providing comprehensive and structured onboarding training, offer ongoing coaching and mentorship for new hires, and ensure access to the right sales enablement resources and tools to support their learning and selling activities. Let's illustrate this metric with an example.

A company hires a new sales representative, John, and wants to track how long it takes for him to become fully productive. They define "fully productive" as the point at which John starts generating sales and meeting his sales targets consistently. John's onboarding process begins on his first day and lasts for 90 days. After the onboarding period, John takes an additional 60 days to ramp up and start meeting his sales targets consistently.

To calculate the time to onboard John, add the duration of the onboarding process and the ramp-up period:

Time to Onboard = Onboarding duration + Ramp-up duration = 90 days + 60 days = 150 days

- **Sales confidence:** This gauges the level of confidence and belief that sales representatives have in their ability to achieve their sales targets and successfully close deals. As a subjective measure, it is often assessed through surveys or feedback sessions with sales reps. This metric offers valuable insights into the mindset and motivation of the sales team. High sales confidence often correlates with improved sales performance, as confident sales reps are more likely to approach prospects with enthusiasm and conviction, leading to better customer engagement and increased success in closing deals. Conversely, low sales confidence may signal potential issues that need to be addressed, such as inadequate sales training, lack of support from the product marketing/sales enablement team, or challenges with the product or service. Product marketers and sales enablement leaders can leverage this metric to identify areas where sales reps may need additional support or resources to boost their confidence. This could involve implementing targeted training programs, coaching sessions, or incentives to keep the team motivated and focused on achieving their sales goals.

For example, a company administers a quarterly survey to its sales team to assess their confidence in achieving their sales targets and overall job satisfaction. During the survey, sales reps are requested to rate their confidence on a scale of 1 to 5, with 1 representing "not confident at all" and 5 indicating "extremely confident." For example, the survey results might be as follows:

Sales Representative A: Sales Confidence Rating – 4

Sales Representative B: Sales Confidence Rating – 3

Sales Representative C: Sales Confidence Rating – 5

Sales Representative D: Sales Confidence Rating – 2

The average sales confidence rating can be calculated by summing up all the confidence ratings and dividing by the total number of sales reps:

Average Sales Confidence Rating = (4 + 3 + 5 + 2) / 4 = 14 / 4 = 3.5

As we've explored the various success indicators that gauge the effectiveness of your sales enablement program, let's now distill these insights and wrap up this chapter by summarizing the key takeaways from this chapter.

Summary

In this chapter, we've embarked on a journey of discovery, unraveling the essential pillars that form the bedrock of a successful sales enablement program. We delved into three top critical components that can make all the difference in your sales enablement efforts: sales enablement collateral, the power of sales enablement tools, and the vital metrics that hold the key to measuring success. Understanding and optimizing these elements enables you to pave the way for a thriving sales enablement program that empowers your sales team to achieve better results.

As we step into the final part of this book, a critical subject awaits us: stakeholder management. Throughout this part, our primary focus centers on effectively handling both internal and external stakeholders. This skill is the art of nurturing robust relationships and maintaining clear communication with all involved parties throughout the product journey, be it within or beyond your organization. Internally, we'll delve into cultivating productive alliances with product development teams, grasping their insights, and ensuring harmonious alignment between marketing, sales, and customer success teams. Externally, we'll explore the intricacies of engaging with analysts, whose impartial perspectives and evaluations hold significant sway over market perceptions and product positioning. With actionable insights and best practices in hand, we'll navigate this chapter together, honing the craft of stakeholder management and propelling our product to new heights of success.

Part 4 – Impactful Collaboration and Value Creation

In the realm of product marketing, adept stakeholder management stands as a crucial cross-functional skill. In this part, we'll explore the significance of two distinct stakeholder groups – internal and external. By skillfully leveraging these relationships, we will uncover the secrets to orchestrating a triumphant product launch and unlocking exponential growth. Understanding the art of engaging both internal teams and external partners holds the key to unleashing the full potential of product marketing.

This part has the following chapters:

- *Chapter 11, Ensure Internal Stakeholders Buy-In*
- *Chapter 12, Analyst Relations (AR)*

Ensure Internal Stakeholders Buy-In 11

Imagine orchestrating a grand performance, where every instrument contributes significantly to creating a masterpiece. In the world of product marketing, stakeholder management plays a similar role – harmonizing the efforts of different players toward a common goal.

Stakeholder management is a process of building and nurturing relationships with various individuals and groups to drive them toward the business goals. These stakeholders can include internal teams (such as product, sales, and customer support) as well as external parties (such as customers, partners, and industry influencers).

Effective stakeholder management ensures that all parties involved are aligned and are contributing their expertise and efforts toward a shared goal. This could encompass successfully launching a product, positioning it effectively, or sustaining its growth in the market. It requires strong communication skills and adeptly maneuvering through diverse perspectives while keeping the customer at the forefront. In this chapter, our focus will be on internal stakeholder management as we delve into addressing several key questions, including the following:

- What are the responsibilities of both PMMs and PMs, and where do their roles overlap?
- How can you obtain buy-in from sales, customer success, and marketing teams?
- How do you establish connections with the C-suite, and what are the key areas to focus on when connecting with them?

Let's start with collaborating with PMs.

Collaborating with PMs

When collaborating with PMs, a question that often arises for us as PMMs is where we stand within the product organization and how we can integrate effectively. This is particularly pertinent for inbound PMMs who have a stronger involvement in product development. Notably, both PMs and PMMs' roles extend to customers, as they are both tasked with comprehending customer needs.

Throughout various stages of product development, PMs engage with customers to gain a deeper understanding of their needs and identify problems to solve at scale. Simultaneously, PMMs engage with customers and conduct customer surveys not only to refine messaging and positioning but also to uncover unmet needs and gain a deep understanding of the jobs to be done. This is an example of where the roles of both PMs and PMMs might overlap. It's precisely at this intersection that they need to create a clear plan delineating responsibilities, aiming not only to prevent duplicated efforts but also to avoid customer frustration resulting from multiple contacts by different parties. To gain a clear understanding of your role as a product marketer within the product organization, it's essential to delve into the primary focus areas of PMs and their key motivations.

As you can see in *Figure 11.1*, PMs are highly focused on product vision, product strategy, product roadmap, and more. PMs are consistently engaged in defining the product's direction both in the immediate and long-term contexts. They serve as the driving force behind collaboration with engineers and product designers, ensuring that the product's features are aligned with its intended purpose. This involves making informed decisions about what features to prioritize and actively refining the product roadmap based on user feedback and market dynamics.

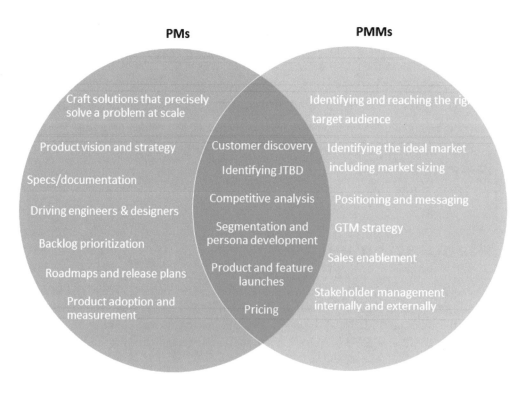

Figure 11.1 – Key focus areas of PMs and PMMs

Source: https://aatir.substack.com/p/why-did-airbnb-combine-product-management

Here comes the question: how as a product marketer can you bring value to the table and be a valued member of the product organization? As a product marketer, you are like the strategic allies that PMs can count on for a range of impactful contributions. You're like the *sleuths* who dive deep into market insights, getting a real feel for what customers truly desire. Providing PMs with an idea of what's trending on the market and what competitors are up to helps them make sure the product development decisions are spot-on and resonate with the people who matter most – the customers.

But it doesn't stop there. When it comes to building the roadmap – the grand plan for the product's journey – you are like the translator. You take the technical features and capabilities and turn them into compelling stories of how these features solve real-world problems. You're also the go-to person for gathering feedback from different teams, so the roadmap becomes a well-rounded masterpiece that aligns perfectly with the bigger picture.

Let's talk vision – you know, imagining the future of the product. As a product marketer, you're like the dreamer who doesn't just see what's right in front of you but can also glimpse what's down the road. With insights into where the market is headed and what customers will want, you can team up with PMs to sketch out exciting features and enhancements that keep the product ahead of the curve.

Crafting a winning strategy that aligns with clear objectives, achieving a product-market fit through customer validation, executing a flawless GTM plan, embracing a customer-centric approach to build loyalty and referrals, and maintaining agility by monitoring and adapting to market dynamics are all key components of effective product marketing. And when it's time to spread the word, you step in as the storyteller. You serve as the link that ties together the intricate technical specifics with the rest of the team. You're great at translating all the geeky stuff into clear, catchy messages that everyone – from the engineers to the sales teams – can understand. All of these elements are essential for consistently driving revenue to your products in line with your company's broader goals.

In a nutshell, when product marketers and PMs team up, it's like a powerful duo working together to transform great ideas into successful real-world products. Their combined efforts have the potential to turn concepts into actual products that make a significant impact. This partnership shines because they bring their skills and knowledge together, each playing an important role at different stages of the product's journey.

Think of this collaboration as a symphony of smart thinking, creativity, and clear communication. Both roles are like the choreographers behind a perfectly coordinated dance that combines understanding what people want, knowing the technical details, and telling a compelling story. When product marketers and PMs join forces, they pool their strengths to navigate the complex process of creating products that people love.

Let's delve into the strategies for fostering effective collaboration with PMs.

Building effective collaboration between PMs and PMMs

Effective collaboration between PMMs and PMs is indispensable for optimizing outcomes within a product team. As mentioned earlier, this partnership ensures a unified vision and strategy, where PMMs contribute market insights and customer understanding to refine product roadmaps curated by PMs. This customer-centric approach integrates feedback from interactions and research, resulting in products that genuinely cater to user needs. The synergy between PMMs and PMs also strengthens go-to-market strategies, allowing for compelling value propositions and targeted messaging that resonate with the intended audience. Additionally, the collaboration establishes a feedback loop for iterative improvements, responds to market shifts, and promotes data-driven decisions. Through seamless communication and shared metrics, this collaboration leads to holistic product development that stands out in competitive markets and delivers substantial business value.

Fostering Effective Collaboration with PMs

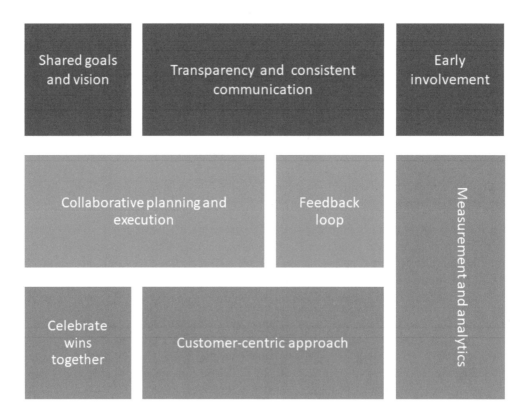

Figure 11.2 – Fostering effective collaboration with PMs

Let's take a deeper look into how PMMs together with PMs establish and achieve effective collaboration:

- **Shared goals and vision**: Align on the overall product vision, goals, and target audience. Ensure both PMMs and PMs understand the customer needs, pain points, and market trends.

- **Transparency and consistent communication**: Establish open lines of communication between you and PMs. Hold regular cross-functional meetings to discuss strategies, updates, and challenges. Share insights from customer interactions, marketing campaigns, and competitive analysis.

- **Early involvement**: Get involved in the early stages of product development to provide market insights and validate product concepts. Engage PMs in the planning of marketing campaigns to ensure alignment with product features and benefits.

- **Collaborative planning and execution**: Work together with PMs to create GTM strategies that align product launches with marketing efforts. Collaborate on messaging, positioning, and target audience segmentation. In addition, collaborate with PMs on competitive analysis to identify the strengths and weaknesses of the product. Use this analysis to inform both product improvements and marketing messaging. Moreover, work together with PMs to create various types of content, such as whitepapers and case studies, to emphasize the product's value proposition. Ensure marketing materials accurately represent the product's features and benefits. Furthermore, partner with PMs to create sales enablement materials that provide sales teams with the information and tools they need to effectively sell the product. Address common objections through product and messaging adjustments.

- **Customer-centric approach**: Use customer feedback to guide both product development and marketing strategies. Share customer success stories and testimonials to highlight the value of the product.

- **Feedback loop**: Establish a feedback loop between you and PMs to refine product and marketing strategies based on real data. Work together to create various types of content, such as whitepapers and case studies, all of which emphasize the product's value proposition. Adjust product features and marketing tactics based on user feedback and market response.

- **Measurement and analytics**: Define shared KPIs that measure the success of both product and marketing efforts. Analyze data together to identify areas for improvement and optimization.

- **Celebrate wins together**: Celebrate successful product launches and marketing campaigns as joint achievements. Reinforce the value of collaboration and teamwork.

Unfortunately, things don't always go smoothly, and conflicts might arise between product marketers and PMs, often due to differing priorities or perspectives. However, these conflicts shouldn't be seen as roadblocks but rather as opportunities to uncover solutions that work for both sides. As product marketers, it's our responsibility to tackle these conflicts head-on, transforming them into opportunities for effective collaboration with PMs.

Collaborating with marketing, sales, and customer success teams

Throughout this book, we've witnessed the remarkable evolution of the product marketing role, transcending its conventional confines. Nowadays, product marketers work with different stakeholders and join forces with various teams throughout the whole customer journey. This alignment, where product, marketing, sales, and customer success come together, is the most important aspect of creating an exceptional customer experience.

Within this collaborative ecosystem, product marketing serves as the essential link in a chain, connecting every element of the customer's interaction with the product. It's not merely about creating compelling marketing campaigns; it's about ensuring that the product aligns with market needs, resonates with the target audience, and ultimately ensures the revenue goal is hit.

In this evolved landscape, the focus on commercialization takes center stage. Product marketers are not only crafting strategies but also actively participating in the execution of those strategies. It's about translating market insights into concrete sales tactics, working shoulder to shoulder with sales and customer success teams to ensure that the revenue goal is not just met but exceeded.

While the partnership with PMs remains crucial, the collaboration with sales and customer success teams becomes equally pivotal. These partnerships facilitate the entire product life cycle, from conceptualization to successful launch and ongoing customer satisfaction. As product marketers, we excel in navigating this intricate web of collaboration, where our role isn't confined to marketing alone; it's about driving adoption and ensuring revenue goals are hit.

Aligning product marketing, marketing, sales, and customer success

Aligning product marketing with other departments is crucial for achieving success. To foster alignment, several key strategies can be implemented. Firstly, engaging with stakeholders across functional teams is vital to determine the optimal position for product marketing within the organizational structure – whether it's under marketing, product, or sales. Establishing a clear positioning for product marketing and promoting this concept among teams ensures a shared understanding of its value.

Another approach to alignment involves integrating product marketing into the project process. Collaborating on the data aspects of projects ensures its integration into standard procedures throughout the organization. This involves collecting data from company intranets, strategy documents, and department-level goals. Identifying existing methods and gaps is also crucial, streamlining focus and achieving quick successes.

For specific teams, different considerations come into play. For marketing, constructing a compelling product narrative and exploring collaboration with external agencies, such as PR firms or website designers, is essential. Establishing foundational documents, such as campaign kickoffs, launch tiers, and positioning materials, aids customer marketing inquiries. Similarly, for the sales team, ensuring they effectively utilize provided tools, content, and collateral is vital. Collaborative marketing efforts and co-marketing strategies can also be explored. Customer success teams need sufficient knowledge to assist clients efficiently. This involves tailoring strategies through cooperation with internal departments for optimal customer and team engagement, leading to enhanced revenue.

Within this framework, there are diverse strategic programs where product marketing collaborates with teams such as marketing, customer success, and sales. These initiatives encompass battle cards, win-loss programs, customer interviews, and customer-centric content, among others. Battle cards provide comprehensive insights for sales teams to proficiently communicate new product features to clients and enhance customer interactions. Win-loss programs, a collaborative endeavor with sales, deeply educate sales teams about factors influencing successful or unsuccessful deals. Customer interviews play a pivotal role in collecting firsthand feedback on product experiences, facilitating a two-way exchange of insights among product marketing, sales, and customer success teams. Additionally, creating customer-oriented content effectively conveys product information to clients.

These examples underscore multifaceted programs that collectively establish productive collaboration among product marketing, sales, and customer success teams. Each initiative contributes distinct insights and resources, culminating in a harmonious alliance that fosters heightened customer engagement, continuous improvement, and overall business growth.

Getting buy-in and earning the trust of each team

Teamwork involves dealing with complexities similar to navigating a winding path in a forest. It's not always as straightforward as carrying out a simple task, particularly when the goal is to maintain synchronization among all team members. Envision assembling an intricate puzzle to establish a coherent team framework. It's analogous to cooking, where every ingredient must complement the others perfectly. However, there's an added aspect: you must consider who's in charge, who's influencing decisions, and who's expressing the most impactful opinions.

After that, the challenge involves combining the different ideas of each team member. It's like putting together a complex puzzle, where every piece adds to the final picture. You're in a brainstorming phase gathering various viewpoints and integrating them into a coherent plan that aligns with the company's goals.

As you navigate through this complex situation, it might feel like skillfully juggling multiple tasks in a demanding environment. You have many responsibilities to handle, including timelines, communication, and feedback loops. It's like carefully balancing fragile objects on sticks while ensuring progress is maintained.

On the other hand, simplifying teamwork and effectively managing diverse stakeholders becomes significantly more attainable by implementing certain strategies. First, it's crucial to establish your core team and identify key stakeholders right from the start. Clearly defining roles and responsibilities is essential. Creating well-defined timelines and milestones in collaboration with your cross-functional partners is also crucial, as these decisions will have downstream effects.

Consistent communication plays a pivotal role. Regular updates and interaction help garner enthusiasm and alignment among everyone involved. Data plays a significant role as well – it's a persuasive tool to gain support from stakeholders. Keeping thorough meeting notes ensures that everyone stays informed with the latest information.

Conducting virtual kick-off meetings involving all stakeholders is a valuable practice. This is where responsibilities are synchronized, and the project's bigger picture is presented. Before delving into detailed plans and roadmaps, it's wise to preemptively list potential risks and obstacles.

Introducing elements of gamification can also be effective. Sending countdown reminders to teams and organizing virtual launch celebrations involve everyone and can boost morale.

Lastly, when forming the team, ensure representation from key stakeholders or their representatives. This approach helps avoid having too many decision-makers, streamlines progress, and keeps things moving efficiently.

Fostering Effective Collaboration with Internal Stakeholders

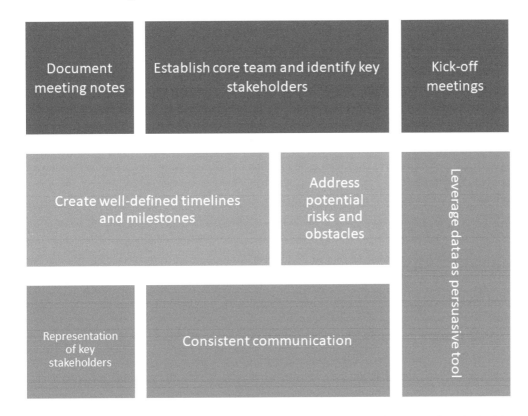

Figure 11.3 – Fostering effective collaboration with internal stakeholders

As all the strategies in *Figure 11.3* come together, teamwork starts flowing better, and managing everyone involved becomes a lot more satisfying. Now that we've got these important pieces in place, we're ready to dig deeper into the exciting stuff: connecting with the big decision-makers in the C-suite.

Engaging the C-suite

In the ever-evolving landscape of product marketing, skillfully communicating your objectives and intentions to both upper management and team leaders necessitates a deliberate and tactical strategy. A cornerstone of this effort lies in comprehending the viewpoints and preferences of these decision-makers. Through a thorough exploration of their concerns and aspirations, you can adeptly shape your messaging to deeply resonate with their interests.

A pivotal point to successful communication lies in the seamless alignment of your product marketing objectives with the overarching business goals. Articulate how your strategic initiatives intertwine with revenue growth, customer satisfaction, or other pivotal performance metrics. Highlighting this alignment underscores the pivotal role that your efforts play in propelling the organization toward its broader aspirations.

Crafting a compelling narrative is equally essential. Distill your product marketing objectives into a concise yet persuasive story, emphasizing the value proposition that your goals bring to the table. By framing your intentions within the context of tangible benefits and outcomes, you can effectively address specific challenges that the organization faces.

Data and insights serve as potent allies in this communication endeavor. Support your goals with concrete market research, robust customer feedback, and pertinent performance data. This substantiates the potential impact of your initiatives and lends a data-driven credibility to your proposals.

Adaptation is key when tailoring your message for various audiences. The C-suite's focus on high-level business impact warrants a distinct communication approach compared to the granular details that team leaders seek. Ensuring your message resonates with each group's distinct concerns and priorities is pivotal to fostering engagement and alignment.

Visual aids, such as charts and presentations, provide a tangible means to convey complex information. Employ these tools strategically to enhance comprehension, enabling your stakeholders to grasp intricate details effortlessly.

Opening the channels for dialogue is paramount. Encourage questions, feedback, and suggestions from the C-suite and team leaders, demonstrating your receptiveness to collaboration and refinement. This dialogic approach not only garners a deeper understanding of their perspectives but also reinforces your commitment to a shared journey.

Underpinning your communication with persuasive techniques further enhances its impact. Leverage storytelling, logical reasoning, and even emotional appeals to influence the decision-making process and engender support for your goals.

The path to success in communicating your product marketing goals is an ongoing journey. Regular updates are instrumental in maintaining alignment and fostering a sense of involvement among stakeholders. By showcasing milestones achieved and proactive adjustments made based on feedback, you exhibit an unwavering commitment to the shared trajectory.

In essence, effective communication of your product marketing goals to the C-suite and team leaders demands a multifaceted approach that combines strategic alignment, compelling storytelling, data-driven substantiation, and ongoing engagement. Through this orchestrated effort, you weave a cohesive narrative that not only garners support but also fortifies the collaborative spirit required for shared success.

Summary

In this chapter, we engaged with various internal stakeholders, starting from the product teams, which require a more tailored strategy, and moving through marketing, sales, and customer success, ultimately culminating with interactions at the C-suite level. Throughout the chapter, we learned that transparent communication, well-defined timelines, established goals, and robust measurement mechanisms are consistent necessities across distinct stakeholder management scenarios. These essential components collectively contribute to facilitating successful collaboration in achieving objectives, all while maintaining a steadfast commitment to prioritizing the customer's needs.

In the upcoming chapter, our attention will shift toward the realm of external stakeholder management, with a specific focus on industry analysts. We will delve into the reasons behind the necessity of cultivating prosperous relationships with analysts and effectively engaging with them. Additionally, we will delve into the strategies and unveil methods for leveraging their potential to propel a product launch to success.

Analyst Relations (AR) 12

An analyst relationship entails the interaction and connection that a company maintains with industry analysts. These analysts are experts specializing in the research and provision of insights concerning specific markets, technologies, trends, and companies. Cultivating a positive analyst relationship requires fostering open communication, sharing pertinent information, and actively seeking feedback and perspectives on various aspects related to the company's products, services, strategies, and market positioning. However, it's important to note that analysts may not be relevant to all industries. Some sectors, such as advertising, may have industry bodies but lack specific analysts covering that sector. Similarly, for consumer products such as the iPhone, industry bodies or dedicated analysts are typically absent. In such cases, the role of providing insights and evaluations is often fulfilled by tech product reviewers. This chapter is relevant to influencers who interface with and influence the industry, encompassing analysts, industry bodies, or key opinion leaders with a broad reach.

Typically, companies engage with analysts from reputable research firms, such as Gartner, Forrester, and IDC. The process of building and nurturing a robust analyst relationship can yield an array of advantages, including heightened market visibility, validation of company strategies, bolstered credibility, and invaluable feedback to inform decision-making and product development endeavors.

For product marketers, the endeavor of building analyst relationships involves establishing and nurturing connections with industry analysts to amass insights and a comprehensive understanding of the market. The outcomes of effective analyst relationships encompass valuable feedback, market validation, and well-informed insights that actively shape your product development and marketing strategies.

In this chapter, our primary focus shifts toward cultivating analyst relationships as we shall address a series of significant inquiries, including the following:

- What constitutes the role of product marketing in AR?
- How can we secure buy-in from analysts and enlist their support?
- What strategies are effective in constructing and monitoring an analyst's plan?

Let's start with the role of product marketing in Analyst Relations (AR).

The role of product marketing in AR

Product marketing holds the responsibility of effectively communicating the value, features, and benefits of a company's products or services to its target audience. Within the context of an AR program, your involvement becomes vital in nurturing positive relationships with industry analysts. You bear the responsibility of adeptly executing a robust AR program, which holds the potential to yield a multitude of benefits. These include achieving more deals and driving increased sales, acquiring deeper competitive intelligence, and enhancing sales enablement. Furthermore, this program facilitates market testing, knowledge expansion, and a heightened **share of voice (SOV)** within the market. Let's delve into the benefits of cultivating a strong relationship with analysts.

How can analysts help?

The establishment of strong and meaningful relationships with analysts holds a strategic role within the realm of PMMs. This significance arises from the profound influence that these relationships exert on the overall success of a product. By engaging with analysts, PMMs gain privileged access to a wealth of comprehensive insights embedded within the market's dynamic landscape. These insights encompass trends that are shaping the industry, the competitive forces at play, and the intricate tapestry of customer preferences.

Intriguingly, the endorsement garnered from analysts translates into a substantial enhancement of a product's credibility. As these relationships flourish, the positive rapport established contributes to an increased likelihood of receiving commendatory reviews and recommendations. This, in turn, elevates the product's reputation, a valuable asset in attracting potential buyers who are drawn to well-regarded offerings.

Beyond this, analysts possess an exceptional capacity to influence industry perceptions of a given product. This goes beyond mere understanding, extending into a realm where PMMs actively participate in shaping the narrative around their offerings. By fostering and nurturing these bonds, PMMs wield the power to not only absorb insights but also actively guide how analysts communicate the strengths of their products to the broader market.

Strategically, the counsel proffered by analysts plays a critical role in PMMs' decision-making processes. This advice navigates PMMs through the complex landscape of product positioning, the identification of target markets, and the formulation of astute go-to-market strategies. The alignment of decisions with the ever-evolving trends of the market is facilitated by this partnership with analysts.

In practical terms, these relationships serve as valuable resources for sales support, enriching the interactions between sales teams and potential customers. The insights and data provided by analysts become integral in addressing customer queries and concerns, enhancing the overall customer experience.

Adding another layer of value, analysts offer invaluable feedback that PMMs can incorporate into the ongoing enhancement of their products. This feedback loop becomes an iterative process, allowing PMMs to refine and improve their offerings based on the expert observations of these industry influencers.

Moreover, the symbiotic relationship between PMMs and analysts extends its influence into the domain of product development. Analyst insights help PMMs guide product roadmaps, ensuring that the products align with the ever-evolving needs and preferences of the market.

Furthermore, analysts serve as early indicators of shifts within the industry landscape. Their keen observations enable PMMs to anticipate market changes and trends, empowering them to adapt strategies proactively.

Benefits of PMMs Building Strong Analyst Relationships

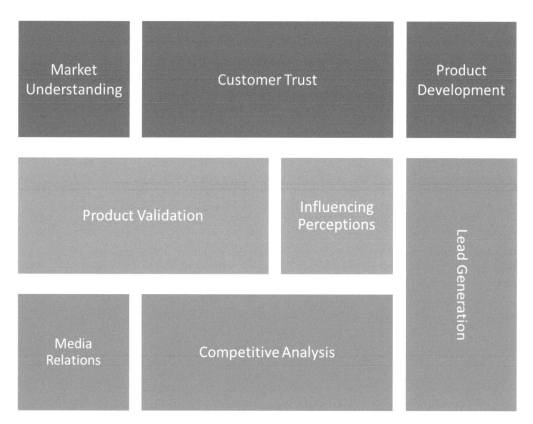

Figure 12.1 – Benefits of PMMs building strong AR

To unlock the wealth of benefits that arise from nurturing a close relationship with analysts, it's vital to craft and run an effective AR program. Think of this program as your trusted companion on the journey to engage with analysts, fostering meaningful interactions and harnessing their insights to improve your products and fortify your position in the market. Let's explore the intricacies of building a successful AR program in detail.

How to create a successful AR program

Creating a successful AR program involves a strategic process that significantly impacts a company's product success. The initial step is to make a deliberate decision to invest in AR, recognizing that it requires substantial effort and financial resources, and might not yield immediate results. This decision hinges on evaluating the right time to invest, considering two dimensions: the company's market presence and product maturity.

Aligning internal stakeholders around AR expectations follows, requiring clarity on the program's purpose, specific goals, and necessary investment levels. This alignment is crucial for defining the scope and potential outcomes. Moreover, setting the expectation that the AR program doesn't involve payment for favorable outcomes is vital, ensuring a genuine and unbiased relationship with analysts.

The program's potential benefits are then scrutinized, including competitive intelligence, messaging validation, product feedback, merger and acquisition insights, market validation, and inclusion in comparative reports. Each benefit underscores the importance of the AR program in shaping a company's strategies and decisions.

Moving forward, identifying two to three influential analysts becomes paramount. The selection process involves tiering and ranking analyst fit by evaluating their influence and alignment with customer trust. Engaging with these analysts is a methodical approach that incorporates periodic interactions, such as inquiry calls to gather feedback on messaging, positioning, and roadmaps, briefing calls to present updates and new features, and strategy sessions for in-depth discussions on subjects vital to the company's direction.

To extract value from the AR program, leveraging analysts' reports, expertise, and insights is crucial. This is achieved through integrating key findings into content, hosting educational webinars with analysts as speakers, and providing analysts with information for their own presentations, reinforcing the company's reputation as an industry leader.

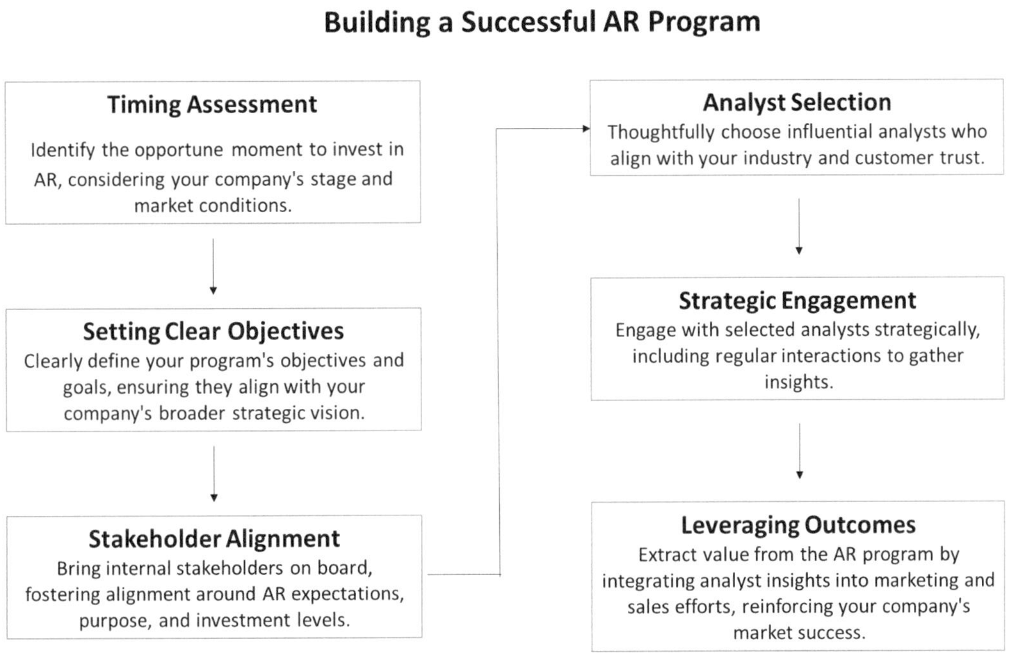

Building a Successful AR Program

Timing Assessment
Identify the opportune moment to invest in AR, considering your company's stage and market conditions.

Setting Clear Objectives
Clearly define your program's objectives and goals, ensuring they align with your company's broader strategic vision.

Stakeholder Alignment
Bring internal stakeholders on board, fostering alignment around AR expectations, purpose, and investment levels.

Analyst Selection
Thoughtfully choose influential analysts who align with your industry and customer trust.

Strategic Engagement
Engage with selected analysts strategically, including regular interactions to gather insights.

Leveraging Outcomes
Extract value from the AR program by integrating analyst insights into marketing and sales efforts, reinforcing your company's market success.

Figure 12.2 – Building a successful AR program

Building an effective AR program involves recognizing the right time to invest, defining clear goals, aligning internal stakeholders, carefully selecting influential analysts, engaging in strategic interactions, and leveraging the program's outcomes in marketing and sales efforts. This comprehensive approach ensures that the relationship with analysts contributes significantly to a company's success in the market.

AR program – best practices

AR programs are essential for enhancing your company's visibility and influence in the market. To create an effective AR program, it's crucial to diligently apply key best practices, including the following important ones:

- Have a clear program objective: A clear understanding of program objectives is fundamental, accompanied by the establishment of a regular communication schedule for sharing updates with the chosen analyst community. Preparatory calls play a vital role, facilitating agreement on speakers' topics and enabling thorough rehearsals for key presentations.

- **Dedicate the right budget to your AR program:** Allocate an appropriate budget for your AR program by considering several key elements. These encompass membership fees, event participation, and personnel costs. The membership fees levied by analyst firms such as Gartner and Forrester can fluctuate substantially based on the type and tier of analysts relevant to your market. Typically, these fees are annual and grant access to analysts, reports, and additional resources.

   Budgetary considerations extend to analyst-hosted events. Larger firms often organize events and meetups, potentially necessitating expenses for attendance and representation. The suitability of such investments depends on your market stage, with start-ups potentially opting for more cautious expenditure.

   Moreover, the personnel aspect merits attention. Reflect on the time investment required from you as a product marketer for analyst interactions, information gathering, and market research.

   Once these elements are outlined, crafting a budget for your AR program becomes feasible.

- **Craft a compelling analyst briefing presentation with consistent messaging:** Involves several key considerations that contribute to its quality and impact. Firstly, ensure the presence of a coherent narrative that seamlessly aligns with your messaging and positioning strategies. This narrative should tie back to the core essence of your product or solution, reinforcing your unique value proposition.

   Your analyst presentation should prominently reinforce consistent messaging and highlight what sets your offering apart from other solutions on the market. Emphasize your distinctive qualities and explain why the market finds them compelling. Demonstrate your differentiation by showcasing real-world instances where your product has made a significant impact. Provide proof to support your statements by sharing tangible examples of how your solution has been successfully adopted by a quantifiable number of clients. Present the outcomes they've achieved, underscoring the transformational effects of your product. In addition, explicitly connect the dots between your solutions and their broader industry implications.

- **Metrics to share with analysts and capture their attention:** Equip your analysts with metrics that capture their interest and revolve around indicators directly linked to your company's growth and impact. Embrace metrics such as the **Year-over-Year (YoY)** growth rate, YoY revenue increase, **Return on Investment (ROI)**, customer base increase, churn rate, and other metrics related to growth and ROI. These metrics serve as robust benchmarks to vividly illustrate your company's trajectory of expansion. If your company is in its start-up phase, certain factors hold particular appeal to analysts, such as fundraising initiatives and the augmentation of your workforce. These elements can significantly enhance their perception of your company's potential and prospects.

- **Maintain a long-term perspective and establish consistent communication:** Sharing a roadmap outlining your company's future plans showcases your commitment to growth, but it's crucial to strike a balance between highlighting potential and setting realistic expectations. Honesty and transparency are essential; while expressing confidence, avoid making rigid promises that could backfire if circumstances change. Analysts will hold you accountable for delivering on your roadmap, so be prepared for questions if goals aren't met. Remember that roadmaps are subject to change due to various factors. If setbacks arise, communicate transparently and offer alternative strategies.

- **Foster ongoing relationships with analysts**: Regularly involve yourself in substantial conversations, exchange deep-seated insights, and take the initiative to actively seek out analysts' expert knowledge and perspectives. These substantial relationships with analysts help you open the gateway to enhancing your company's position and driving more sales.

Fostering and maintaining strong relationships with industry analysts is instrumental in acquiring valuable insights and a comprehensive understanding of the market. Effective analyst relationships yield invaluable feedback, market validation, and well-informed insights that directly influence your product development and marketing strategies. This underscores the importance of crafting the right AR program, allocating appropriate budgets, and consistently conveying the appropriate messages to maximize the benefits of your AR program.

Summary

In this chapter, we delved into the creation of an impactful AR program, revealing its potential to grant product marketers unique access to a wealth of comprehensive insights. We explored how analysts possess the remarkable ability to shape industry perceptions of products. Furthermore, we offered valuable best practices and insightful tips for constructing a robust AR program, guaranteeing its effectiveness.

As we wrap up this chapter, we bring the final curtain down on the last section of this book. The journey through these pages has been a deliberate endeavor to provide you with a comprehensive understanding of the key functions and activities of product marketing. The insights woven into these chapters have been meticulously crafted to offer not only assistance but also a reservoir of practical utility. May this book act as a foundation upon which you can continue to explore and master the intricacies of the product marketing role.

Index

A

A/B testing team 64

Airbnb 96-97

Alphabet 33

analyst relationship 259

Annual Recurring Revenue (ARR) 112

AR program 262-264

    best practices 265

average order value (AOV) 41

B

behavioral segmentation 131

Bottom of the funnel (BOFU) 47

    post-purchase behavior 48

    purchase decision 47

buyer personas 137, 139-143, 145-146, 168-169, 173

    creating 127, 134, 136-137, 139, 141-142, 144-146, 179-180, 195-198, 202, 217, 223, 238

C

C-suite 256-257

    engaging 252, 257

call-to-actions (CTAs) 41

click-through rate (CTR) 204

common distribution methods 192, 194

direct sales 181, 192-193, 195

exploring 192, 206

indirect sales 193

compelling messaging 153, 162, 167

buyer personas 137, 139-143, 145-146, 168-169, 173

crafting 153, 159, 165, 167, 169, 176

measuring 167, 172-173, 203-204, 206, 208, 210, 213, 246

optimizing 167, 172, 174

refining 167, 172

rolling out 174

target audience 153-154, 159-160, 162, 164-172, 176, 178-182, 184, 186, 188-189, 194-198, 201-202, 206, 208-209, 212, 214, 217-218

testing 160, 171-173

Competitive intelligence (CI) 68

competitive positioning 153, 158, 161-163, 165

content distribution 198, 200-201, 203

considerations 179, 181, 209

content strategy 177, 182, 197-198, 218

content development 198

content types 201

creating 127, 134, 136-137, 139, 141-142, 144-146, 179-180, 195-198, 202, 217, 223, 238

Continuous Integration (CI) tools 20

conversion rate (CVR) 41, 173, 203

Cost Per Acquisition (CPA) 111

customer acquisition cost (CAC) 203

customer advisory board (CAB) 101

customer lifetime value (CLTV) 133

customer research 85-91, 93-94, 96, 113

types 53, 59, 61, 68, 88, 97, 103

Customer Satisfaction (CSAT) 97

customer segmentation 127-136, 149

behavioral 135-136

firmographic 131-132, 135

geographic 131-132

improving 56, 74, 83, 130, 136, 145

needs-based 131

post hoc 130

steps 132, 140, 149

value-based 132

customer success teams 252

collaborating with 247

D

distribution strategy 177, 181-182, 192, 194-198, 201-202, 216, 218

adjustment 208

customer buying behavior 181

evaluation 177, 192, 194, 198, 203, 213, 215-216

summarizing 233, 246

Driver, Approver, Contributor, Informed (DACI) 58

E

effective messaging 153, 166-167, 176

automation technologies 174-175

key elements 154-155, 166-167, 170

empathy maps 139

F

flywheel model 48

G

General Manager (GM) 40

global product launch 216

go-to-market (GTM) 56

GTM life cycle 56

    launch phase 57-58

GTM strategy 107, 177-185, 187-188, 192, 194, 198, 200-201, 203-209, 214, 217-218

    components 177-178, 182, 194, 205-206, 218, 220, 223, 246

    messaging 177, 179-180, 182, 188-189, 197-199, 201-202, 204-205, 208, 217, 222, 237

    positioning 153-158, 161-165, 167-169, 175-177, 179-180, 182-184, 187-188, 190, 205

    pricing 177, 180-182, 184, 188-189, 194, 215-216, 235

    product-market fit 190

    target audience 153-154, 159-160, 162, 164-172, 176, 178-182, 184, 186, 188-189, 194-198, 201-202, 206, 208-209, 212, 214, 217-218

H

Harvard Business Review (HBR) 68

HubSpot 130, 144-145

I

ideal customer profile (ICP) 134

inbound product marketing 17, 25, 27, 29-31, 33-34, 37

    Key tasks 30

Intercom 94

J

JBTD 146-147

    versus personas 148

K

Kano method 120

Key Performance Indicators (KPIs) 44

key performance indicators (KPIs) 103

L

learning management systems (LMSs) 128

lifetime value (CLTV) 215

lifetime value (LTV) 41

M

market requirement documents (MRDs) 101

market research 53-60, 65-68, 84-85, 87, 90, 101, 180, 182-184, 187-188, 192, 197

    need for 81

    types 53, 59, 61, 68, 88, 97, 103

marketing qualified leads (MQLs) 45

Middle of the funnel (MOFU) 47

    evaluation of alternatives 47

    information search stage 47

minimum viable product (MVP) 187

Monthly Recurring Revenue (MRR) 112

N

narrative design 153, 163-165, 176

Net Promoter Score (NPS) 97

net promoter score (NPS) 191

NPS metric 109

    promoters 110

O

Objectives and Key Results (OKRs) 44

outbound product marketing 26, 39, 45

    and customer journey 45

    critical activities 40

    GTM campaign timeline 41

    marketing plan 42-43

    messaging and creatives 41

    sales enablement plan 44

P

pay-per-click (PPC) 43

persona-based selling 146

    pricing strategy 146

    product development 29-33, 127-129, 136, 138-139, 144, 147, 149

personas 127, 136-137, 139-149

    using 128, 130, 132, 134, 136, 139, 142, 145-146, 149

positioning 153-158, 161-165, 167-169, 175-177, 179-180, 182-184, 187-188, 190, 205

    key components 155, 159-160

primary research 60-62, 64

    methods 58-62, 64-65, 70, 84, 86-89, 91

product launch 108, 178, 204-206, 212-213, 215-218, 246

    alignment 116-117, 123, 187-188, 190, 199, 206-208, 218, 220-221, 246

    blueprint 178, 205

    goals 87-88, 91-92, 98-99, 109, 181, 184, 194, 198-199, 203, 205-206, 209-212, 218, 221-222, 232, 244

    metrics 181, 183-184, 187, 189-191, 201, 203-204, 208, 210, 212-216, 218, 222, 233, 239, 246

    tiering 210-211

product marketer 17, 19, 22-25

    role 17-27, 259-260

product marketing 259-260, 265

Product Marketing Managers (PMMs) 106

product roadmap 115-118, 120, 122-126

    advantages 116

    communicating 122-125

    role of product marketing 115, 117

Q

qualitative data 62, 64

quantitative data 64

Quibi 18

R

Responsible, Accountable, Consulted, Informed (RACI) 207

return on investment (ROI) 129, 204

RICE model 119

ROI 109, 111, 113

S

sales 249, 251-253

sales qualified leads (SQLS) 46

Salesloft 132

search engine optimization (SEO) 144, 182

secondary research 59-60, 65

serviceable addressable market (SAM) 184

share of market (SOM) 184

share of voice (SOV) 260

Slack 33

small- and medium-sized businesses (SMBs) 184

stakeholder management 247, 257

strategic narrative 163

strong value proposition 159, 176

substitute analysis 75

SWOT analysis 75-77, 79, 82, 84

    opportunities 54, 56, 60, 68-70, 73, 75, 78-79, 81

    strengths 55, 62, 68, 73, 75, 77, 79

    threats 77, 79

    weaknesses 55, 73, 75, 77-79

T

Top of the funnel (TOFU) 46

    problem/need recognition stage 46

total addressable market (TAM) 129, 183

    calculating 183-184, 215

U

user experience (UX) 136

user research 87

    goals 87-88, 91-92, 98-99, 109, 181, 184, 194, 198-199, 203, 205-206, 209-212, 218, 221-222, 232, 244

    methods 58-62, 64-65, 70, 84, 86-89, 91

    scope 96

V

value proposition 153-167, 169, 172, 176

value-added resellers (VARs) 193

Verily Life Sciences 33

VoC metrics 109

    CSAT 100-101, 110

    NPS 100, 105, 110, 112

VoC program 85, 95-98, 100, 102-103, 105-106, 109, 111-113

    building 87, 96, 105-106

    principles 103, 105

Voice of Customer (VoC) 85

W

Waymo 33

win/loss analysis 80-81

Y

year-over-year (YoY) 112

Z

Zendesk 53

Zoom 86

‹packt›

www.packtpub.com

Subscribe to our online digital library for full access to over 7,000 books and videos, as well as industry leading tools to help you plan your personal development and advance your career. For more information, please visit our website.

Why subscribe?

- Spend less time learning and more time coding with practical eBooks and Videos from over 4,000 industry professionals
- Improve your learning with Skill Plans built especially for you
- Get a free eBook or video every month
- Fully searchable for easy access to vital information
- Copy and paste, print, and bookmark content

Did you know that Packt offers eBook versions of every book published, with PDF and ePub files available? You can upgrade to the eBook version at packt.com and as a print book customer, you are entitled to a discount on the eBook copy. Get in touch with us at customercare@packtpub.com for more details.

At www.packt.com, you can also read a collection of free technical articles, sign up for a range of free newsletters, and receive exclusive discounts and offers on Packt books and eBooks.

If you enjoyed this book, you may be interested in these other books by Packt:

The Art of Crafting User Stories

Christopher Lee

ISBN: 9781837639496

- Leverage user personas in product development for prioritizing features and guiding design decisions
- Communicate with stakeholders to gather accurate information for writing user stories
- Avoid common mistakes by implementing best practices for user story development

- Estimate the time and resources required for each user story and incorporate estimates into the product plan
- Apply product frameworks and techniques for user story prioritization and requirement elicitation
- Benefit from the experiences, insights, and practices of experts in the field of user story mapping

Unleashing the Power of UX Analytics

Jeff Hendrickson

ISBN: 9781804614747

- Understand the significance of analytics in successful UX projects
- Apply design thinking as a problem-solving tool in a UX practice
- Explore taxonomies, dashboards, KPIs, and data visualizations to understand data enterprise in depth

- Discover key considerations to determine which UX analytics tools are best for your projects
- Craft a North Star statement and understand how it guides your work
- Design and deliver the best research findings collateral
- Get to grips with heuristics and performing the effective evaluations

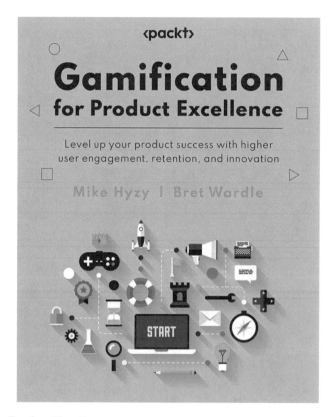

Gamification for Product Excellence

Mike Hyzy, Bret Wardle

ISBN: 9781837638383

- Explore gamification and learn how to engage your user with it
- Gain insights into the functionality and implementation of different gamification frameworks
- Master specific game elements and mechanics that can be used to improve user experiences
- Design a successful gamification strategy to test your hypothesis and develop a business case

- Implement and test the prototype you've created with users for feedback
- Say the right words to sell your gamification strategy to stakeholders
- Use design thinking exercises and game elements to improve the product management process

Packt is searching for authors like you

If you're interested in becoming an author for Packt, please visit authors.packtpub.com and apply today. We have worked with thousands of developers and tech professionals, just like you, to help them share their insight with the global tech community. You can make a general application, apply for a specific hot topic that we are recruiting an author for, or submit your own idea.

Share Your Thoughts

Now you've finished *Cracking the Product Marketing Code*, we'd love to hear your thoughts! Scan the QR code below to go straight to the Amazon review page for this book and share your feedback or leave a review on the site that you purchased it from.

https://packt.link/
r/1837632766

Your review is important to us and the tech community and will help us make sure we're delivering excellent quality content.

Download a free PDF copy of this book

Thanks for purchasing this book!

Do you like to read on the go but are unable to carry your print books everywhere?
Is your eBook purchase not compatible with the device of your choice?

Don't worry, now with every Packt book you get a DRM-free PDF version of that book at no cost.

Read anywhere, any place, on any device. Search, copy, and paste code from your favorite technical books directly into your application.

The perks don't stop there, you can get exclusive access to discounts, newsletters, and great free content in your inbox daily.

Follow these simple steps to get the benefits:

1. Scan the QR code or visit the link below

https://packt.link/
free-ebook/
978-1-83763-276-3

2. Submit your proof of purchase
3. That's it! We'll send your free PDF and other benefits to your email directly

Made in United States
Troutdale, OR
07/28/2025

33236524R00164